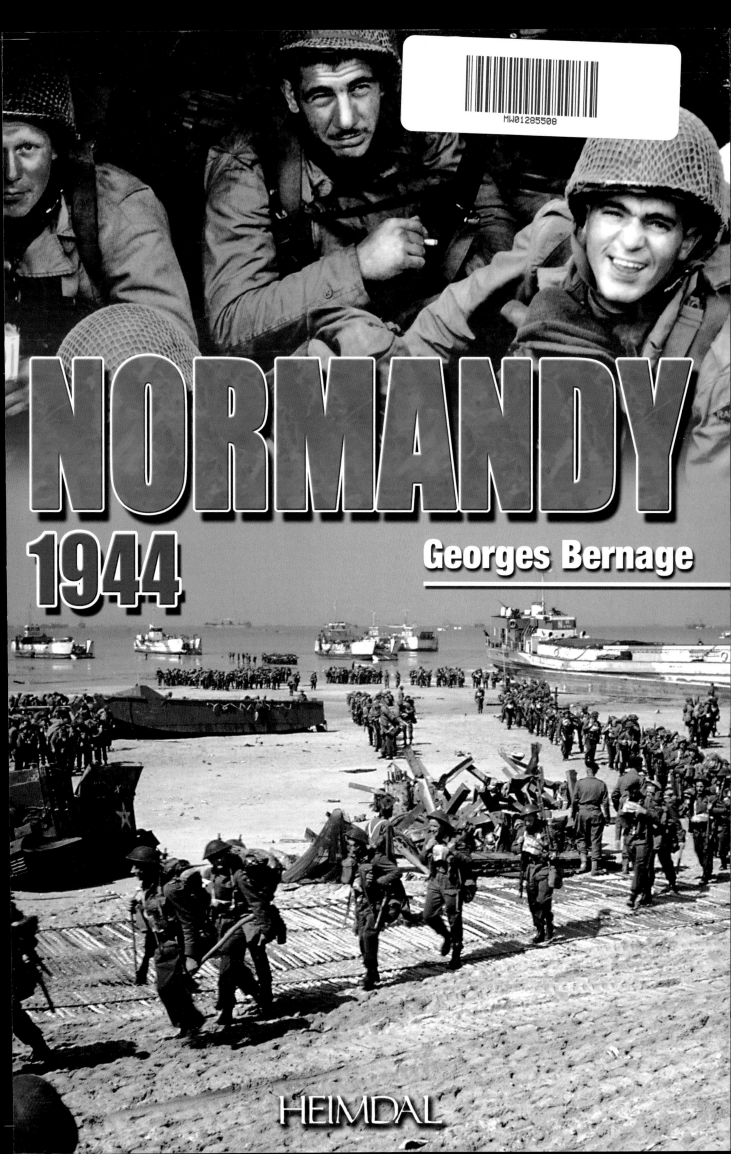

NORMANDY
1944

Georges Bernage

HEIMDAL

- Written by Georges Bernage
- Design and layout: Georges Bernage
- Graphic editing: Christel Lebret and Nicolas Bucourt

Editions Heimdal
BP 61350 - 14406 BAYEUX Cedex
France
Tél. : 02.31.51.68.68 - Fax : 02.31.51.68.60 - E-mail : Editions.Heimdal@wanadoo.fr
site internet : www.editions-heimdal.fr

ISBN 9-78-285-04-85-162

Inroduction

This publication is the result of forty years of work, research and, above all, talking with hundreds of people who lived through the events, allied and German veterans and civilians.

Among the latter I would like to especially mention Bill Millin, with whom I walked where he had been on 6 June, as well as spending entire evenings in conversation at the château de Damigny when he stayed there. Remaining in the same sector, I also met each year, when they were there together, the legendary figures of John Howard and Hans von Luck. There were also other British and Canadian veterans such as Eric T. Lummis, Dick Atkinson, Lockie Fulton, Stuart Tubb, Ross Hill, Bruce Egleston, Chesters Rutherford, Gordon Brown, S. Radley Walters. There were American veterans such as Ted Liska, John Allsup, William Tucker, Laughlin E. Waters, as well as German veterans, Gerhardt Bandomir, Wilhelm Kirchhoff, Franz Gockel, Heinz Harmel, Hubert Meyer, Rudolf von Ribbentrop, Hans Siegel, Otto Funk, Reinhold Fuss, Herbert Walther, Willi Fischer, Heinz Freiberg, Günther Gotha, Heinz Schiemann, Werner Zimmermann, Fritz Porochnowitz, Leopold Heindl, Willi Scharz, Karlheinz Marckert, Karl Willer, Erwin Wohlgemuth, Willi Arnold and many others, not forgetting Polish veterans like Edouard Podyma, Stefan Barylak or Michal Kuc, and the French veterans of Commando Kieffer.

There were also a vast amount of civilian eye-witness accounts! Above all I would like to mention Monique Corblet de Fallerans, Bernardin Birette, abbé Launay and Roger Delfortrie, but there were many others who can be encountered throughout my many publications.

Normandy 44 is a summary grouping together some of the most striking photos, generally linked to the text with very accurate captions and extremely precise maps that allow the reader to follow the text step by step.

Finally, the text itself, after the two big classics of the decades of the past, The Longest Day and Invasion! They're coming! , allows us to follow operations as they unfolded with a strong human dimension thanks to many eye-witness accounts. Once more, historical reality is stronger than fiction. We invite you to take a look.

Georges Bernage
Historian and publisher

NB: This work also owes thanks to that which is constantly undertaken by *Normandie 1944 Magazine*, published by Editions Heimdal.

Guide

For readers who are not specialists in military history, here are a few guidelines to help you.

The basic infantry combat unit is the platoon (Zug in German), with around forty soldiers led by a second-lieutenant or lieutenant. A company (150 to 200 men) has three combat platoons, a command platoon and a support platoon (mortars, machine-guns). It is commanded by a captain (Hauptmann in German, but led by a Major in the British Army).

A battalion (900 to 1,000 men), commanded by a major (Germany and USA) or a lieutenant-colonel (British Army), has three combat companies, a command company and a support company.

The regiment, led by a colonel, has three battalions, a command company and support companies with a strength of 3,000 to 4,000 men. The division has various regiments and battalions with a strength of 12,000 to 18,000 men, depending on the country and type of division.

German units were designated alternately with Roman and Arab numerals, a practical method that prevented confusion. Thus, the 1st platoon was I.Zug, a 1st company, 1.Kompanie and a 2nd battalion, II.Bataillon, whereas the 3rd infantry regiment was Infanterie-Regiment 3, with the Roman numeral added after, here too in order to avoid any confusion. As for the 3rd army corps, it was III.Armee-Korps and the 7th army, 7.Armee.

The companies of American and British units were designated by letters, A Company for the 1st, or D Company for the 4th company and so on. The battalions were designated by Arab numerals in these armies. Thus, to sum up, in the German army, the 2nd battalion of Grenadier-Regiment 1058 is II./1058, whereas in the US Army, the 3rd Battalion of the 505th Parachute Infantry Regiment is 3/505 PIR.

Is everything clear now? Let's go and discover these pages of an exceptional story!

The eve of battle

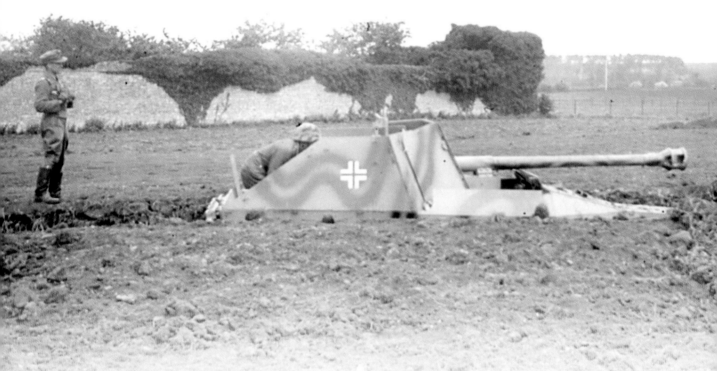

Cairon, May1944, Leutnant Höller (wearing a Einheitsfeldmütze, cap) is about to carry out a firing exercise with his troop. The vehicle, a self-propelled gun on a French tank chassis, is armed with a 7.5 cm gun. Its driver's hatch is opened and it is partially buried in a protective ditch. (Coll. H. Höller via J.-C. Perrigault.)

On Monday 5 June 1944, a strong wind was blowing clouds across a sky where blue was rarely glimpsed. Everything was quiet in Normandy. Today, yet again, the Allies had not been able to land. The sky would be filled with heavy cloud the following night, yet...

There was not much at hand in Normandy in order to deal with a possible invasion: a few static infantry divisions that were often understrength and with little combat experience, as well as soldiers who were either too young or too old. There was just one armoured division, the 21.Panzer-Division, deployed between Caen and Falaise, plus a tank battalion issued with obsolete equipment based in the Cotentin. Much stronger forces were concentrated east of Normandy, in the south, and north of the river Seine.

The **21.Panzer-Division** was a reconstituted unit taken from the 5.Leichte Division, this unit had been created in North-Africa in August 1941 and had fought well before being wiped out in Tunisia in May 1943. Some of the Division's personnel had managed to be evacuated and they would form the core of this new unit. The Division would be commanded by Generalleutnant Edgar Feuchtinger and would stand apart from the fact that it was mostly re-equipped with captured French materiel, reconditioned thanks to skill of Major Becker. The panzer regiment would initially be equipped with French S35 tanks. The 8th anti-tank companies of the two grenadier regiments (inclu-

ding the 8./192 in which Leutnant Höller served, and the 8./125) were equipped with half-track chassis on which armour plating was fitted, and an excellent German anti-tank gun, the 7,5 cm Pak 40. This hybrid, but efficient combination, was named Selbstfahrlafette für 7,5 cm Pak 40 auf Somua MCG S307 (f), we can see above one of these machines commanded by Leutnant Höller and a profile on page 107.The artillery regiment (Panzer-Artillerie-Regiment 155 commanded by Oberstleutnant Hühne) also had homemade armoured guns using French materiel. Thus, 12 German 10,5 cm lFH 18/4 guns mounted on French Lorraine half-track chassis (Geschützwagen Lorraine-Schlepper see opposite page), as well as 6 German 15 cm s.FH13/1 guns, also on Lorraine chassis, equipped the 2nd battalion (Hauptmann Thanneberger). The 3rd battalion (Hauptmann von Ziegeser) also had the same equipment. Note that this regiment's 10th battery (10./155) had four French Unic chassis each fitted with 24 Russian Katioucha (Stalin's Organ) type rocketlauncher ramps. As for the assault gun group, Sturmgeschütz-Abteilung 200, placed under the command of the famous Major Becker, it had been formed at the beginning of 1943 by transforming sixty Hotchkiss H-39 and Somua tanks into assault guns. The chassis of these French tanks were salvaged and fitted with German 7,5 cm and 10,5 cm howitzers (10,5 cm FH 18/40), a very powerful gun protected by an armoured housing. After having proved themselves on the Eastern Front, these

Inspection of Panzer-Artillerie-Regiment 155. In the foreground is a 10,5 cm lFH 18/4 auf Geschützwagen Lorraine-Schlepper (f). (Coll. Hans Höller/J.-C. Perrigault/Heimdal.)

21. Panzer-Division emblem.

hybrid guns were integrated into the new division and would also prove their worth in the coming battle, causing heavy losses to the British tanks.

On 5 June at Cairon, Leutnant Hans Höller, a former member of the Afrikakorps (1) who maintained good relations with the local population, had been worried for several days; allied observation planes had been flying over their positions without any threat whatsoever from a Luftwaffe that was totally absent from the skies. At the same time, on the eastern bank of the Orne, Major Hans von Luck commanding Panzergrenadier-Regiment 125 from his HQ at Bellengreville; his men would soon be attacked from the sky (see chapter 3).

On the Calvados coastline, the 716.Infanterie-Division, commanded by Generalleutnant Wilhelm Richter, only had a strength of 7,771 men on 1 May 1944. It was lacking approximately 50% of its strength and comprised mostly of men unfit for front line service. One of its units, south-west of Graye-sur-mer, was reinforced by Ost-Battaillon 441, Russian volunteers who had arrived in the sector on 19 March 1944 and who had not come there to fight Canadians, their future opponents. Another battalion of former Soviet soldiers, Ost-Bataillon 642, was positioned on either side of the Orne estuary. One of the division's officers, Hauptmann Henry Kuhtz, a veteran of the Eastern Front, arrived here on 19 January 1943 to take command of the 10th company of Grenadier-Regiment 736, the 10./736, between Courseulles and Berniéres. The days were taken up with strengthening coastal positions and carrying out exercises. On 26 February, wrote in his diary: We continued extending WN28, WN29 and WN31 (Courseulles). It is a huge undertaking. Let's hope (&) that we will be ready in time.

However, to the west of the department, a new division which was deployed inland, was brought

Leutnant Höller was born on 20 July 1921 at Pottschach, in Austria. He commanded one of the troops of 8.(s.)/192 led by Oberleutnant Braatz. He is seen here wearing the double-breasted feldgrau Feldjacke worn by assault gun troops, with Litzen (collar tabs), he has been decorated with the Iron Cross 2nd Class and the Verwundeten-Abzeichen since the African campaign, the cuff title of which he is wearing here. The Iron Cross 1st Class, seen here, was awarded to him for his action during the fighting at Bénouville on 6 June 1944, by the Kommandeur of II./Panzergrenadier-Regiment 192, Major Zippe. (Coll. H. Höller via J.-C. Perrigault.)

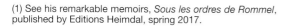

(1) See his remarkable memoirs, Sous les ordres de Rommel, published by Editions Heimdal, spring 2017.

© Thierry Vallet / 2012

21. Panzer-Division

© Thierry Vallet / 2012

Above: Panzer IV Ausf. H of 1. Kompanie from the Panzer-Regiment 22. Note the white numbers and the brush-applied camouflage. This tank was destroyed in a fixed position north of Caen. (Thierry Vallet.)

Opposite: French Somua S35 tank which equipped most of the regiment's II.Abteilung. (Profile Thierry Vallet.)

up to the coast in the sector which would be that of Omaha Beach. This would be a total surprise for the Americans who had not picked up its presence. This 352.Infanterie-Division, commanded by Generalleutnant Dietrich Kraiss, was more powerful than the 716. Infanterie-Division. One of its artillery groups, the 1st (I./AR352), was led by Major Werner Pluskat, seen in The Longest Day and would not be where he said he would be on D-Day. Also, a few days before these decisive events of Pentecost 1944, he made some odd comments to the officers of his unit, saying that when the decisive moments came, they should first think of saving their own skins.

Did the Germans know?

The German high command believed that the landings would take place in the Pas-de-Calais, contrary to Hitler and Rommel who saw Normandy as more of a possibility (1). Thus, Hitler moved up to the coast the 352nd division, opposite the future Omaha Beach sector, just before the landings, as we have seen. In the Cotentin, the 91. (Luftlande) Division, arrived mid-May 1944, forcing the Americans at the last moment to totally modify their airborne operation plans; their 82nd and 101st Airborne Divisions would be grouped together, instead of being dropped on each side of the peninsula, something which would complicate cutting off the Cotentin. However, as Rom-

Crépon, 4 September 1943, a platoon of the 10th company Gren.-Rgt. 736 ,716th infantry division. The crew of a Granatwerfer (mortar type 8-cm-s-GrW34) seen here with their field equipment. Note the numerous helmets fitted with wire and the folding entrenching tool of the soldier carrying the mortar barrel. (Photo H. Kuhtz via P. Cherrier.)

Opposite: The same place today. (E. Groult/Heimdal.)

There are numerous accounts that show some soldiers on the coast knew - see the account by Bernardin Birette in chapter 4. The information made its way up the chain, but it is obvious that it was blocked .

Even more surprising is the account by Rudolf von Ribbentrop, son of the Reich Foreign Minister, at the time commander of a company of Panther tanks with the 12.SS-Panzer-Division Hitlerjugend. At the end of the morning on 3 June 1944, he had received a lung wound caused by an allied fighter-bomber as he was driving along a road in the Eure following a night exercise. He was taken to the Bernay hospital. It was there that, on 4 June, he received a visit from the chancellor of the German embassy in Paris, sent by his father to report

mel was insisting on moving up the 2.Panzer-Division, it instead remained in Picardy, closer to the Pas-de-Calais than Normandy. As for the 116.Panzer-Division, deployed to the west of Rouen, it remained at the disposal of the men behind the plot to kill Hitler... until 20 July! (2) Was this due to high command self-deception or deliberate sabotage?

(1) As shown by Chester Wilmot, in *The Struggle for Europe*, and Hubert Meyer in *12.SS-Panzer-Division*, Heimdal, pp.25, 92 and 93.

(2) Written account sent to G. Bernage by General von Schwerin, on 9 February 1977.

Above and opposite: A short rest for the 10./736 in Crépon, September 1943. C Company of the Green Howards passed through this village on 6 June 1944. (H. Kuhtz via Paul Cherrier.)

Major Werner Pluskat (in the centre wearing an armband) was commander of the 1st artillery group (battalion) of the 352. ID (I./AR 352). His HQ was in the château d'Etreham. His forward observation post (B-Stelle) was in WN 59, at Sainte-Honorine-des-Pertes. This photo was taken after fox hunting by the group's officers, the day after Pentecost in the Saint-Lô area. On the left we can see lieutenant Bernhard Frerking who commanded this group's 1st battery. On this day, eight of his officers (Major Pluskat, captain Wilkening, commander of the 3rd battery), the commander of the 2nd battery and four lieutenants, spent the evening at lieutenant Frerking's HQ at Houtteville. (Coll. Heimdal/H. Severloh.)

on his son's condition: *"He told me that the latest information suggested the allied landings for 5 June. When he bid me farewell on the morning of 5 June, before driving back to Paris in his Holzhocker car, I jokingly said that nothing had happened, to which he snapped back, and with cause, The day is not finished! It was during the night of 5 to 6 June that they came ! Rommel, the army commander in charge of us, was with his family in Germany."* (3)

Thus, the Germans knew, but... Some of the high command wanted the defeat of the 3rd Reich and of Germany and to this end, knowingly helped the Allies in their enterprise. We have all heard about Operation Walkyrie, the plot of 20 July 1944 against Hitler. However, without going into the details, we should remind ourselves of the role played by Admiral Canaris, head of the German

Above: Spring 1944, Sainte-Mère-Eglise, German soldiers collecting water from the same pump seen opposite and filling the A.Brohier-marked water cart. American paratroopers would have their photo taken there on 6 June... (ECPA)

W5, 20 May 1944: On this day, two weeks before D-Day, a ceremony took place at W5 which would be in the thick of the action during the landings at Utah Beach. On this day, Generalleutnant von Schlieben, commander of the 709. Infanterie-Division, awarded the Knight's Cross of the Iron Cross (Ritterkreuz) to Leutnant Arthur Jahnke, who was in command of this position. This young officer of the 3./919 had won this decoration whilst in command of the 5th company of GR 572 of the 302.ID on the Eastern Front at the beginning of 1944. He had fought valiantly with the 6th army in the region of Nikolaievsk. General von Schlieben is seen here awarding this prestigious decoration (opposite, bottom left), before inspecting the men accompanied by Leutnant Jahnke. We see here Leutnant Janhke with some of his men (below) at the end of the ceremony. (ECPA.)

(4), Hubert Meyer accurately points out how, according to Chester Wilmot, the fake intelligence deliberately sent by the Fremde Heere West service led to decisive errors. Despite the incredible courage of the German soldier, who held out for almost three months in the Normandy bocage, the allied command had a top secret weapon: this being some elements of the German high command.

Abwehr counter-intelligence, who deliberately misled the high command, but also that of General Speidel, Rommel's chief-of-staff who explained, after the war, his role in the blocking crucial intelligence. In his book on the 12.SS-Panzer-Division

(3) Rudolf von Ribbentrop, *Mon père, Joachim von Ribbentrop*, Heimdal, 2016, pp. 323 and 324.

(4) Cf. Supra.

Above: Badge worn on the left sleeve by Georgian volunteers, ex Soviet soldiers.

Opposite: In this photo, part of a set taken by the French photographer Zucca, during a general inspection of Ost-Bataillon 795 by general Hellmich in the Hague area of the Cotentin, we can see one of this unit's second-lieutenants using a binocular telescope. The Georgien badge is visible on his sleeve. These men, hailing from the far-off Caucasus, were the first men to face American paratroopers who dropped over the Cotentin. (BHVP.)

American paratroopers ready for the big jump

On the other side of the Channel, the American paratroopers were ready to go to war, as were the seaborne troops that had been prepared by long months of training in the USA and in Britain. However, on the eve of the biggest invasion of all time, there was a growing sense of worry. What if this operation failed? In the months since February, Air Chief Marshall Sir Trafford Leigh-Mallory, commander of the Overlord air forces, had been warning Eisenhower, the Supreme Commander of the operation. Up until 30 May 1944, the Air Chief Marshall had been warning the Supreme Commander about the likely massacre of 'the two superb airborne divisions.' He even believed that there would be the terrible figure of 50% casualties for the paratroopers and 70% for the glider pilots and the men they were flying in. However, supported in his determination by Lieutenant-General Bradley, commander of the American forces involved in the operation, Eisenhower did not bend but still feared sending his paras towards certain death. On Monday 5 June, the operation having been postponed for 24 hours due to bad weather, Eisenhower gave the order to start Operation Overlord

He then set off to visit some units that were to go into action. Leaving his headquarters at Southwick House in Portsmouth, his personal secretary, Kay Summersby, and driver, took him first to see the 50th Infantry Division, who were due to land at Gold Beach. The Supreme Commander then arrived, at around 8pm, in Newbury, near Greenham Common. There he met paras of the 2nd Battalion, 502nd Parachute Infantry Regiment,101st Airborne Division, before the big jump. Eisenhower was accompanied by photographers and cameramen, to make sure that the moment was kept for posterity. Excitement immediately grew to fever pitch, Ike is here! The paratroopers moved towards Ike who spoke to some of the men gathered around him, talking to First-Lieutenant Wallace C. Strobel, who also happened to be celebrating his birthday. Indeed, he was born on 5 June 1922 at Saginaw, Michigan, and today was his 22nd birthday. At around 8.30pm, Lieutenant Moore captured this historic moment with a few photos that would become famous. Strobel remembered that: The photograph was taken shortly before we left the zone where we had been confined to for five days for security reasons. *"We had blackened our faces and hands with soot and cooking oil so that we would be less visible at night and not reflect any moonlight. We were all psychologically ready for the operation. The containers, which had to be fixed to the planes, held our machine-guns, mortars and ammo. The had been prepared earlier and given the number of our plane, then taken to the planes. Our plane's number was 23. This explains why I am wearing the number 23 around my neck in the photograph. The planes and the sticks were identified in this way so that we could easily find the planes, crews and containers of each stick. We were waiting for the order to make our way to the planes when word began to spread that Eisenhower was around."* (4)

(5) See the article by Stéphane Jacquet, in issue N°2 of *Normandie 44 Magazine*, Heimdal, pages 10 to 19.

5 June 1944

General Dwight D. Eisenhower in conversation with 1st Lt. Wallace C. Strobel, of Easy Company, 2nd Battalion, 502nd PIR, 101st Airborne Division Screaming Eagles. The photo was taken by Lt. Moore. Stood around General Eisenhower are men of E Company 2/502nd PIR .
From left to right around the General:
A: Cpl. Hans Sannes*,
B: Bowser
C : Pfc. Ralph Pombano*,
D: Pvt. Schuyler W. Jackson,
E: Cpl. William E. Hayes,
F: Frakes*,
G: 1st lt. Strobel,
H: Pfc. Henry Fuller,
I: Pfc. W. Boyle,
J: Pfc. Noll*. (NARA.)
*: Not identified with certitude.

Lord Lovat, a legendary figure

Simon Shimi Lovat was the 15th Lord and 4th Baron of his lineage. He was also the 25th Chief of Clan Fraser. His ancestors, hailing from Anjou with William the Conqueror, were named Frésellière, a name that became Fraser when they settled in Scotland where they formed a clan. Born on 9 July 1911 at Beaufort (a French name) castle in Scotland, near Inverness, he became a second-lieutenant in 1930 with a small territorial unit, the Lovat's Scouts, a sort of private army made up of gamekeepers from the family estates. The following year his father died and he became the 15th Lord Lovat and 25th Chief of Clan Fraser. Mobilised in 1939 as Captain of Lovat's Scouts, he volunteered for the first commando units and was attached to N°4 Commando, which he commanded with the rank of major during the raid on the Lofoten islands on 3 March 1941. He then took part in the Dieppe raid of 19 August 1942, leading the same unit. Promoted to brigadier and in view of the Normandy landings in 1944, he took command of the 1st Special Service Brigade, comprising of several commando units that would see action on Sword Beach. He was later badly wounded in the airborne bridgehead at Bréville. He did not return to the front and died on 16 March 1995 at Beauly near Inverness.

Brigadier Simon Christopher Joseph Fraser, The Lord Lovat (1911-1995)

Lovat's Scouts cap badge. (Coll. G.B.)

Opposite: Bill Millin playing the bagpipes for the Commandos on the football field at Tichfield. (IWM)

Below: 4 June 1944, Lord Lovat speaks to his men shortly before embarking for the crossing towards Sword Beach.

The Commandos

The Commandos were a special type of unit created by the British. Lord Lovat commanded the 1st Special Service Brigade, grouping together several commando units that would land on Sword Beach: the N° 45th Royal Marine Commando, N°3, N°4 Commando and 1st B.F.M.C. (Commando Kieffer). On Sunday 4 June, the Commandos were grouped together near Southampton. Present was the Lord Lovat's personal bagpiper, Bill Millin who was under the direct orders of Shimi Lovat and who would thus have the privilege of being the only piper on the front line. Millin said that: *"I spent my time playing the bagpipes for the various units in the brigade, taking care not to force my loud music on them as I well understood that they wouldn't like that... Luckily for me, most of the men in the 1st Special Service Brigade liked this sort of music and the men always gave me a polite welcome whenever I popped in to see them. Sometimes I even suspected that they were pretending to be polite due to the fact that I was the official brigade piper and also Lovat's personal player. The Brigadier was hugely popular with the men, especially those of N°4 Commando which was mostly made up of French soldiers."* (5)

On 4 June, Lord Lovat spoke to his commandos prior to the embarking for Normandy. He first spoke to them in English: *"The bigger the challenge, the better we play. Our task appeared a tough assignment, but we held the advantage both in initiative and fire support. It was better to attack than defend. The enemy coastline would be flattened and defences pulverized before we arrived. Once N°6 Commando, which is to take the head of the Brigade, is through the Atlantic Wall the momentum of our advance inland must be kept going at the double to reach the airborne division. Dropped overnight, the paras would be holding the high ground over the canal and river bridges north-east of Caen: we were not going to let good men down... there would be no pause to slow the speed of our thrusting attack. I allowed three hours to reach the Orne bridges and all afternoon to make good the high ground beyond. We would be dug in before dark to meet inevitable counter-attacks... It was going to be a long day."* If the bridges had been seized intact, the rubber dinghies - which weighed men down - could be cast aside. The bri-

gade was going to make history and I had complete confidence in every man taking part! I ended with the suggestion, "If you wish to live to a ripe old age - keep moving tomorrow.» And so we stood across the sea to France." The speech in French was shorter and quicker... the Commandos then went to embark at Warsash on 5 June, on the river Hamble. Bill Millin said that: *"Once on board, I put my haversack in the hold. It was a tiny and very uncomfortable space. I went back on deck and tried to attract the gaze of Shimi Lovat. He no doubt wanted me to play a piece of Scottish folk music, but at that moment he was talking with the naval officer in command of the flotilla. I found myself on the landing craft that was to lead the way down the river, along the Isle of Wight, and finally across the waters of the Channel. Someone came up to me to say that the Brigadier wanted me to play something when we sailed down the river. I looked over to Lovat who was standing on the poop deck, he nodded to me to take position at the bow of the landing craft. The boat was sliding gently over the water when I began to play 'The Road to the Isles'. The armada was en-route to its destiny!..."*

Above: Warsash on the River Hamble, 5 June 1944, men of N°3 Commando embark on the LCIs of the 201st Flotilla, just opposite 'The Rising Sun pub. The Commandos are embarking with their folding bicycles. (IWM)

Below: A photograph taken by Captain Leslie Evans from LCI N°519 which transported the HQ of the 1st Special Service Brigade. LCI N°502 transported Lord Lovat and Piper Bill Millin. The ship was captained by Lieutenant-Commander Rupert Curtis, commander of the 200th Flotilla, the LCIs of which can be seen crossing the Channel in single file. LCI N°503, 504, 505, 516 and 521 carried N°6 Commando, led by Lieutenant-Colonel Derek Mills-Roberts. LCI N°501, 509, 512, 535 and 538 transported N°3 Commando command by Lieutenant-Colonel Peter Young and LCI N°517, 518, 528, 530 and 532 transported the 45 Royal Marine Commando of Lieutenant-Colonel Charles Ries.

(5) Taken from his memoirs, *La Cornemuse du D-Day*, Editions Heimdal, p.68.

2

Paras in the Cotentin

Paras in the Cotentin

The US airborne assault as it is portrayed in the West Point museum. One can make out in the background the east coast of the Cotentin with Utah Beach and the flooded areas behind the line of dunes. On the right, one can see the Merderet marshes on each side of La Fière. The countryside is portrayed fairly accurately. (Coll. Airborne Museum, Sainte-Mère-Eglise.)

At around 8pm on Monday 5 June, 20-year old Bernardin Birette,the son of farmers living at the Heguerie farm at **Audouville-la-Hubert**, halfway between Sainte-Mère-Eglise and the sea, found himself with Edouard Pergeaux near the Vierge crossroads. Two 'flaks' (German anti-aircraft personnel) turned up on bicycles and stopped near the electrical transformer opposite the statue of the Virgin. One of them climbed up to the trans-

The Vierge crossroads. On the evening of 5 June, the Germans dismantled the fuses on the electricity poles. (Heimdal)

former, cut off the electricity and then removed two fuses which he passed down by rope to his colleague; he then climbed back down and got back on his bicycle. It was an unusual thing to do. Bernard Birette, surprised, shouted out to the German who replied, as he pedalled off Mouzieur fini elektrik! But why, continued the young Norman farmer. As he made his way off, the German shouted back: Maybe big problem tonight! Bernardin remembered the RAF attack on the battery at Saint-Martin-de-Varreville eight days earlier and at that very moment, the early dusk was upset by the low-level passage of four British fighters and the sound of machine-gun fire coming from the direction of Chef-du-Pont a few minutes later.

A few kilometres away, at **Sainte-Mère-Eglise**, at around 9pm, German soldiers were having fun on their bicycles in trying to beat the record for the fastest lap around the church; they were part of Grenadier-Regiment 1058, one of the regiments of the 91.Luftlande-Division that had recently arrived in the centre of the Cotentin. Present there was sergeant Rudi Escher and his group of six men; they belonged to the regimental headquarters company which was based in the château of Fauville, a kilometre south of the town. Sergeant Escher (24), enlisted in October 1939, had joined his new regiment seven weeks earlier. Like most

Sergeant Rudi Escher.

The Saint-Méen altar in the church at Sainte-Mère-Eglise hides the staircase leading to the church tower that would become part of D-Day history. (Heimdal)

of the men in his group, including corporal Rudolf May (22), he had fought for two years in Russia.

Since 2 June, sergeant Escher and his men had been tasked with watching the sky from which spies and paratroopers might come. They carried out this task from the church tower, climbing up via a hidden door placed behind the altar, dedicated to Saint-Méen and which led to a spiral staircase. The bicycles were stored in a room situated opposite the church doorway. It was now **11pm** (German time, 10pm for the Allies). Corporal Rudolf May climbed up to the top of the church tower accompanied by a young soldier aged 18; they took up position behind the stone railings on the southern side, opposite the square and settled down for their period of sentry and observation duty. Rudi Escher and four other soldiers, including Alfons Jaki, remained below, at the foot of the church. The night was quiet and calm.

During this time, 18 pathfinder teams of the 82nd and 101st Airborne Divisions, who would mark out the drop zones, were on their way. Each team was led by a lieutenant and comprised of four operators for two Eureka beacons and four men tasked with covering the operators and securing the drop zone. At **12.16am** on 6 June, the first Pathfinders landed on the soil of Normandy. This was a team of the 502nd PIR, made up of 19 men, including Captain Frank Lillyman and three members of the intelligence platoon of the 101st Airborne Division, whose mission was to reconnoitre the battery of Saint-Martin-de-Varreville; they hoped that they had dropped on the future DZ A. A few minutes later, the other teams of the 82nd and 101st Airborne Divisions prepared to jump. However, luck was not on the side of these Pathfinders. Clouds and ground fog prevented the pilots of IX Troop

German soldiers in front of the church in Sainte-Mère Eglise. (Coll. H.J. Renaud.)

Carrier Command from finding their way. Due to flak, the drops were made at altitudes that were too high or low and at a higher speed than planned for in training. This led to teams being scattered and the loss of equipment when leaving the plane. Captain Lillyman and his three teams were gathered in the same sector, less than two kilometres north of of DZ A, at Saint-Germain de-Varreville. These teams were able to quickly set up their Eureka beacons and Holophane lights. All the teams of 505th PIR (82nd Div.) reached DZ O near Sainte-Mère-Eglise. However, for the others, the Pathfinders of 501st PIR landed on enemy positions and had to fight before they could even unharness themselves from their parachutes. And, due to being scattered, many teams did not know if they had reached their objectives. Things had not gone to plan and there was chaos on most of the drop zones.

Shortly after the Pathfinders had taken off, 13,000 American paratroopers of the two airborne divisions took to the sky and headed for Normandy. 432 planes had been allocated for Mission Albany, the transportation and drop of the 101st Airborne, they took off half an hour after the planes

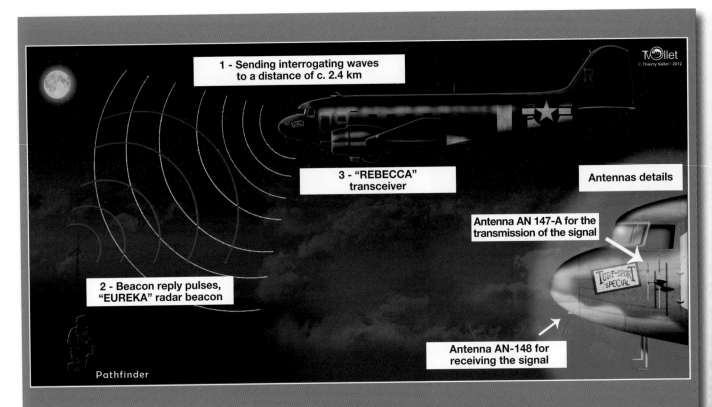

1 - Sending interrogating waves to a distance of c. 2.4 km

3 - "REBECCA" transceiver

Antennas details

Antenna AN 147-A for the transmission of the signal

2 - Beacon reply pulses, "EUREKA" radar beacon

Antenna AN-148 for receiving the signal

Pathfinder

Rebecca - Eureka system

Created and designed by the British but made by the US Army especially for D-Day, these devices had remained a secret up to that point. It worked by sending radio frequency impulses between the planes, equipped with the Rebecca device (transceiver) and the Eureka (transponder) which guided the plane, with great accuracy, towards the desired zone. The devices only worked if the plane received the transponding impulses according to a code that was only known by the plane. Once over the ground, Eureka was used as a straightforward transmitter-receiver between the crew and the ground crew, with the possibility of sending short messages, also in Morse code.

The 3.5 metre high antenna could be folded up with the mast, supports and pegs. According to American instruction booklets, the entire beacon weighed 12.5 kg with bag and harness.

carrying the Pathfinders. The 502nd PIR and the artillery men of the 377 PFAB had to jump over DZ A, between Turqueville and beach exits N°3 and 4, but only one battalion, the 2nd, was concentrated. Only 15 sticks landed on DZ C near Sainte-Marie-du-Mont; others landed near Sainte-Mère-Eglise. The 501st PIR experienced similar problems to DZ D. The code name for the transportation and drop of the 82nd Airborne Division was Boston. This mission took off ten minutes after Albany. Here too, the drop was somewhat scattered and was even worse, due to flak, for the 507th PIR who were supposed to reach DZ T (Amfreville). Only two or three sticks landed on, or near, the drop zone. 50 sticks landed less than a kilometre away and 22, more than three kilometres. Some sticks would be dropped more than twenty kilometres from their objective, like the 180 paratroopers dropped over Graignes. The scattering of all the US airborne troops in the first hours of the landings might appear to have been a terrible failure, but over the following days it became an advantage on the ground. The German troops would overestimate the enemy strength and were unable to organise effective counter-attacks against hidden paras, the number and movement of which could not be judged.

Although regrouping for the Americans was virtually impossible, for the Germans it was total confusion. Before the arrival of this aerial arma-

Photo of Rudolf May taken before he passed away.

da, shouting was heard in **Sainte-Mère-Eglise**, as night fell around 11pm. A fire had broken out at Madame Pommier's house and was first spotted by a German sentry. Four firemen brought out the pump from its store room. Then, as they arrived in the church square, several planes flew over; they ducked, no bombs! They carried on their way and set up the pump. The two fast and alternate peels of the church bell brought out the local inhabitants who headed towards the glow of the fire; some brought their buckets. Most of the people in the human chain that was made to help put out the fire were women. The Mayor, Alexandre Renaud joined in. German soldiers supervised the gathering of around sixty people. Suddenly, a larger formation of planes was heard in the sky. It was lit up by the flames and under fire from flak firing towards the white stripes painted on the wings and sides of the planes. Up in the church tower, Rudolf May watched this sudden intrusion in the quiet night. He could make out things falling from the sky; they were containers. He also saw the inhabitants trying to put out the fire which was spreading to a small barn next door. In the sky, a C-47 of the 81st TCS became lost in the bank of clouds and was heading towards Cherbourg, harassed by flak. Its navigator, Bob McInnes, saw the fire and dropped his paras too far away. Then, other planes suddenly appeared, flying at a very low altitude. The sound of the engines grew to such an extent that they smo-

thered that of the church bells. White dots left the fuselages, making the Germans open fire. The civilians fled in panic, the women screaming; the group broke up, shouting out: Parachutists! Parachutists! It was **12.15am** (allied time 1.15am local time). Two sticks of 506th PIR jumped over the town; at least four of these men were killed by ground fire. The population was terrified. The first paras hit the ground and were chased by the Germans. Twenty minutes later, a stick of F Company, 505th PIR jumped over the town; six or seven paras were killed on their way down. Sergeant Ray was the only one to land amidst the Germans; he fell, hit by a burst of submachine-gun fire, but before dying, he managed to kill his adversary. Pfc. Blakenship disappeared into the burning house; his body would be identified by an officer later that afternoon. According to John Steele, another para named White, also fell into the flames, but his name is not on the list of soldiers killed in Normandy.

Pfc. John Steele fell towards the square, wounded in the foot by a flak splinter; he drifted towards the church tower and his parachute became stuck on the north side (whereas the dummy is today hung on the south side, opposite the square. Pfc. Russell also hit the church and found himself stuck on the lower part of the roof. Spotted by a German, he thought his time had come, but Sergeant Ray had landed just before him and killed the German, perhaps Alfons Jakl (see further on) before being killed himself. Without losing any time? Russell undid his harness and ran away from the town.

In another C-47 bringing in a stick of I Company, 505th PIR, Pfc William Tucker, 20, saw tracer fire all around him and heard Ray Krupinski, behind him in the plane, shout out: Son of a bitch, I've been hit again! He landed near a tree in the Haule park, close to the house on fire. He undid his harness and saw Pfc. Everett Gillilard arrive, a para from his company. All around him he could hear metal crickets clicking. Three of four men were soon around him as planes flew very low overhead.

Above. Paratroopers of 3/506 PIR in a C-47. The photo was taken on 4 June and the men have not yet blackened their faces. (Heimdal)

Above: Aerial photo taken of Sainte-Mère-Église shortly after 6 June. (USAF) You can compare it with the Heimdal map **opposite**.

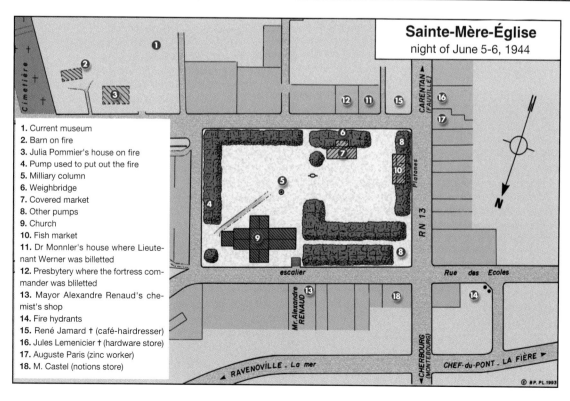

Sainte-Mère-Église
night of June 5-6, 1944

1. Current museum
2. Barn on fire
3. Julia Pommier's house on fire
4. Pump used to put out the fire
5. Milliary column
6. Weighbridge
7. Covered market
8. Other pumps
9. Church
10. Fish market
11. Dr Monnler's house where Lieutenant Werner was billetted
12. Presbetery where the fortress commander was bliletted
13. Mayor Alexandre Renaud's chemist's shop
14. Fire hydrants
15. René Jamard † (café-hairdresser)
16. Jules Lemenicier † (hardware store)
17. Auguste Paris (zinc worker)
18. M. Castel (notions store)

The church of Sainte-Mère-Eglise.

Above: The presbytery where the German Town Major for Sainte-Mère-Eglise was billeted. (Heimdal.)
Below: The store room for the fire fighting equipment in rue des Ecoles in Sainte-Mère-Eglise. (Heimdal.)

group, one man had been killed, private Alfons Jakl (buried at the Orglandes cemetery). After the firefight, the German soldiers grouped together in ranks of three south of the square, holding this area before pulling back to the town centre, unsure of the situation and fearing being surrounded before daybreak. Making the most of a slight pause, the Sainte-Mère-Eglise garrison left the town via the main road leading south. Rudi Escher's group was back together. The six men recovered their bicycles in the store room and went towards the south as far as the château of Fauville.

Other elements of the 505th Parachute Infantry converged towards their objectives. The first paratroopers of the 2nd Battalion (2/505) hit the soil of Normandy at **9 minutes to 1**. Their leader, Lieutenant-Colonel Vandervoort, injured his ankle upon landing and began gathering his men together, using his rifle as a crutch. An ammunition cart was found to carry the commanding officer then the group, now comprising of 400 men (there would be 575 by the evening of 6 June out of the Battalion's 630), moved off towards its objective, the area of Neuville-au-Plain, two kilometres north of Sainte-Mère-Eglise. This village was supposed to cover the town from the north.

The paratroopers of the 3rd Battalion 3/505) arrived from the west of Sainte-Mère at 3 minutes past 2. Their leader, Lieutenant-Colonel Krause, with only 158 paras, entered the town, which had been abandoned by the Germans, and set up defences.

To the south, in the sector of **Sainte-Marie-du-Mont**, the **101st Airborne Division** was also very scattered. The divisional commander, Major-Gene-

William Tucker in 1944 and 1993. (Coll. G.B.)

Sergeant Robinson took command of this plane's stick and they left the town, surprised by the thickness of the hedges, Five or six feet high, covered from top to bottom with a jungle of bushes and rows of trees. The paratroopers had not been prepared to meet this type of countryside. Regrouped on the outskirts of the town, they were then led by lieutenant Walter Kroner whilst waiting to retake the town that the Germans were going to leave...

During this time, Rudolf May and his young comrade were in the church tower. Having seen John Steele pass by like a shadow, they first thought he was dead, then they heard him talk. The young grenadier thought he could easily shoot him but Rudolf May told him to be careful. Are you mad, if you shoot you'll give us away! John Steele took 45 minutes to cut away his parachute suspension lines and slid down to the square where he was captured by the Germans; he managed to escape a few days later.

With all the planes, paratroopers raining down from the sky and a C-47 crashing (where today's Sainte-Mère hotel-restaurant is), the Germans realised that this was a serious event. In sergeant Escher's

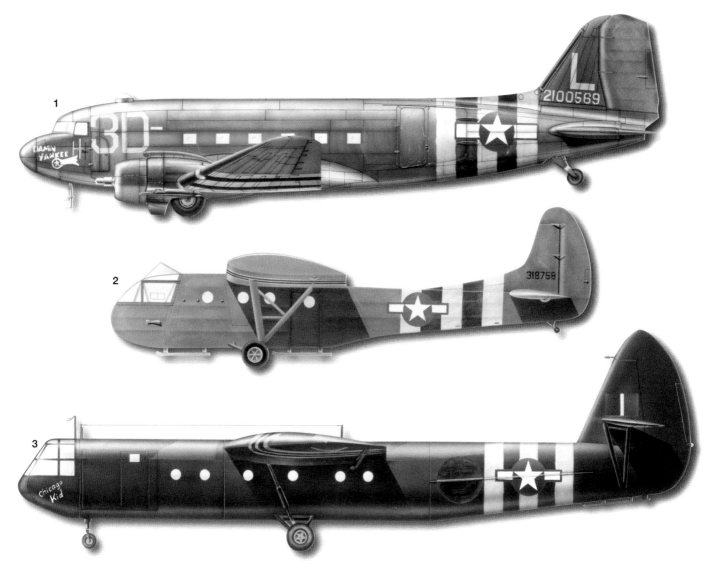

ral Maxwell D. Taylor, was between Saint-Marie-du-Mont and Vierville with men of the 501st PIR; he joined up with Lieutenant-Colonel Ewell, commander of the 3/501 and had only gathered together 90 men. Paras of the 506th PIR (their sector) would defend the divisional headquarters near Hiesville, whereas Major-General Taylor decided to march with Ewell towards one of the beach exits, Exit N°1 near Pouppeville. On their way there, the group was reinforced by isolated men and a group led by Colonel Turner. Major-General Taylor then said: *"Never have so few been led by so many..."* They soon arrived at Exit 1, cleared for the landings. North of the 101st sector, the 502nd PIR of Colonel Van Horn Moseley, who had broken a leg during the jump, arrived at DZ A, near the Saint-Martin-de-Varreville gun battery. The leader of the 2/502, Lieutenant-Colonel Steve A. Chappuis, had also broken a leg, albeit less seriously. Lieutenant-Colonel Cassidy (1/502) marched towards this battery, that he was tasked with destroying, and came across Captain Lillyman, the leader of the Pathfinders. They arrived together at the position of the gun battery and found that it was empty. They then marched towards the north and arrived at Foucarville where Cassidy set up road blocks to cover the northern front of the paratroopers' sector. As for Lieutenant-Colonel G. Cole (commander of 3/502), he was tasked with marching to Exit 3, clearing it then holding on, but he landed too far west, near Sainte-Mère-Eglise. He first marched towards the battery with a force

1. Flight tested as early as 1935, the C-47 was ordered in large quantities by the US Army Air Forces in late 1941.

2. 13,039 Waco CG-4 were made and it was massively used by the two airborne divisions.

3. The Airspeed Horsa AS 51 could transport many more men and equipment than the Waco. This is why it was also used by the Americans. (Profiles by V. Dhorne/Heimdal)

Major-General Maxwell Taylor, commander of the 101st Airborne Division (US Army)

of nearly 80 men. However, there was a firefight with the Germans and Major Vaughn was killed. He also saw that the battery was abandoned and quickly reached Exit 3 at 7.30am. Captain Robert L. Clemens went to Exit 4, a little further north.

1. Brig.Gen. Don Pratt deputy commander of the 101st Airborne Division, seen here looking at maps. (Private collection)

2. England, 25 May 1944. From left to right 1st Lt. John L. May (Pratt's aide de camp), Brig. Gen. Donald F. Pratt, Lt. Col. Mike Murphy (pilot), Lt John M. Butler (co-pilot) in front of Brig. Gen. Don Pratt's glider, The Fighting Falcon. Only Murphy and May survived the crash. (Private collection)

3. The crash site of the Fighting Falcon and the memorial to Brigadier General Don Pratt. (E. Groult/Heimdal.)

4. Captain Charles O. Van Gorder in front of the wreck of the glider that carried Don Pratt. On the right one can see a long wooden stake that the paras used to try and prise the glider from the hedgerow it was stuck in. (Milton Dank)

Two generals die during the night

At around **4am**, other elements of the two divisions arrived by glider. This was the case of Brigadier-General **Don Pratt**, the deputy commander of the 101st Airborne Division who arrived in a glider named The Fighting Falcon. Flying the glider was a high-ranking officer, 34-year old Lieutenant-Colonel Mike Murphy who had been a test pilot and who had been chosen to fly the general due to his flying skills. He was followed by another glider flown by Lieutenant Victor Warringer, transporting part of the 101st medical team (the 326th Medical Company), including Captain Charles O. Van Gorder. The two gliders were on their run in over Hiesville above LZ E. There was a strong 18 to 20 knots side wind. Mike Murphy landed in a field covered with a heavy morning dew and the gliders aquaplaned. The Fighting Falcon and the second glider crashed into a hedgerow and line of trees 250 metres from the D329 road (south-west of Hiesville). Brigadier-General Pratt and Lieutenant Butler were killed instantly and Lieutenant-Colonel Murphy's right femur was broken. It was **8 minutes past 4**.

In the same sector, the paratroopers of Easy Company would destroy the 105mm guns of the Holdy battery in a feat of arms that became famous. Whereas south-east of Sainte-Mère-Eglise, Brig-Gen. Pratt was killed when his glider crashed, another general would also die that same night. In the very early hours of 6 June, with the paratroopers of the 82nd and 101st Airborne Divisions dropping over the Cotentin, General **Wilhelm Falley**, commander of the 91.(Luftlande) Infanterie-Division, whose headquarters was at the Bernaville château, near Picauville, was taking part in a Kriegspiel at Rennes, accompanied by other staff officers. Told of the unfolding events in his sector, Falley quickly left in his car accompanied by his aide de camp, Major Bartuzat, and his driver. However, Falley did not know that his headquarters was then only a few hundred metres from the drop zone of the 508th PIR and that since 2.15am, groups of paratroopers were trying to regroup in the sector. Among the latter was Lieutenant Malcolm Brannen of the headquarters company of the 3rd Battalion, 508th PIR. who had gathered together men of his regiment. Corporal Schlegel of the same company was also there, along with ten other paratroopers. The two groups were moving without having linked up. At dawn, the general's staff car was approaching the château when it was ambushed, killing the general and the major and capturing the driver. The 91.ID had lost its commander.

For the German high command, the alert had started at 11pm (10pm English time) when yet another air raid had finished off churning up the terrain of the gun battery (1./1261) of Saint-Martin-de-Varreville. This was the end of the alert for the commander of German coastal defences in the sector, lieutenant-colonel Günter Keil; he commanded Infanterie-Regiment 919, the companies of which were deployed from the Baie des Veys, in the south, to Aumeville-Lestre, in the north. His headquarters was north-east of Montebourg. He went to bed and was woken up by his adjutant, lieutenant Saul, who informed him that paratroopers had been dropped. The maximum alert was given, Alarmstufe III; but the telephone lines had been cut. He could not alert his units.... all he had left were dispatch riders to spread the alert. However, the rider he sent to colonel Triepel, commander of the coastal artillery unit (HKAR 1261) was shot at by paratroopers and had to turn back. Lieutenant-colonel Keil had no idea what had happened to his units and could not issue his orders. He was reduced to commanding the headquarters company (captain Simoneit) at Montebourg, with his 56 men and ten customs personnel, strengthened by 90 men from the combat school!...

Generalleutnant Wilhelm Falley. (Photo Coll. Charita/ Heimdal.)

Opposite: During a trip to Normandy, via Caen and Saint-Sauveur-le-Vicomte, Feldmarschall Rommel stopped at Picauville where he was greeted by Generalleutnant Falley at his headquarters in the château of Bernaville. Rommel is seen here on the large steps of the château as he leaves his host. (BA)

Above: The same spot today, the shutters are closed. (E. Groult/Heimdal)

Keil would prove his worth over the following days, but for now, he was cut off, even if the beaming Leutnant Wappaens had just brought in his first prisoners. However, this officer was shot in the heart and killed a short while after.

With the 101st!

Fighting was also taking place at **Sainte-Marie-du-Mont**, a central locality in the 101st Airborne's sector. Jean Lelarge, who was 13 at the time, saw the arrival of the paras: I thought that the planes were flying very low. A group of men jumped out and their parachutes opened, they swung two or three times then they were on the ground; no doubt so that they would not remain targets in the sky for long. I realised that if I could see all of this in detail, whereas it should have been pitch black, it was because the sky was lit up like plain day by flares that were also falling, attached to parachutes. This locality would become an essential junction with the coast.

The 101st Airborne Division was tasked with clearing four beach exits but also, to the south of the sector, the bridges over the Douve south of Saint-Côme-du-Mont, at Barquette and Port. Capturing these bridges was essential in order to pursue the attack towards Carentan and link up with the men landing at Omaha Beach. This was the mission of the 3rd Battalion of the 506th PIR and 501st PIR. The latter was led by the colourful Colonel Howard Johnson. He made his men yell *"We are the best!"* As General Marshall, Chief-of-staff of the US Army (1), recounted. The men did not obey Johnson because they liked him or that they knew in combat he would turn out to be a leader like no other,

capable of making the right decisions. He was a tyrant and his requests, like his eccentricity, created fear rather than respect. A man serving in his headquarters said the following: *"He was friends with any man capable of gritting his teeth and marching as long as he was not blind; The maximum, the impossible, these were his objectives. The regiment thrived and grew strong because his tyranny was tempered by a team of young officers whose command capabilities in combat were probably without equal throughout the rest of the army."* With his light blond hair, sunburned face and steely gaze, Colonel Johnson, nicknamed 'Skeets', was a character that seemed to be straight out of an American action movie. However, he was, as we have seen, a leader of rare energy. He did not put up with any lateness or human frailty. When selecting the first men for his unit, he decided on one essential point; their aggressiveness. He asked himself the following questions when deciding whether to keep the men he was offered: Do they have the physical aptitude, are they mentally agile, are they aggressive, can they kill? According to Captain Laurence Critchell (2), who was one of his headquarters officers: *"Johnson wanted killers; he wanted to fight a bigger force; he wanted a regiment that could become a single weapon."* They would turn out to be 'killers' who took no prisoners during this decisive night, but this was also because they could not deal with them. However, fate would not be on the side of Colonel Johnson; first he struggled gathering up his men that had been scattered all over the place, in order to head to his objective, the La Barquette lock, a crossing point at the base of the Cotentin peninsula. At dawn, he at last had one hundred and fifty men with him. Wading through the marshes, they reached the canal at 4am and took up positions on their objective two hours later. They ambushed a column of German paras and inflicted heavy losses. However, La Barquette did not give Johnson the adventure that he expected; the lock was a cul-de-sac and the advance on Carentan would be via the road, further to the west and which would see the exploits of another leader, Lieutenant-Colonel Robert C. Cole, com-

Generalleutnant Wilhelm Falley's grave in the German cemetery at Orglandes, block 10/grave 267. (Photo B. Paich.)

Colonel Howard Johnson.

(1) In *Invasion aéroportée en Normandie*, Payot, Paris, 1968.
(2) L. Critchell, *Four Stars of Hell*, Battery Press.

The flooded zones were a deadly trap for many paratroopers who were caught in their suspension lines and drowned. (US Army)

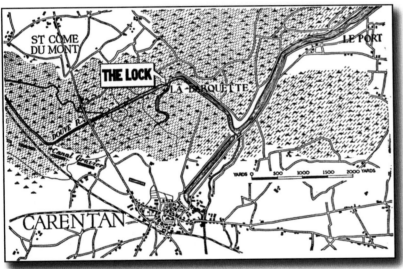

Opposite. This American map shows that the lock at La Barquette did not lead anywhere, stuck in the middle of the marshes between the vital road going to Saint-Côme-du-Mont in the west, and the vital small bridges leading to Port (in the east) and from there to Brévands in order to go around Carentan via the north which would be the case. The only good thing about the lock was that it could be used to slowly lower the water level... Colonel Johnson, who wanted to be the first, found himself in a dead end.

Below, left: The La Barquette lock today, looking towards the mouth of the Douve. Carentan is to the right of of the path, on the left, that Johnson used. (E.G./Heimdal)

Below, right: On this 1944 aerial photo, taken once the waters had receded, we can see the La Barquette lock viewed from Carentan and looking towards the north, along the high ground of the peninsula overlooking the floodable low ground. Saint-Côme-du-Mont can be seen bottom left. We can make out the tree-lined path taken by Johnson, on the right, and the houses in which his men sheltered. (Coll. M. de Trez-Dead Man s Corner.)

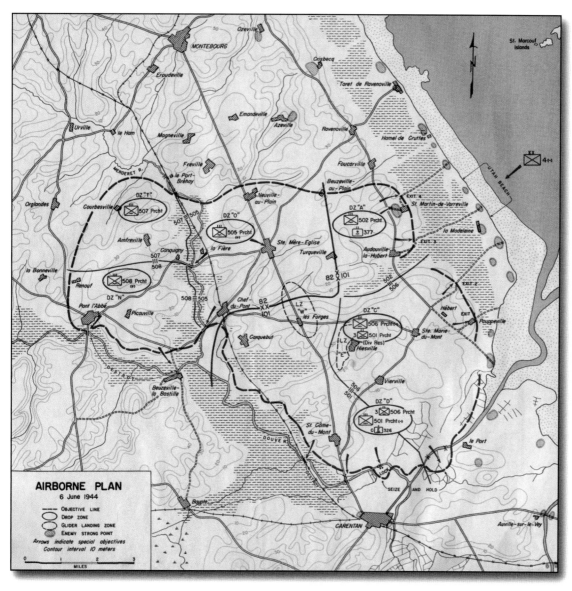

This map of the airborne assault plan shows the zones allocated to the two airborne divisions and their objectives. For the 101st, along with the clearing of the four beach exits (N°1 to 4), the 3/506 had to take the crossing over the Douve next to the small village of Port, whereas the 501st PIR was tasked with taking the sector of Saint-Côme-du-Mont and the La Barquette lock. The three divisional drop zones are indicated, as well as the landing zones for the gliders. The red patches indicate German positions. (US Army)

mander of the 3rd Battalion, 502nd Parachute Infantry Regiment.

With the paratroopers of the 101st Airborne holding positions north of the marshes in the south, in preparation for the advance towards Carentan, in the north and west, those of the 82nd Airborne would prepare jumping off positions.

At **4am**, a convoy of 52 gliders from Ramsbury, brought in some help for the paras of the 82nd who were on the defensive in the Sainte-Mère-Eglise sector. One of the gliders, carrying medical supplies, crashed into a wall of the hospice, whereas another, transporting a 57mm gun, hit the school. The gliders were bringing in A and B Battery of the 80th Antitank Battalion of the 82nd Airborne Division, which was equipped with 57mm anti-tank guns. They would reinforce the road blocks around the town. Commenting on the role played by the glider pilots, whose craft were crashing into the hedges, Brigadier-General Gavin exclaimed: Those guys aren't paid enough!

Before long, after the sun began to rise and with quiet reigning over the town of **Sainte-Mère-Eglise**. A few inhabitants began to emerge from their doors and chat in low voices about what they thought of this exceptional night. According to the Mayor's son, Henri-Jean Renaud. Lieutenant-

This modern-day winter photograph shows conditions identical to those of 1944. The map shows the officially flooded areas (blue lines), but the waters were much more widespread than those shown on the map. Carentan was practically surrounded by water. The low valleys, like the one south of Vierville, were also flooded. Aerial observation had shown the flooding and it was a source of worry for the Allies. However, reeds had grown in these wet zones, giving a green hue to the water and thus minimising the danger. Also, as this photo shows, where the poles emerge from the waters, the latter was often only ten centimetres deep, but the presence of numerous unseen canals created formidable and deadly traps for paratroopers burdened with equipment. In 1944, this area was full of mosquitoes due to the permanent presence of water in these marshlands. (E.G./Heimdal)

Alexandre Renaud, mayor of Sainte-Mère-Eglise in 1944.

Henri-Jean Renaud in June 1944.

Lieutenant-Colonel Krause, commander of the 3rd Bn. 505th PIR. He landed a kilometre to the west of Sainte-Mère-Eglise. He sent a message from the town at 5am on 6 June. (US Army)

Colonel Krause, commander of the **3rd Battalion of the 505th PIR**, had landed during the night a kilometre to the west of Sainte-Mère-Eglise, right in the field that had been selected as the assembly point for his stick. On the ground, resistance was non-existent. Once gathered together, the men of his stick were split into four groups and sent off in opposite directions to reconnoitre the terrain, with the order to return within forty-five minutes. The reconnaissance groups thus brought in a group of ninety paratroopers guided by a local man who was obviously drunk and who pointed out to them that the German garrison in the town of Sainte-Mère-Eglise had left to make their way to a quartermaster transport unit's camp.

Krause then quickly reorganised his unit into two companies and marched off towards the town, using the hedgerows to conceal his men. Upon arriving on the edge of Sainte-Mère-Eglise, he ordered six platoons to set up road blocks at the various access points to the town, except for the one he intended to use himself. When he considered that these combat groups were in position, he left with his group towards the town centre in order to destroy the German communication centre linked with Cherbourg. Capturing the town was straightforward. Thirty Germans were captured and eleven killed as they tried to escape.

At 5am, Krause sent a runner to the regimental commander, Colonel William Ekman, with the following message: I am in Sainte-Mère-Eglise! then, an hour later, a second runner was sent with a new message I hold Sainte-Mère-Eglise! However, neither of the runners found Ekman. But the second runner came across Major-General Ridgway and handed over his message. On this morning there were many messages which did not reach their destinations. However, this one had the consequence of making, until 12 pm, Colonel Ekman, who was less than one kilometre from Sainte-Mère-Eglise, believe that the town was still in German hands.

The 2nd Bn. **(2/505)**, commanded by Lieutenant-Colonel Benjamin Vandervoort, had carried out one of the rare grouped landings (27 out of its 36 sticks landed on or near the DZ). At dawn, he had managed to gather up some 575 paratroopers out of the 630 that made up his battalion. Unluckily, Vandervoort had broken his ankle upon landing and had to be moved about in a cart that was found. His mission was to 'mop up' the northern entrance to Sainte-Mère-Eglise on the RN13 road, from where a German counter-attack was expected.

At **6.15am**, when he finally established radio contact with Ekman, he found out that he was in Neuville. He was without any news for two hours.

Sainte-Mère-Eglise

The photos shown on these two pages are particularly famous. They have been published many times and have contributed to the huge fame of the small town of Sainte-Mère-Eglise. Cornelius Ryan's book and the film it later inspired, 'The Longest Day', would place this small Cotentin town into the pantheon of places touched by history. At Sainte-Mère-Eglise and Sainte-Marie-du-Mont, the paras had landed during the night amidst the houses. At Sainte-Mère-Eglise, the conditions had been rendered more dramatic by the fire at Julia Pommier's barn, lighting up the arrival of the paratroopers and, above all, by the presence of civilians who had come to help put out the fire and who witnessed the events, and the Germans who immediately opened fire on the paras. However, the Germans got the situation under control. But before sunrise, they evacuated the town and at dawn, Lieutenant-Colonel Krause's 3/505 penetrated into the town and set up positions, dealing with a German counter-attack from the north in the afternoon. Also, from 11am onwards, the town came under German artillery fire.

This photo was published in a small American propaganda booklet for the French public and contained photos taken by Weston Haynes. In the booklet, this photo is shown with the following caption: The Germans had been ordered to behave well. But before running away, they looted this store and killed the owner. In fact, there was no looting by the occupying forces in Sainte-Mère-Eglise. Jules Lémenicier and his family were still present at 11am on 6 June 1944, playing cards with neighbours when the owner was killed by harassing fire. At 11am, a German shell exploded in the middle of the street. Jules Lémenicier died from wounds received by shell splinters. One can see the numerous traces caused by shell splinters on the shop front. Note also the 'quincaillerie' sign (ironmonger) and the petrol pump, the only one in the town. (Coll. Heimdal.)

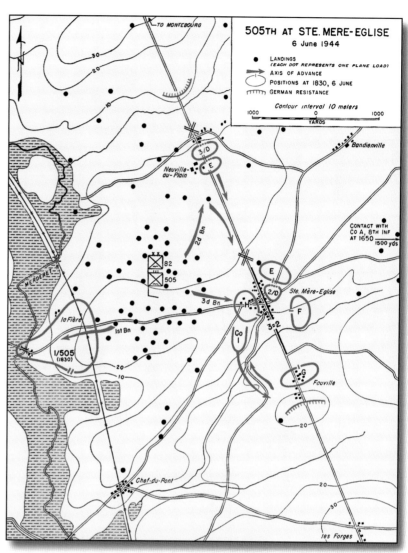

505TH AT STE. MERE-EGLISE
6 June 1944

- LANDINGS
  (EACH DOT REPRESENTS ONE PLANE LOAD)
- AXIS OF ADVANCE
- POSITIONS AT 1830, 6 June
- GERMAN RESISTANCE

Contour interval 10 meters

1000 0 1000
YARDS

Above: The caption for this photo, taken on 7 June says, American infantry flush out a German sniper in the church tower.... (Coll. Heimdal)

Below: This famous photo shows a paratrooper running towards the church door. Was this a reconstitution for the war correspondent's camera? There were indeed Germans in the church tower and, during the night, Rudolf May threw a grenade near the church door. However, all of the Germans, including those in the tower, had left before dawn. This scene is, therefore, of a man running out of prudence towards a church that is now empty. (NA/Heimdal.)

This map shows the landing zones of the 505th PIR, mostly to the west of Sainte-Mère-Eglise, as planned. Each dot represents a stick dropped by a plane. The 3/505 of Lieutenant-Colonel Krause headed for Sainte-Mère-Eglise. The 2/505 of Lieutenant-Colonel Vandervoort made for Neuville-au-Plain, before going back to Sainte-Mère-Eglise. As for the 1/505, it reassembled in order to march towards La Fière. German resistance stiffened north of Neuville-au-Plain and south of Fauville. (US Army map colourised by Heimdal)

The 2nd Battalion, 505th PIR was led by Lieutenant-Colonel Benjamin Vandervoort. At dawn and with a broken ankle, he managed to gather together 575 paratroopers of this battalion. (Coll. D. François.)

Above and opposite: 6 June, near Saint-Marcouf, wary paratroopers question civilians. They had been warned about civilians who could also be collaborators... In the photo opposite, the marking on the helmet designates a lieutenant. (US Army)

At **8am**, he received orders, counter-orders and disorder, par for the course when operating in enemy territory. It was Ekman who first stated that he had not heard from the 3rd Battalion. Then, at **8.10 am**, he ordered him to: Turn back and take Sainte-Mère-Eglise!; at **8.16 am**: Come back to Neuville, I think that the 3rd Battalion is in Sainte-Mère-Eglise!, at **8.17 am**, Ignore previous message, make your way to Sainte-Mère-Eglise! Vandervoort, being careful after all these contradictory messages (do not forget that he was moving about with a broken ankle), decided to retrace his steps, but left behind a group of forty paratroopers led by Lieutenant Turner Turnbull of D Company, to set up a threadbare defensive position at Neuville-au-Plain.

Turnbull was a 'half-Cherokee', nicknamed 'The Chief' in his company, and respected for his warrior attributes, something that he would go on to prove over the following hours.

At around **9.30am**, the 3/505 was attacked south of Sainte-Mère-Eglise by two Georgian companies, supported by three light tanks and two self-propelled guns. They were repulsed by the men of the 3rd Battalion, with Vandervoort arriving at that time with his 2nd Battalion (2/505). After talking with Krause, the newly arrived men ensured the defence of the northern part of the town.

During this time, the Turnbull group was doubling over to Neuville which it captured within a few minutes. The village was unoccupied and Turnbull took up positions north of it along some high ground, lined with a hedgerow which gave him a 500-metre field of fire to the north. He placed a

group of ten men with a machine-gun in an orchard on the edge of open ground situated to the west of Neuville. His defences were completed by a bazooka man and two infantrymen in houses along the RN 13 road.

Twenty minutes later, the men in position behind the hedgerow spotted a long column of German infantrymen, singing as they marched along the road. Vandervoort, now in a jeep that had been flown in with gliders transporting his division's heavy equipment a few hours earlier, arrived at that moment. The jeep had in tow a 57mm gun. Whilst the gunners were taking up position in order to strengthen the strong point, Vandervoort and Turnbull were talking when a Frenchman turned up on his bike. The latter pointed a finger down the road behind him. In the distance, the two officers could make out men marching their way. The man said that they were German prisoners being escorted by paratroopers. It was true that Vandervoort could see a few men in paratrooper uniform waving orange triangles, but the perfect marching order of the column made him uneasy. When the column was less than 800 metres away, Vandervoort had no doubt as to what was taking place opposite him. He ordered the machine-gunner to open fire. In a flash, the men opposite scattered on both sides of the road and began firing back. The Frenchman took advantage of this and disappeared. This was a company of Grenadier-Regiment 1058 of the 91. (Luftlande) Infanterie-Division, comprising of 190 men. Turnbull's men, still hidden behind their hedgerow to the west, pinned the Germans down along the road, but the latter tried to go around their flanks.

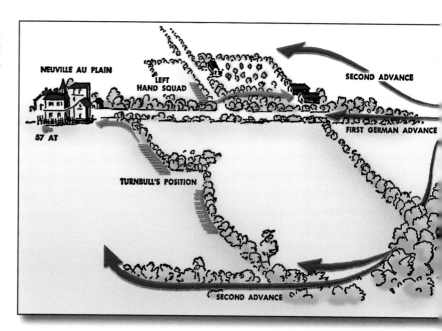

Top: This sketch, from one in General S.L.A. Marshall's book, shows the Germans' two attempts to outflank Turnbull's position. Note also the position of the 57mm anti-tank gun. (Heimdal, from S.L.A. Marshall)

Above: A chenillette used by the Germans and destroyed in the Neuville sector. A glider can be seen behind the hedgerow. (US Army)

E Company of the 506th PIR (101st Airborne) were supposed to have reached DZ 'C' near Sainte-Marie-du-Mont but were instead ten kilometres north of their objective. They made their way through the dense bocage in order to reach their sector. Along the way, they met up with another group led by Major John P. Stopka (502d PIR), consisting of troopers from various units (including members of the 377th Parachute Field Artillery Battalion from the 82nd ABN Div.) Together, these men took up positions in a farm at the crossroads controlling access to the beach at Ravenoville.

Led by Major Stopka, the paratroopers took over the Marmion farm south of Ravenoville where they captured some German soldiers and a precious chenillette equipped with a trailer. They pose here with their spoils of victory. The paratrooper holding the flag is James W. Flanagan, of C Company, 502d PIR. (NARA)

Vandervoort sent a runner to Turnbull asking *"Are you alright? Do you need any help?"* The man was able to return with the assurance that things were fine: *"Ok, everything is under control, don't worry about me!"* Vandervoort placed his trust in the reputation of The Chief .

Shortly after the start of the fight, a German self-propelled gun, coming from the direction of Cherbourg, appeared at a distance of less than 500 metres and opened fire. When it opened fire a second time, the bazooka man was killed at the defensive position situated along the side of the road. Its fifth shell nearly hit the anti-tank gun and the gunners fled into a house. Then, a few minutes later, the gunners returned to the gun and hit the self-propelled gun twice. A German assault gun then appeared, a Sturmgeschütz which they managed to damage.

The German infantry used the cover of the hedgerows to try and outflank Turnbull's positions, using mortar fire support. By mid-afternoon, eighteen Americans had been killed or wounded.

La Fière sector

The 505th PIR, commanded By Colonel William Ekman, was probably the luckiest airborne regiment of those that jumped on 6 June. They were able to regroup easily and carry out all of missions that they had been tasked with.

The plan was for the 1st Battalion **(1/505)** to leave the drop zone and take the causeway at La Fière on the Sainte-Mère-Eglise/Pont-l'Abbé road by the Merderet river. In reality, only one company had been tasked with this mission, 'A' Company.

The La Fière causeway was a strategically vital area, it was 800 metres long and surrounded by marshes and flooded zones several metres deep. It was one of the only places in which the Merderet could be crossed.

Lt. John Dolan of 'A' Company, followed by elements of 'C' Company and a few paratroopers of the 507th, was the first to arrive with his company in the sector. Near the bridge was a manor house and farm, occupied by a group of Germans who had fortified the barns and main house. It took several hours for Dolan and his men to push the enemy out of this strong point.

A few engineers of 307th Glider Engineer Battalion arrived with a 57mm gun. Dolan set up his defensive perimeter around the bridge, the manor and along the river.

The Germans appeared on the other end of the causeway at Cauquigny. They numbered approximately 250 and were supported by artillery, heavy calibre mortars, but above all, were preceded by two Renault tanks which were then followed by a third. A furious firefight broke out on both sides of the Merderet as control for the causeway heated up with dead men falling on both sides.

Thanks to two bazooka teams positioned on each side of the bridge, the three tanks were knocked out. The Germans withdrew in disarray, but counter-attacked again, without success, at the end of the afternoon.

Major F.C. Kellan, commanding the 1st Battalion of the 505th, was killed on 6 June, as well as his successor, Major James Mc Ginity also killed the same day. This left Lieutenant Dolan in command of the battalion in the sector of La Fière. A little further south, at Chef-du-Pont, a bridgehead had been established opposite the marshes.

The paras finally held out against the German counter-attack in this 'first battle of La Fière'. There would be a second, three days later. For now, the paratroopers held a sector between the Merderet in the west, the Carentan marshes to the south, the coast and the northern edge of Sainte-Mère-Eglise towards Montebourg which would be solidly held by Lieutenant-Colonel Keil. This bridgehead was where the paratroopers and the 4th Infantry Division would link up. (3) The chaos caused by scattered drops disorganised the paras, but even more so the Germans who formed isolated pockets in the bridgehead. The largest of these pockets was that formed by the 795th Georgian battalion, made up of soldiers hailing from the far distant Caucasus and which was the main adversary of the American paratroopers, putting up a fierce fight...

(3) See chapter 4.

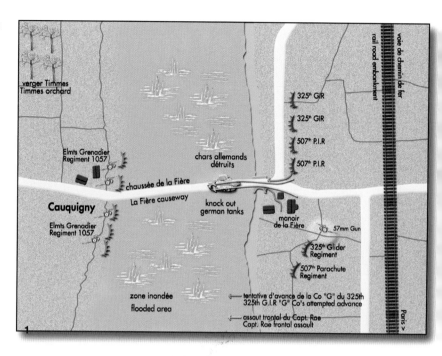

1. Sketch of the battle of La Fière, 6 June 1944, showing the forces present. (Heimdal)

2. Aerial photograph taken looking east, showing the manor of La Fière on the east bank in the foreground. The Germans were on the west bank, beyond the flooded areas which are marked in blue.

3. The manor of La Fière seen today from the same angle. (E.G. Heimdal)

3

The wings of Pegasus

Pegasus, the winged horse, emblem of the 6th Airborne Division. (Nicolas Bucourt collection)

Seen here in front of their Albermarle aircraft, pathfinders of the 22nd Independent Parachute Company synchronise their watches. From left to right: Lieutenants De La Tour, Wells, Vischer and Midwoop. De La Tour would be killed in Normandy. (IWM)

Everybody was ready for the big jump. The Royal Air Force had placed, for the operation, 423 aircraft of fifteen squadrons of N°38 and N°46 Group. On the evening of 5 June, Air Chief-Marshal Sir Trafford Leigh-Mallory, commander of all the air forces for Operation Overlord, visited each of the airfields from where the British and Americans would depart. All of the men had been well-trained but many had never seen action before. At fifty minutes before midnight, Squadron Leader Merick took off from Harwell with the first of the six Albermarles transporting the 22nd Independent Parachute Company. Flying with him was Air Vice-Marshal Hollinghurst. The moon was bright and the sky clear. (IWM)

Monday 5 June had not been a very nice day for Major von Luck, commander of a grenadier regiment, the 125th of the 21.Panzer-Division. The weather in Normandy had not been at its best and it had rained all day with strong gusts of wind. However, now, in the evening, the weather at last began to clear up. Von Luck was in a house on the edge of Bellengreville (to the west of Vimont), south-east of what would become the British airborne bridgehead. In front of him were documents and maps in preparation for his regiment's exercises. His deputy officer, lieutenant Helmut Liebeskind (1), was at the regimental HQ in the centre of the village. Both were waiting for a report from the II Battalion (II./125) which at that time was carrying out a night exercise in the Troarn-Escoville sector towards the coast. During this time, the I Battalion, equipped with half-track armoured vehicles, was in a holding position to the rear. Hans von Luck had been trained by Rommel when he was an officer cadet, before Hitler took over power, and he had been imbued with the offensive spirit. Thus, von Luck ordered his battalions to attack immediately and individually in the event of an allied landing, without taking into account orders from the high command.

Further away, at the Ranville bridge, spanning the Orne, were two civilian guards on duty that night, Adolphe Houlbey (59) and Pierre Avice (67). They were with German sentries who were, on average, aged fifty. To the west was the metallic outline of the lifting bridge at Bénouville. Based at the latter was a small German garrison armed with a flak gun and a machine-gun. There were two cafés opposite each other on the west bank: the 40-year old Louis Picot's café (to the north), and that of the Gondrée family, to the south. The area between the two bridges was marshy.

(1) He would go on to be a Bundeswehr general after the war.

Major Hans von Luck was close to the airborne bridgehead and the first to intervene against it. (Heimdal.)

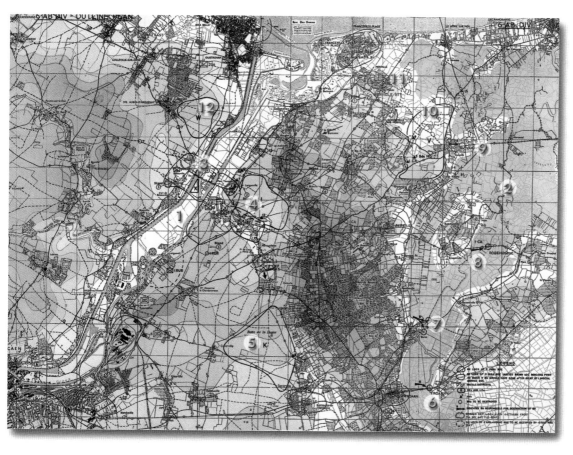

1 The Orne and the canal to the west. 2 The Dives and the flooded zone and marshes to the east. 3 LZ X and the bridge at Bénouville, LZ Y and the Ranville bridge. 4 Ranville and DZ N of the 5th Brigade. 5 LZ K and DZ K, to the south for the gliders and reinforcements, plus the 3rd Brigade. 6 The Troarn bridge. 7 The Bures bridges. 8 The Robehomme bridge. 9 The Varaville bridge. 10 Drop Zone V. 11 The Merville battery. 12 LZW: 6th Airlanding Brigade.

Glider N°3 on its run in. It made a bumpy landing at 18 minutes past midnight. (Taken from a painting at the Mémorial Pegasus)

Metal cap badge of the' Ox and Bucks' (Oxfordshire and Buckinghamshire Light Infantry).

In England, the men of the 6th Airborne Division were getting ready for the big jump. The Royal Air Force had set aside 423 aircraft for the operation. On the evening of 5 June, Air Chief Marshal Sir Trafford Leigh-Mallory, commander of all the aerial forces for Operation Overlord, had visited each of the airfields from which the British and American paras would depart. All of the men had been well-trained, but many of them had not been in action before. At fifty minutes before midnight, Squadron Leader Merick took off from Harwell with the first of the six Albemarles carrying paras of the 22nd Independant Parachute Company, who were tasked with marking out the drop zones. He took with him Air Vice Marshal Hollinghurst. The moon was bright and there was a clear sky.

Pegagus Bridge

One of the first men to board the gliders was Major John Howard, commanding the 'coup de main

party' of the 2nd Ox and Bucks (Oxford and Buckinghamshire Light Infantry) for the attack due to take place around midnight. He had been tasked with taking the Bénouville and Ranville bridges, the control of which would allow the linking up of the Sword Beach and airborne bridgeheads. This was a vitally important operation, the success of which lay in the precision with which the glider pilots would land close to the objectives. Six gliders were used; three for Landing Zone X near the Bénouville lifting bridge and three for Landing Zone Y near the Ranville swing bridge. Thus, Major Howard and his men would now climb into their gliders. Glider N°1 was flown by Jim Wallwork and carried the Major and Lieutenant Brotheridge; another man, Corporal Wally Parr, had written the name of his wife on the glider, Lady Irene. Lieutenant Brotheridge had to cross the bridge to reach the western side with N°1 Platoon. In glider N°2, Lieutenant Wood (N°2 Platoon) was tasked with wiping out the defences on the east bank. In gli-

The lifting bridge at Bénouville seen from the west bank of the canal. This is a pre-war photo. (Archives du Calvados)

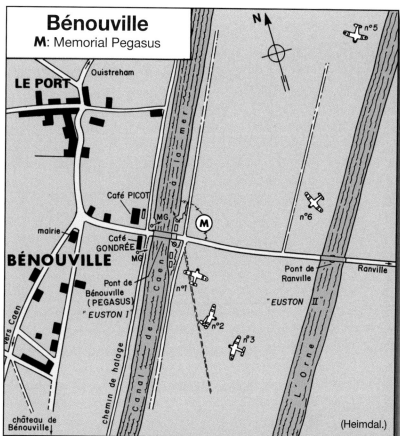

Bénouville

M: Memorial Pegasus

(Heimdal.)

Above: This aerial photo allows us to see clearly gliders N°1, 2 and 3, as well as the German trenches in front of the entrance to the bridge. (R.A.F.)

Below: In this extract from a painting, we can see that glider N°1 landed very close to the bridge. We can see the Gondrée café on the other side of the canal. (Memorial Pegasus)

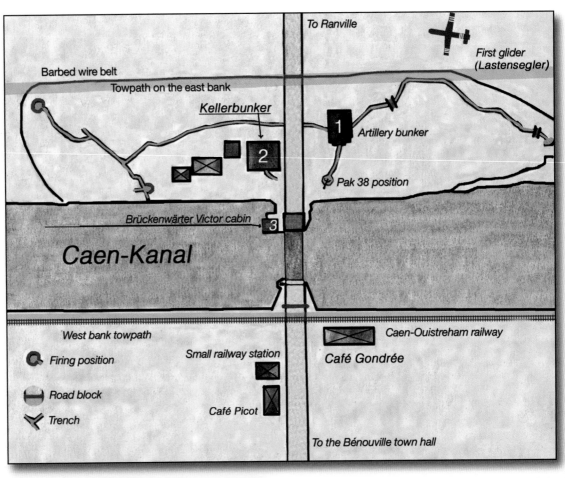

Map of Wn 13, defending the lifting bridge at Bénouville, the future Pegasus Bridge, showing the positions as remembered by Obergrenadier Römer. (E.G./P. Cherrier/Heimdal.)

To Ranville

First glider (Lastensegler)

Barbed wire belt

Towpath on the east bank

Kellerbunker

Artillery bunker

Pak 38 position

Brückenwärter Victor cabin

Caen-Kanal

West bank towpath

Caen-Ouistreham railway

🔘 Firing position

Small railway station

Café Gondrée

Road block

Café Picot

Trench

To the Bénouville town hall

Obergrenadier Helmut Römer was part of the small garrison of the 3.Kompanie of Gren.-Rgt. 736 in position near the bridge at Bénouville and led by a sergeant. His account gives a different version to those seen up to now. There was no German resistance. He was skeptical that Unteroffizier Hickmann could have killed Mr. Picot as he was on the other side of the bridge. As for Dan Brotheridge, he was accidentally shot by one of his comrades as the Germans did not have time to open fire. As for Helmut Römer, he was terrified and hid behind Sambucus bushes with two other comrades, before being taken prisoner... (Coll. H. Römer.)

der N°3, Lieutenant Smith (platoon n°3) had to reinforce N°1 Platoon on the east bank. This was Operation Euston I which landed on Landing Zone X. Euston II was for Landing Zone Y and the Ranville bridge, under the command of Captain Priday (glider N°4) which landed on Landing Zone X, with Lieutenant Fox (N°5) and Lieutenant Sweeney (N°6).

At **10.56 pm**, Wallwork signalled to the pilot of his Halifax tug aircraft that his glider N°1 was ready. He then took off. The five other gliders followed, each one at a minute's interval. They would arrive over the objective in approximately one hour and twenty minutes before the pathfinders who would mark out the drop zones.

Flying glider N°5 was S/Sergeant Stan Pearson who remained in contact with the Halifax pilot, W/O Peter Bain via intercom. The latter asked Pearson, *"Is everything alright back there?"* The Normandy coast was reached shortly after midnight (English time, one o'clock for France). Peter Bain asked, *"Can you see the mouth of the Orne?"* Stan and his co-pilot replied in the affirmative. Bain released the cable as they were flying level over Cabourg. Stan Pearson pulled on the controls of his Horsa and turned to 187 degrees. However, Stan and Len realised that they were too heavy and that their speed was too high. They passed by the orange flashes of a flak battery then, having descended to 4,000 feet, it became obvious that with their heavy load they would not reach the Ranville bridge so they took up a new heading. At 3,000 feet (around 1,000 metres), they spotted flashes on the ground in the canal bridge sector (Euston I); they said to Lieutenant Sweeney that there appeared to be fighting underway near the Bénouville bridge. Gliders N° 1, 2 and 3 were already on the ground and their men in action. Glider N°1 had at last arrived five minutes earlier. This glider, flown by Jim Wallwork, was also heavily loaded. On its approach, Wallwork's stomach tightened, the glider was at high speed with the bridge appearing and the ground rising up to meet it; on the left were trees and to the right a marshy area. The barbed wire belt was right ahead; the nose of the glider was designed to crumple. If the Germans had put poles in the ground then they would pull the wings off, slowing down the Horsa. But it was going too fast, he had to slow it down with the brake parachute, a risky manoeuvre. They were on the ground, the parachute opened, forcing the rear of the glider upwards with the front wheel collapsing. The glider bounced, the three wheels torn off! The impact was hard. A second order was shouted out and the co-pilot, Ainsworth, pressed the parachute release. The glider hit the ground again, on its skids , throwing up a shower of sparks, then its nose crashed into the barbed wire. The violent impact detached the seats and the two pilots were thrown through the perspex windscreen. Other men inside were also thrown out. Major Howard had fainted. On the bridge, the German sentry, Helmut Römer (of the 3./716), heard a crash but thought that it had been caused by a bomber's wing falling to the ground. He did not sound the alert, something which saved the British.

Despite the impact, the landing was a work of art in terms of accuracy. The men came to after eight or ten seconds. They jumped out of the glider. All was quiet. Lieutenant Brotheridge sent three men off to destroy the concrete bunker housing a machine-gun, north-east of the bridge. It was at this time that Glider N°2 arrived, one minute after

the first! S/Sergeant Boland had to manœuvre to avoid the first glider and the fuselage broke in half. The only victim of these landings was a man who drowned in the marshes. The men jumped out and joined those of Major Howard. The latter sent them to clear a trench from where fire was coming from on the other side of the road. Glider N°3 then arrived with its parachute deployed. It bounced and arrived with a great crash on its skids. Lieutenant Sandy was thrown clear and knocked out. The time was **12.18 am**.

In the meantime, on the bridge, the German sentry, seeing Lieutenant Brotheridge and twenty men heading towards him, ran off to the western entrance in order to sound the alert. Another German took out his pistol and was killed by a Sten bullet fired by Brotheridge; the first German to die. At the same time, the three men who had been sent to knock out the concrete bunker threw in their grenades, causing loud explosions. With their mission accomplished, the three men took up position near the Gondrée café whilst engineers began cutting the wires of the detonation charges for blowing the bridge, but this was an unnecessary precaution as the demolition charges had not been installed. The first gunshots alerted the Germans and, at the same time as Lieutenant Brotheridge appeared at the end of the bridge, he was hit in the neck by a bullet. But the bullet did not come from the right direction. Brotheridge had time to

Cap badge of the Parachute Regiment. (Coll. N. Bucourt.)

In fact,the accuracy of the landings of the three gliders was helped by a Eureka beacon placed in the Bénouville château by the Resistance...

Paras seen here climbing on board an Albermarle, a transformed bomber on which roughly painted 'invasion stripes' have been added. This aircraft could carry a stick of ten paras and their equipment. These men were part of the first wave, dropped over Normandy at 12.20 am. The Albermarle planes, used for this very first drop, carried men of the 22nd Independent Parachute Company and those of the Advance Parties.

The paras seen here are on a Stirling aircraft heading for Normandy. As Major-General Gale said Go to it!

Terrence Otway of the 9th Battalion, tasked with taking the Merville battery.

throw a grenade into the defensive position. The other position was cleared by Corporal Billy Gray. Opposite him, a German NCO, sergeant Hickmann, fired back, emptying his MP 40 magazines, but the young soldiers with him, lacking experience and softened by life in Normandy, were frozen with fear by this attack that came out of the night, and did not support him. The German NCO had to pull back with his four soldiers. The firing continued against other soldiers in the area. The shooting even affected the civilians. Louis Picot took the risk of standing outside his café and when he saw the British on the east bank, cried out Vive les Anglais! This expression of welcome was cut short by a burst of fire from a nearby German soldier. Lieutenant Sandy Smith had also reached the end of the bridge and he killed a German who was about to throw a grenade. Spotting Georges Gondrée climbing up out of the cellar of his café, where he had taken shelter with his family, Smith fired a burst towards the outline which appeared behind the window. Georges was not hit and he went back to the cellar. At **12.21 am**, the three platoons of Major Howard had cleared Bénouville, the German defenders were either dead or had run away. The survivors who were still hiding in the little bunkers did not stand a chance; no prisoners would be taken, satchel charges and phosphorous grenades mopped up the last positions. The wounded Lieutenant Brotheridge would die shortly afterwards and Lieutenant David Wood was wounded by a burst fired by an isolated soldier. At **12.22 am**, Major Howard controlled the entire position and set up his HQ in a trench at the north-west angle of the bridge. In the Euston II sector, glider N°6 (Lieutenant Fox, flown by S/Sergeant Roy Howard) had made a text book landing near the Ranville bridge. Glider N°5 (Lieutenant Sweeney) landed a little further north. As for glider N°4, bringing in Captain Brian Priday, it ended up 13 kilometres away, where the pilot had found two bridges, but at Périers-en-Auge! The Ranville bridge was captured quickly and the good news was immediately sent to Major Howard. Thus, the coup de main party had been a fabulous success. Corporal Tappenden, Major Howard s radioman, could now send into the night the message that signalled Ham and Jam announcing the success of the operation.

The Pathfinders arrive

As Major Howard, still alone with his men, established himself on the captured position, the Pathfinders arrived to mark out the drop zones. Six Albermarle planes dropped 60 paras of the 22nd Independent Parachute Brigade over three zones (N,V, K) which had to be marked out. Only those dropped at 12.20 am by two aircraft at Zone N (Ranville) carried out their mission to the full. They marked out Drop Zone N with their Eureka radio beacons, the signals of which would be picked up by the Rebecca receivers of the planes in the second wave. The Pathfinders planned for Zone K (Touffréville) jumped too short from one of the planes, meaning that 13 sticks were dropped on **Zone N**, those of the second plane arrived correctly to mark out **Zone K** planned for the 3rd Brigade. For **Zone V** (between Varaville and Merville), planned for Lieutenant-Colonel Otway and his men, the drop was not bad but the containers and equipment were lost in the marshes. The leading elements of the 3rd and 5th Brigades (200 men), who arrived with the Pathfinders (60 men), reinforced Major Howard s 140 men in this airborne bridgehead.

The paras arrive

It was **12.45am** when the sky was filled again with throbbing engines. The second wave had left England with 110 Stirling and Albermarle aircraft and six Horsa gliders of 38 Group. There were also 146 C-47 planes and six gliders of 46 Group. 5,000 paras were on their way.

The good job done by the Pathfinders in marking out Drop Zone N brought Brigadier Nigel Poett's 5th Brigade to its objective. Over the space of twenty minutes, 123 planes dropped 2,026 men and 702 containers on DZ N. Brigadier Poett, dropped with the leading elements, at the same time as the Pathfinders, had reached the bridge over the Orne approximately half an hour after hitting the ground after having experienced some difficulty in finding his bearings in the middle of the night. He was then informed by Lieutenant Sweeney of the fantastic success of the coup de main party. At that time, the sky began to fill with the throbbing sound of dozens of approaching aircraft. At **12.50 am**, the 5th Brigade paras jumped over Ranville at DZ N. However, the German garrison in the sector was now on the alert and soon, with the drops, mortar and machine-gun fire began to be directed towards the drop zone. Two Stirlings were hit by flak and crashed with the men they were carrying, but thirty-one aircraft had dropped their paras. Their rallying was not easy. Major Taylor, commanding A Company, 7th Battalion, and whose rallying call was 'Double Nigel, double!' (he had the same first name as Brigadier Poett), had to reach the Orne bridge where he was to meet up with the Brigadier. He went into a small farm house and later said: *"You know how it is when you ask your way in the countryside, you always come across the village idiot. I did not come across the village idiot, but I found the most elderly inhabitants. They were, of course, frightened and I had to convince them that we were not Germans on exercise. They at last realised who we were, their shyness disappeared and they were very happy to see us. They had no idea."* (2)

Lieutenant-Colonel Pine Coffin, commanding the 7th Battalion, was also having difficulty in finding his way: It was a most desperate feeling to know that one was so close to it (the DZ), but not knowing in which direction it lay.... it was impossible to pick a landmark though until a chance flare, dropped by one of the aircraft, illuminated the church at Ranville... Private Chambers blew the regimental call with his bugle, a small horn, in order to rally the men of his battalion! At 2.15 am, the Lieutenant-Colonel only had 40% of his battalion's men with him and a few containers. However, Major Howard's whistle sounded through the night from the other side of the Orne. Lieutenant-Colonel Pine Coffin was reassured, he knew now that the coup de main party had succeeded. He made his way with his men to the Major. Shortly before **3 am**, the 7th Battalion paras crossed the two

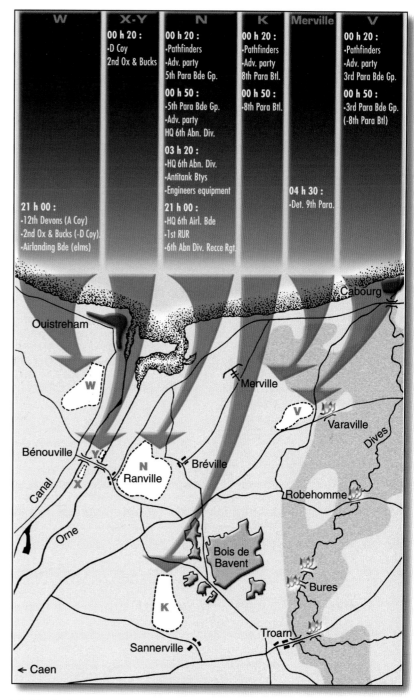

W	X·Y	N	K	Merville	V
	00 h 20 : -D Coy 2nd Ox & Bucks	**00 h 20 :** -Pathfinders -Adv. party 5th Para Bde Gp.	**00 h 20 :** -Pathfinders -Adv. party 8th Para Btl.		**00 h 20 :** -Pathfinders -Adv. party 3rd Para Bde Gp.
		00 h 50 : -5th Para Bde Gp. -Adv. party HQ 6th Abn. Div.	**00 h 50 :** -8th Para Btl.		**00 h 50 :** -3rd Para Bde Gp. (-8th Para Btl)
		03 h 20 : -HQ 6th Abn. Div. -Antitank Btys -Engineers equipment		**04 h 30 :** -Det. 9th Para.	
21 h 00 : -12th Devons (A Coy) -2nd Ox & Bucks (-D Coy). -Airlanding Bde (elms)		**21 h 00 :** -HQ 6th Airl. Bde -1st RUR -6th Abn Div. Recce Rgt.			

Major General Richard Gale.

Brigadier Nigel Poett 5th Brigade

Lieutenant-colonel Pine Coffin 7th Battalion

bridges and took up defensive positions on the west bank, prepared by the Ox and Bucks, but also on the east bank where the paras and Major Howard's men still only numbered 270 to secure the bridgehead.

(2) An account from *Ready for anything*, Page 155.

(3) In *Red Berets*, Page 161.

Brigadier James Hill,
3rd Parachute Brigade.

At the southern part of the bridgehead, another 5th Brigade battalion, the **12th**, led by Lieutenant-Colonel Johnson, was tasked with taking and holding Bas de Ranville. Dropped at 12.50 am, the men were scattered and some only reached their units several days later! One hour after the jump, only 60% of the men had been assembled but Bas de Ranville was taken without any difficulty. Among these paras was Lance Corporal Frank Gleeson of C Company, who had made a problem-free jump (probably at the site of today's camp site near Mariquet). *"I was looking towards the north to find my bearings, I was alone. Suddenly, out of the night, I found myself in front of a big horse. He then joined up with his C Company and went with them to their position south of Bas de Ranville. An old man was watching from behind a first floor window of his house. Then, upon arriving south of the hamlet: We stopped and dug our foxholes. Two hours later, an officer turned up: according to him, our positions were not in the right place. He made us move forward two hundred metres. It was daylight and the Germans were watching out for the slightest sound or movement. It was difficult to dig new positions in these conditions."* (4)

Led by Lieutenant-Colonel Peter Luard, the **13th Battalion** was also very scattered. They were tasked with holding Ranville and covering the approaches to the bridges from the south-east and between the Orne and the Bois de Bavent. The recognition signal was a hunting horn and, by **1.30 am**, only 60% of the men set out to undertake their mission. The paras were also tasked with removing the 'Rommel's asparagus' in order to clear the terrain for the supply gliders due to arrive at 3.35 am.

As for Brigadier James Hill's **3rd Brigade**, it was tasked with tough missions; the taking of the bridges over the Dives at Varaville, Robehomme, Bures and Troarn, and the blowing up of five bridges in order to protect the east of the airborne bridgehead from German counter-attacks. The low-lying and partly marshy Dives valley, to the east of the 6th Airborne Division sector, had been flooded by the Germans by opening up a system of locks. However, this flooded zone was crossed by roads that could allow the Germans to bring up reinforcements from the 711th division. The Brigade was also tasked with destroying the German battery at Merville.

To the south, engineers of the 3rd Para Squadron, led by Major J. Rosevaere (Royal Engineers), sped through **Troarn** under German fire, in a jeep towing a trailer filled with explosives. They reached the bridge and blew it up five minutes later. In the centre, Lieutenant-Colonel Pearson (8th Battalion) led 120 paras and engineers through Bavent in order to reach the **Bures** road bridge and rail bridge.

Captain Jukes led the assault group towards these two objectives at **6.30 am** and blew up both bridges. To the north, the engineers of the 3rd Platoon, 3rd Para Squadron of the 1st Canadian Parachute Battalion, destroyed the **Robehomme** and **Varaville** bridges, a mission which was carried out with few losses. All of the elements engaged then withdrew to the Bavent defensive sector. At 12.20 am, the 9th Parachute Battalion of Lieutenant-Colonel Terence Otway, was dropped in the DZ V sector near the Merville battery. However, here

too the drop was very scattered. At 2.50 am, only 150 out of the 600 paras dropped, rallied the rendezvous at Varaville and Otway only arrived at 3 in the morning. The battery had four 100 mm guns which could threaten Sword Beach; the British intelligence services believed that the guns were of the even bigger 150 mm calibre. Fierce fighting broke out when the paras reached the battery, with German artillery men and a reinforcement company of IR 736. The paras lost 5 officers and 65 other ranks killed or wounded. Otway and his men withdrew to Plein at **6 am**, the mission having failed. (see the book: Helmut von Keusgen, *Pegasus Bridge-Merville Batterie*)

By **3 in the morning**, Major-General Richard Gale was in command at his headquarters in Ranville, in the midst of the 5th Brigade paras. He now waited to be joined in the bridgehead by Lord Lovat's commandos!

Despite the counter-attacks launched at the very beginning of the morning and the failure at the Merville battery, the establishment of a British airborne bridgehead had been a success, solidly assuring the eastern part of the allied sector east of the Orne.

(4) As recounted by F. Gleeson to the author.

Opposite: Alarm! An officer from Kampfgruppe Luck will send his men to counter-attack the paras. (BA)

Opposite: As soon as the first para drops were made, Major Hans von Luck (seen here on the left with the binoculars), commanding Panzergrenadier-Regiment 25, then Kampfgruppe Luck, intervened immediately in order to place his units on the alert and sending them to counter-attack, to the east of the Orne, against the airborne bridgehead. He is seen here with his adjutant (right), lieutenant Helmut Liebeskind. (BA)

Below: The Germans begin rounding up their first British para prisoners. (Heimdal Collection)

Above: Para POWs are taken away in a truck. (Heimdal Collection)

Below: A rare colour photo of a Horsa glider taken by a German war correspondent. (Heimdal Collection)

4

Utah, or "Hutte à biches"

In long lines, ships of all types head towards the coast along designated channels, thanks to a remarkable and highly complex organisation. The barrage balloons protect the fleet from any eventual German air attack. (US Navy)

As the gliders brought in the supplies to the paras advancing in the maze-like bocage of the Cotentin, a small force was preparing itself to take the only obstacle situated in front of Utah Beach: The **Saint-Marcouf islands**. This tiny archipelago was made of two main islands. The western island was a sort of large rocky outcrop populated by sea birds. On the eastern island, a large fortress rose up, equipped with an access port, which dated back to Napoleon who had never used it. The Americans believed that this archipelago could be sheltering a German garrison, or at least a storeroom for setting off, from a distance, minefields. Elements of the 2nd and 4th Cavalry Squadrons, led by Lieutenant-Colonel E.C. Dunn, comprising of a total of one hundred and thirty men, had the mission of taking these islands. At **4.30 am**, two hours before H Hour, four men, only armed with daggers, swam up to the creeks planned for the landing, but discovered that these two islands had been abandoned by the Germans. The main force landed an hour later and suffered losses due to mines; with a total of 19 men by the end of D Day.

At **5.45 am** (H-45), a quarter of an hour after this first conquest, the landing fleet, Force U for Utah Beach, approached the coast under the command of Rear-Admiral Moon on board USS Bayfield, which had left Plymouth twenty hours before H Hour. He had at his disposal a considerable naval force with the imposing firepower of Task Force 125. Thus, the USS Nevada opened fire on the battery at Azeville (2./1261), the USS Erebus on

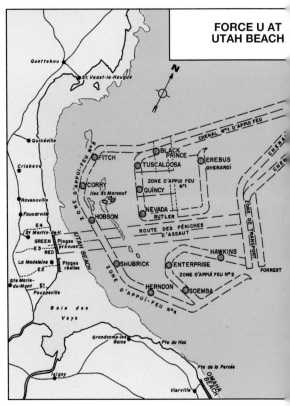

Map showing the approach channels and fire-support zones opposite Utah Beach (Map by B.Paich/Heimdal)

The landing craft each carried 36 infantrymen. They headed towards the beach as part of Force U for Utah Beach. (NA/Heimdal)

the two batteries at La Pernelle (9./1261 and 10./1261), the USS Tuscaloosa and USS Quincy on those at Mont Coquerel (4./1261) and Crisbecq (3./1261), HMS Hawkins on that of Saint-Martin-de-Vareville (1./1261 already wiped out by air attacks), HMS Black Prince on that of Morsalines (6./1261) and HMS Enterprise on the Utah Beach landing zone. The Dutch gunship Soemba would attack more particularly the beach defence positions. The support force also had eight destroyers, USS Forest, Hobson, Shubrick, Cory, Herndson, Fitch, Butler and Gherardi) and two rocket-launcher LCT which would crush the coastal positions (1).

The hell that came from the sea crushed the artillery batteries and coastal positions, especially as, a few minutes later, 276 B-26 Marauder bombers of the 9th US Air Force, dropped 4,404 tonnes of bombs on seven objectives between the beach at Beauguillot (W3), to the south, and the dunes of Vareville (W10) to the north. The effects on the ground were devastating. Thus, at Pouppeville, lieutenant Rohweder, in command of the 2nd company of GR 919, the 2./919, observed in the early daylight the allied ships heading towards two coastal resistance nests; W2a and W3. It was then that the bombers arrived in several waves 'covering the sky' and dropped their bombs on W3, W4, W5 and W7. Leutnant Ritter, commanding W3, managed to get in touch with lieutenant Rohweder to inform him that he only had left one NCO and a private, with just a light machine-gun, sub machine-gun and a 98k rifle! & This position was virtually wiped out but Rohweder ordered him to hold on and promised to help him (2).

At **W5**, which would face the landing, the situation was just as dramatic as that of second-lieutenant Ritter. There, Leutnant Artur Jahnke was opposite the allied fleet in a totally torn up position. As Paul Carell states (3): *"Everything that they had patiently taken months to create was upturned as if it was a toy following the passage of a hurricane. The 7,5 anti-tank gun was just a pile of*

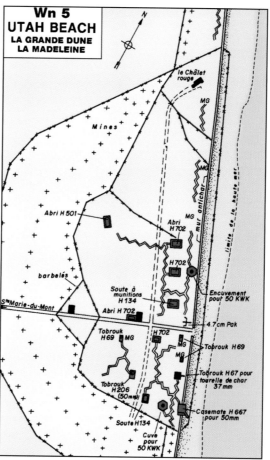

Wn 5
UTAH BEACH
LA GRANDE DUNE
LA MADELEINE

W5 (or Wn5) was a 'resistance nest' cut off from the others to the north and south. There was not a continuous strip of coastline. (BP/Heimdal)

(1) note that USS designates a US Navy ship and HMS one of the Royal Navy. The USS Nevada had ten 14-inch guns (355 mm) and sixteen 6-inch guns (152 mm), the USS Tuscaloosa and USS Quincy had nine 8-inch guns (203 mm) and eight 5-inch gins (127 mm) I HMS Hawkins had seven 7.5-inch guns (190 mm), HMS Enterprise six 6-inch guns (152 mm), HMS Black Prince eight 5.25-inch guns (133 mm) and the Soemba, three 150 mm guns.

(2) All of this information comes from a report made by lieutenant-colonel Keil when he was in captivity.

Leutnant Arthur Jahnke commander of W5. This photo was taken on 20 May 1944. Two weeks later, he and his men would be plunged into hell. (ECPAD)

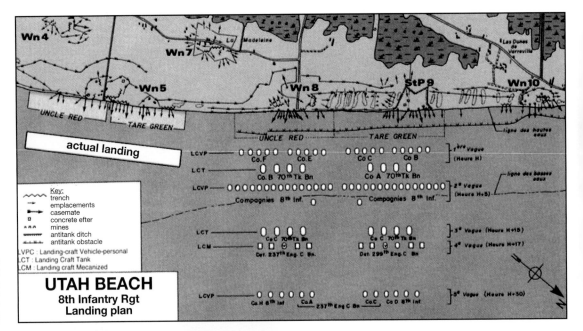

actual landing

Key:
- ∿∿∿ trench
- → emplacements
- ►■ casemate
- □ concrete efter
- ʌʌʌ mines
- ⌐⌐⌐ antitank ditch
- ⊢⊢⊢ antitank obstacle

LVPC : Landing-craft Vehicle-personal
LCT : Landing Craft Tank
LCM : Landing craft Mecanized

UTAH BEACH
8th Infantry Rgt
Landing plan

metal. *The 88 gun was also hit. Two ammunition bunkers had blown up; all of the shooting positions were flattened.* Luckily, the loss of men was light because the attack had surprised the gunners in their shelters and these had stood up to direct hits. However, lieutenant-colonel Keil, commanding Grenadier-Regiment 919 had no contact with his companies and strong points, including the position held by second-lieutenant Jahnke. The French postal services resistance group had cut all the phone lines and all communications were interrupted. *After this bombardment, Jahnke saw a fleet heading toward his position.*" Indeed, although the landing force was supposed to land further north, opposite W8 and StP 9, the current had pushed it 1,800 metres south of its objective. An 'alternative tide' had pushed the amphibious force landing craft towards the south during the rising tide, the current being much stronger and a lot less longer than the falling tide. However, this navigational error paid dividends as this southern sector was less exposed to firing from the Azeville and Crisbecq batteries which were thus at the limit of their range.

Then, from **6.20 to 6.30 am**, the P-47 Thunderbolt fighter-bombers attacked the coastal positions with rockets in order to finish off the job of knocking them out. Let us go back to Leutnant Jahnke caught up in the middle of this hell: *"These planes only attacked the two corner bunkers housing the two 5 cm anti-tank guns. The rockets smashed against the bunkers, exploding against the slits and sight windows."* (4)

Offshore, the assault waves of the 8th R.C.T. (5) of the **4th Infantry Division**, began moving in. This division was commanded by Major-General Barton, with Brigadier-General 'Teddy' Roosevelt as his deputy commander. Twenty LCVP landing craft brought in four 8th Regiment companies opposite this almost annihilated position. Here, the coast was flat, unlike the high coast line at Omaha Beach. These four companies made up the first wave, supported by two DD amphibious tank companies of the 70th Tank Battalion, brought in by LCT, with B Company on the left and A Company on the right.

The beach was in sight, it was low-lying and had few landmarks; the confusion caused by drifting could have resulted in chaos. In fact, three guide boats were supposed to each mark two beach sectors, Uncle Red to the left (to the south) and Tare Green right (to the north). But PC 1261 had

The 4th Division had been considerably reinforced for the landings with the support of other units, including the tanks of the 70th Tank Batalion (with the first wave), the tank destroyers of the 801st TD Battalion (SP) (from 9 to 13 June), the artillery batteries of the 13th FA Obsn Bn, Battery B of the 980th FA Bn (155 mm guns), Battery B of the 65th Armored Field Artillery Battalion, the 915th FA Bn (105 mm guns a unit detached from the 90th Division all of its artillery units were attached to the 4th Division from 6 to 8 June). (DAVA/Heimdal)

sunk early morning and LCC-80 had not been able to make the crossing due to a stuck propeller. These ships were destined for Uncle Red, therefore there were not any patrol craft for this beach sector. On the other hand, LCC-60, with navy officers Sims Gauthier and Howard von der Beek, was able to accurately mark out the other objective thanks to its radar (6). However, due to a heavy swell, the amphibious DD tanks could not be put to sea as planned and the LCTs bringing them in were late and in disorder as they approached the coastline. More than the drifting caused by the currents, it would appear that the presence of the LCTs was the origin of the chaos which pushed the landings further south. This incident held up the first waves.

Thus, at around **6.40am**, ten LCVP, brought in E and F Companies of the 8th Infantry Regiment at the Uncle Red beach sector, south of W5 which had been crushed by the bombardments. At approximately 300 metres from the beach, the commanders of these leading companies fired special smoke projectiles to signal the fleet to lengthen the range of its guns. Brigadier-General Theodore Roosevelt landed with this first wave. Ten minutes later, B and C Companies (1/8) also landed on the right flank of the Tare Green beach sector, opposite W5. They were rapidly followed

by the DD tanks of A and B Companies of the 70th Tank Battalion. Corporal Friedrich was in a Renault tank turret armed with a machine-gun, placed on a concrete bunker, he cut down the landing Engineers with his heavy machine-gun, but the turret received a direct hit from a tank and Friedrich was wounded.

Finally, W5 was taken by this unstoppable assault and the wounded Jahnke was captured. Roosevelt then quickly organised an inland reconnaissance. He spotted the roadway to use for heading inland, this was Exit 2 leading to Sainte-Marie-du-Mont instead of Exit 3 to Audouville-la-Hubert and Turqueville. Teddy Roosevelt then returned to the beach and held a meeting with the leaders of the 1st Battalion (Lieutenant-Colonel Conrad C. Simmons) and 2nd Battalion (Lieutenant-Colonel Carlton O. MacNeely) of the 8th Infantry Regiment, concerning the decision to continue landing on this beach sector which was not part of the plan. Given the first good results

(3) In *Ils arrivent*, Robert Laffont, 1961, pp. 73 and 74.

(4) *Op. cit.*, p.75.

(5) Tactical combat group made up from the 8th Infantry Regiment.

(6) The accounts of these two officers on board LCC-80 were told to Jonathan Gawne in *Jour-J à l'aube*, Histoire et Collections, 1998, p.151.

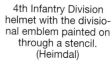

4th Infantry Division helmet with the divisional emblem painted on through a stencil. (Heimdal)

This photo taken in the dunes at Utah Beach shows a meeting of the 4th Division commanders: Brigadier-General Roosevelt, without his helmet (as Sergeant Liska saw him) and Major-General Barton. Brig.Gen. Roosevelt had landed with E Company in the first wave. (Heimdal)

Medics landing and treating wounded on the beach. Out of the 197 losses, the 4th Division only counted 12 killed within the 8th and 22nd Infantry Regiments. (NA/Heimdal)

This photo shows us one of the consequences of the bombardments. A German soldier has been 'buried' in the sand from a dune from which he is trying to extract himself with great difficulty. (DAVA/Heimdal)

and the more favourable situation, the decision was taken to continue. He is believed to have said: *"Our war starts here!"*

The second wave, planned to arrive five minutes later at H+05, and the third at H+15, then came in. Gaps inland had to be made in order to bring in reinforcements; this was the work of the Gap Teams. Thus, at **8 am**, more than 600 metres of beach was free and all of Colonel Van Fleet's 8th Infantry Regiment had arrived. It was even joined, at 7.45 am, by the 3rd Battalion of the 22nd Infantry Regiment, with the rest of the latter arriving at 10 o'clock. By then, Colonel Van Fleet's regiment

had begun moving inland. Its first battalion, the 1/8, advanced on the right towards La Madelaine and W7 on the Exit 3 road leading to Audouville-la-Hubert, with the other battalions advancing in different directions. The third (3/8) advanced straight ahead to Exit 2 and La Vienville where it came under fire from two anti-tank guns, then four 76,2 mm guns of the13./919 led by Oberleutnant Schön, but the Germans withdrew after blowing the bridges. As for the 2nd Battalion, it marched southwards as far as W2a and turned west along the short road leading to Exit 1, then Pouppeville which was reached at midday. In the meantime,

through Exit 1 and Pouppeville, the 2/8 linked up with the paratroopers of the 3/501 (Taylor) and the Ewell column, then made its way to Sainte-Marie-du-Mont. In the centre, after having lost two DD tanks and having got through the obstacle of the artillery guns at Vienville, that they knocked out, the 3/8 linked up with the paras of the 2/506 led by Lieutenant-Colonel Strayer and, strengthened by elements of the 70th Tank Battalion, went to Les Forges. In the evening, these two battalions were holding positions at the important crossroads at Les Forges on the RN13 road, leading towards Sainte-Mère-Eglise in the north, Carentan to the south, and towards Sainte-Marie-du-Mont in the east.

At **12.05pm**, the German artillery to the east of the Baie des Veys (352.ID sector) intervened by opening fire on Utah Beach with the field artillery guns of I./AR 352. However, despite this harassing fire, the advance inland of the troops who had landed was inexorable. Further north, the 1/8, the 1st Battalion of the 8th Inf. Regt., strengthened by A Company of the 70th Tank Battalion, went through Exit 3, already held by the Lieutenant-Colonel Cole's paratroopers (3/502). This battalion, supported by tanks, then advanced beyond Audouville-la-Hubert

Sergeant Ted Liska in Normandy, 1944. (Coll. G.B.)

the landings continued. After the 22nd Infantry Regiment, which was complete at 10 am, the third regiment, the 12th, came ashore at midday. Sergeant **Ted Liska**, who was with D Company of the 12th Infantry Regiment, had landed at 10.30 am. The ramp was lowered and the men waded through the water towards the shore. The water was deep in places and, despite being 1m85 tall, it rose to Sergeant Liska's waist. The beach was strewn with all sorts of debris and the men then had to go between the white lines marking the sector. Further on, Ted Liska spotted Brigadier-General Roosevelt, without a helmet walking with a stick and with the bottom of his trousers out of his boots. The flooded zone then had to be crossed by walking through water again. The link up with paras was then made. Thus, after going

As infantrymen climb up the dunes and head inland, others wait, protected by the anti-tank wall before also receiving the order to move off. The wall is still there. (NA and E.G./Heimdal.)

Units continue to form up at the foot of the anti-tank wall. This was not an unnecessary precaution as the German batteries of Azeville and Saint-Marcouf/Crisbecq were harassing the troops that were landing. We can see here the explosion of a shell. (DAVA/Coll. Heimdal.)

This map shows us the crossing points across the flooded zones used by the three battalions of the 8th Infantry Regiment. Note Exit 2 with the destroyed bridge and the anti-tank gun battery at Vienville. (Heimdal)

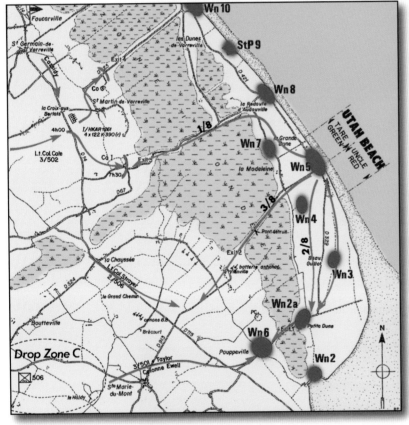

and by the day's end, found itself stuck in front of Turqueville, the locality and surrounding area of which was solidly held by captain Stiller's 795th Georgian battalion.

Let us now go back to **Bernardin Birette** (see chapter 2), in the family farm at **Audouville-la-**

Brigadier-General Theodore Roosevelt Jr., was the son of President Theodore t Roosevelt. He was the deputy commander of the 4th Infantry Division on 6 June 1944. He was serving with this division when he died of a heart attack on 12 July 1944. He is buried in the American cemetery at Colleville. (Coll. Heimdal.)

Hubert. A huge bombardment had shaken the countryside an hour and a half after his return to the farm, with more than 850 bombs falling on the village, killing three civilians and more than one hundred animals... The Vierge crossroads and the Birette family farm were spared. A soldier in German uniform, who was under arrest and held in a farm outhouse, was driven mad with terror and broke down the door. He took shelter in the trench next to Bernardin, the latter's parents and Monsieur Lefrançois. They spent part of the night in this shelter. Bernardin Birette could not help but marvel at the multitude of flares and tracer rounds of all sorts criss-crossing the darkened sky. Then, once the bombardment was over, shadows were seen in the sky. Suddenly, rifles were pointing at the people in the trench; Monsieur Lefrançois realised that they were not Germans and explained to the American paras the reason why the unarmed Georgian was with them. The paras then grabbed the prisoner and moved off we now know that the American paras shot their prisoners during this decisive night (7). Dawn then broke. In order to find a safer place, Bernardin and his mother headed towards the enclosure opposite where they thought they would be better protected from unexpected visitors. They then ran to take shelter in the ditch of the hedgerow overlooking the enclosure. *Wer da!* The order froze them to the spot. Eleven German rifles were pointing at the ditch where they had run to. The faces of the soldiers were full of tension. An NCO came over, it was the adjutant who was billeted at the Birette's house. He immediately recognised Madame Birette and calmed his men down, explaining that this was the owner of the 'Kassel', the name he used for the farm. Madame Birette was Belgian and had, therefore, been a refugee during the First World War; she had retained a good level of Flemish and this helped with the forced cohabitation with her German 'hosts'. Seeing that this was not a safe situation to be in, Bernardin Birette and his mother went back to the farm shortly before 6am. In the farm, the outlines of twelve American paratroopers surrounded Bernardin's father. German and Georgian prisoners, some of whom were wounded, were being guarded in the ditch opposite the farm. Things were quiet and the paras controlled the crossroads. Monsieur Birette noticed that the kitchen window of the house had been broken (he had locked up the house before the night's events). As he approached the window he saw bloodstains. Two wary Americans made him open the house then, making Bernardin go in first, cautiously went in. The bloodstains went up the stairs. With a sub machine-gun resting on his shoulder, the young Birette climbed up the stairs, closely followed by the two Americans. Entering the bedroom, they saw two heavily bleeding Georgians laying between the beds with the two Mausers next to them. One of the men had a torn thigh and could not stand up. The other, with a stomach wound, got up signalling that he surrendered. Then, curiously after having opened his shirt, used his pocket knife to undo a false lining in his shirt, taking out a photo that he held out in front of him. The photo showed a Soviet soldier, wearing a side cap bearing the red star. The paras looked quickly at the photo in disbelief, then hastened the two men downstairs to join the other prisoners. Held up by Monsieur Lefrançois, the Georgian with the shredded leg made his way down the stairs in great pain.

This famous photo, taken at Turqueville on 6 June, shows 101st Airborne Division paratrooper, Wilbur Shanklin of the 506th PIR HQ Company. He is armed with a M1 rifle with affixed bayonet and is equipped with a machete and American and German grenades. A cricket is held by a piece of knotted string from his left shoulder strap. His name, Shanklin, is marked on his M3 knife sheaf. We can also see, on his right shoulder strap, a gas detector armband and the lanyard of the Colt .45. He also carries a German water bottle on his chest. This is one well-equipped para! The surrendering 'German' soldier is in fact Georgian. The photo is from Turqueville which the Georgians of Ost-Bataillon 795 fiercely defended until 7 June. He does not have much equipment: a salvaged belt and an old, patched-up pair of drill trousers. (US Army.)

At around **11 am**, a group of American soldiers from the beach arrived at the farm. One of the them, an interpreter, asked Bernardin Birette to lead them to the German HQ situated in the village of Brocq near Turqueville. The group marched off, but a short while before, the American attached a badge above Bernardin's left breast pocket, telling him that it would prevent him being mistaken for a franc tireur if he was caught by the Germans. The group advanced along a small hedgerow-lined road. The sun was already hot. At the front were two civilians, Maurice Blaizot, Bernardin Birette with the interpreter to his left. Suddenly, as they went around a hedgerow, a grenade exploded near the group. The US soldiers threw themselves to the ground and fired at the ash tree. The two Normans did not move. Luckily, no one was hurt. At the foot of the tree lay a German with six grenades hanging from his belt; he was finished off with the bayonet. Upon arriving at the house used by the local German headquarters, they

(7) Various published accounts by American paratroopers and also in Mark Bando's *Histoire secrète de la 101e Airborne*, Editions Heimdal.

Above: The Vierge (Virgin) crossroads and the Herguerie farm (in the background) at Audouville-la-Hubert. Both were spared any damage by the bombardment during the night of 6 June. (E.G./Heimdal.)

Opposite: The Herguerie farm where the Birette family lived on 6 June 1944. The Georgian prisoners and their German leaders were liquidated by the paras behind the farm at around 3 pm. (E.G./Heimdal.)

found it empty. A few US soldiers entered and crashed about looking for documents. Some appeared at the windows wearing abandoned German caps and goofing around, pretending to be the previous owners to their comrades outside.

Shortly before the group returned to the Birette farm, an American photographer asked them to pose for the American press. Weston Haynes had landed that morning at Utah Beach. He had already photographed the group as they moved off earlier. However, this time he set up his tripod and asked the two civilians to pose alongside the interpreter. Getting into the right pose seemed to take for ever; indeed, they were visible from the high ground of Turqueville where Germans and Georgians were firing in their direction, with the bullets buzzing past their ears. Weston Haynes played around with his tripod and asked Maurice Blaizot to point out where the Germans were; he also asked Bernardin Birette to place his hand on the interpreter's shoulder. Hayes then set up a new pose. Bernardin, by now fed up, said to his friend: *"This is completely mad, he is going to get us killed for a picture!"* The photo was then at last taken.

1. Weston Hayes followed the advance of the seaborne troops. He then took this photo where we can see a group of American soldiers accompanied by two Norman civilians: Maurice Blaizot (in front with the cap) his house had been bombed and he had made his way to the Birette family) who led the GI's to Le Brocq late morning, and Bernardin Birette (in the centre with a beret). This photo was published in a small American propaganda booklet for the French with the accompanying caption: *Essential guides, the French allowed us to find the emplacements of ammo dumps and those of enemy snipers; they did all that they could to help us*. (Heimdal Collection)

2. The famous photo taken whilst under German fire in the hamlet of Le Brocq.

3. Bernardin Birette seen here in April 1993. Nothing has changed (Heimdal)

For the return trip, Bernardin suggested, in vain, a different itinerary avoiding the road overlooked by the Germans.

Back at the farm, Bernardin chatted with the US sentry guarding the thirty German and Georgian prisoners he was standing opposite from. The soldier gave him cigarettes, even though he did not smoke. He did not dare turn them down. To be honest, he felt ill at ease, he knew many of the faces of these prisoners and wounded men as they had carried out jobs together. Several were bleeding out and looked back with blank, white faces. But what if the Germans regained the upper hand...?

At around **3 pm**, a tall paratrooper ran in and put an end to this soul searching. After a brief exchange of words with the sentry, the latter took Bernardin Birette by the arm and led him behind the farm wall. They were barely out of sight when a long burst of fire broke the silence. Back on the road, Bernardin Birette discovered the corpses of these prisoners. They would stay there for fifteen days before a special detail turned up and loaded them into a truck. As the corpses were on a road often used by tanks, the dried up bodies looked like planks. The uncertainty of the fighting and lack of men regarding the number of prisoners in this vital sector appears to be the reason for such an act. It was not the only one. Later, at **Ecoquenéauville**, Weston Haynes continued photographing the American advance towards Sainte-Mère-Eglise.

Thus, in this sector, the main VII Corps objectives had been achieved. The landings had been a success with low casualties 197 for the 4th Division. Also, materiel was arriving in large quantities behind the seaborne troops. The link up between the latter and the paratroopers at the beach exits had played an important role in the advance inland. Also in this sector, the 101st Airborne Division had suffered much heavier losses, especially when the reinforcement gliders arrived at the end of the day, with many of them crashing on Landing Zone E (to the west of Hiesville) due to enemy fire and after 8 pm, there were 258 killed and wounded on Hill 30. Also, although the bridgehead was solid between Sainte-Marie-du-Mont and the coast, to the west the American paratroopers were cut of in groups in the middle of the Germans and the Georgians and a link up had not yet been established with the paras of the 82nd Airborne at Sainte-Mère-Eglise. Finally, the German paras of von der Heydte's 6th regiment had launched a counter-attack in the south, coming up against the 501st paras at Basse-Adeville and reaching Vierville.

The war correspondent Weston Haynes who also landed at Utah Beach on 6 June 1944. He took photographs that would go on to become famous. (Coll. Heimdal.)

This map allows us the see the advance of the 4th Infantry Division on D-Day as far as the hamlet of Les Forges on the RN13 road which was reached by the 2/8 supported by tanks of the 70th Tank Battalion. We can also see the sector still held by the Georgian battalion around Fauville and Turqueville. However, Ecoqueneauville was reached by American troops. Note also the position of Audouville-la-Hubert at a crossroads. The link up was made at Sainte-Marie-du-Mont. However, the 505th PIR was still cut off at Sainte-Mère-Eglise.

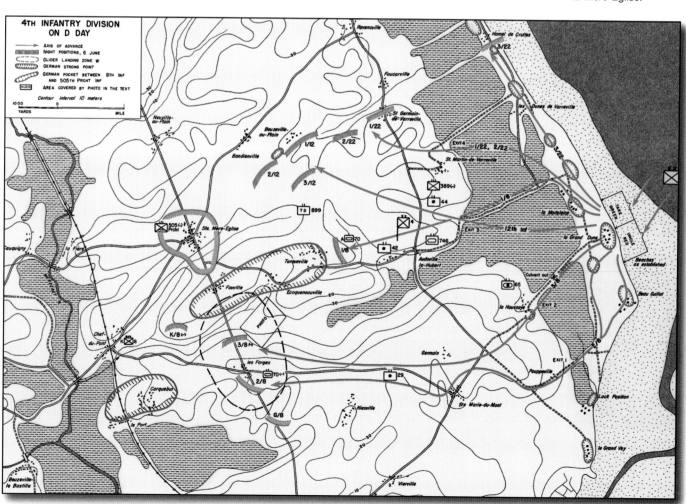

5

Bloody Omaha

This LCVP is landing men of tank N°9 of A Company, 741st Tank Battalion. (NA)

Major Pluskat.

It was 5 am on this 6 June on the high ground overlooking the wide beach which nestled between the cliffs at Colleville to the east, and those of Vierville to the west. The beach was overlooked by fifteen 'resistance nests' -from WN 60 to WN 74, from east to west). The morning had now broken with a light subdued by the clouds and an iron grey sky. The German defenders had been on the alert in this sector since midnight, but this was also the case for some civilians.

Indeed, at midnight, at the farm on the Pissotière track, south of **WN 66**, eleven Reich soldiers of various nationalities were billeted, including a Pole (who spoke good French) and a 'Mongolian'.

Alarm! Albert André, the 16-year old farmer's son was fast asleep and did not hear this word shouted out in the night. The following morning he found out that American paras had been dropped in the sector with a 37 mm gun a drop error or special mission? At midnight, the man on sentry duty in the André family farm sounded gave the alarm. At 12.30 am, four paras had drunk coffee at Gaston Dupont's place (a small house by the Saint-Laurent bend). During this time, eight other paras had taken up positions in the lane running alongside the André family's garden. There, they awaited the eleven 'soldiers of the Reich' as they left to go to their post at WN 66. They were all killed with daggers to avoid any shots giving away

Hans Heinze, not fully awake and feeling grumpy, was at the observation post near Colleville.

Further off, to the south-east, at the hamlet of Houtteville, in the Legrand family house, Oberleutnant **Bernhard Frerking** woke up private **Hein Severloh**: Es geht los! (Here we go!). It had just reached midnight (German time) when Severloh jumped out of his bed. His leader, lieutenant Frerking, commanded an artillery battery, the 1st battery of Artillerie-Regiment 352. This battery was one of the three of the regiment's 1st group. This group was commanded by Major **Werner Pluskat** who was immortalised in the film *'The Longest Day'* on the basis of an account by the latter in which he put himself forward in a way that was somewhat removed from reality. Pluskat had dropped by Houtteville on the evening of 2 June, he had seen lieutenant Frerking along with six other officers, including lieutenant Wilkening (commander of the 3rd battery). Major Pluskat had made a surprising speech on this evening, saying that he was expecting an attack and that his men would then have to pull back as fast as possible. In any case, he was with a woman in Caen on the evening of 5 6 June and not at his observation and command post at Sainte-Honorine-des-Pertes, a far cry from what is is portrayed in the film... Thus, lieutenant Frerking and his servant, corporal Severloh, left Houtteville in a small horse-drawn cart and reached **WN 62** at 12.55 am, where the battery's observation post was placed.

At 5 am on 6 June, after having seen squadrons of bombers passing overhead, the German soldiers in their positions thought that they could make out the outlines of ships. Suddenly, the artificial fog lifted and the biggest armada of all time appeared in front of the frightened faces of Hein Severloh and his comrades. The latter was in an open-air position a few metres from lieutenant Frerking's observation bunker. Corporal Severloh, a country boy from Lower-Saxony and who hated military discipline, had just fed an ammunition belt into his machine-gun, the formidable MG 42 with an incredible rate of fire. He was still unaware of the role he would play in the coming hours...

Suddenly, a rumbling sound came in from the sea as the ghostly outlines of the approaching bombers came in against the grey and cloudy sky. The rumbling now rose to a hellish crescendo. The German soldiers rushed into their shelters. The bombs rained down but 50 metres to the rear of the defensive positions which remained undamaged! The bombs only killed a few cows... At 6 am, the allied naval Bombardment Group opened fire on the coast with the heavy guns of the the two Force O battleships, the USS Texas and USS Arkansas, and those of three battle cruisers, the Glasgow, Montcalm and Georges Leygues, the two latter being French ships. On the coast, a thick, suffocating light grey chalk dust filled the air. The smoke and dust from the debris covered the sky that was lit up flashes of explosions. For Hein Severloh, *"It felt like the whole world was falling into a rumbling, screeching and crackling hell caused by the explosions of the shells. Near to us, the dry grass and bushes began to burn. However, once again, the shells from this drum fire hit the rear of the strong-point and only caused light damage."* This awful crashing did, nevertheless, cause partial and permanent hearing loss to Hein Severloh.

their presence. The eleven bodies were found the next morning in the lane.

The American paratroopers in the Sainte-Mère-Eglise and Sainte-Marie-du-Mont sector had attracted the attention of the German garrisons in the sector; the Cotentin was not far away and flak had been heard. Leutnant **Hans Heinze**, the quartermaster officer of captain Grimme, commander of the II battalion of Grenadier- Regiment 916, had been on the alert since midnight; a few units had sent in reports of parachute drops but it was soon discovered that they were dummies which set off explosions upon landing. However, the battalion's three infantry companies went to their positions.

Leutnant Hans Heinze.
(Coll. G.B.)

Oberleutnanti Frerking
(© HEK).

Hein Severloh in 1944,
aged 21. (© HEK)

And in 2002, aged 79.
(© HEK)

German artillery observation post. That of lieutenant Frerking was a little narrower. (BA.)

Offshore, the landing craft were pushed about by the sea swell caused by the 10 to 18-knot wind, creating waves some 3 to 4 feet (1.2 metre) high and even as high as 6 feet (1.8 metre)! Movement in the transport zone had run according to a complex timetable in order to accurately bring in the hundreds of ships. The big transport ships had put their landing craft into the sea at approximately 10 miles (16 km) from the beaches. The heavy swell had caused delays. Worse still, the strong currents carried the landing craft to the east and many soldiers did not arrive where they were supposed to. Indeed, in this sector there were very strong side currents which led towards the east, gouging out canals on the beach. They reached a maximum speed of 2.7 to 5 knots (8 km) from the shoreline. Strong winds could increase the strength of the currents and this was the case on 6 June 1944. A report from the destroyer, Saterlee, stated that it had to manoeuvre 20 to 30 degrees in the current in order to maintain its line of fire. These particular conditions would push eastwards on average a thousand metres, or more, the majority of the landing craft and they would arrive in total disarray. Thus, E Company of the 16th RCT, supposed to land at Easy Green (opposite Saint-Laurent), had all of its landing craft scattered to the east, along the 16th RCT beaches, as far as Fox Green. For this company, there would not be any organised command. The men landed in unknown sectors where they could not carry out their mission, something which often halted all initiative.

For now, however, the men heading towards the shore were unaware of all of these setbacks the German positions, intact despite the air and naval bombardment, but also these strong currents. They were reassured by the sight of explosions covering the coast, not knowing that they were hitting the rear of the high ground. They had other things to worry about in the rough sea. At the forefront were the LCMs of the 2,000 engineer soldiers of the Special Engineer Task Force led by Lieutenant-Colonel O'Neill; they would be among the first to reach Omaha Beach and were already exhausted by several difficult days spent on their ships following the postponement of the landings. The LCTs were now spread out over never-ending columns in their three mine swept lanes, chugging along at a maximum speed of 7 knots fully-loaded, towing their LCMs which they loaded at H-3 (3.30 am). Some landing craft floundered in the heavy swell and the Coast Guards were at hand to pick up the men in the sea. Lieutenant Rosenbloom (USCG) was captain of Rescue Cutter 16. He gave instructions to his sailors: *"When you get them out of the water, they will try and get rid of their rifles and grenades that are pulling them down. It is up to you to remind them that the war is not over, that we will dry them out and send them back in. Don't have any qualms, when we are full, in leaving men in the middle of the sea, even if they are screaming or about to go under; another cutter will deal with them. Do not pull dead men on board, only their dog tags. Focus on the survivors who will struggle grabbing the ropes and netting, the ship's medic will know what to do next. A big ship could sink at any moment with hundreds of men in the sea. A maximum effort from each of you is now required."*

Thus, the Engineers would be the first men to go in. Team 14 arrived at **6.25 am** at Easy Red in a LCM; it was hit by a shell and all of the sailors were killed. These were the first Americans to die at Omaha Beach and it was the start of hell there. The other teams arrived a few minutes later. Ten men from Team 12 were killed whilst preparing to blow their charges and an LCM, loaded with infantry became stuck on the obstacles, setting off seven Tellerminen. Seven sailors were killed with Team 13 when a shell exploded in the middle of the explosives-laden engineers.

The first wave now came in. The very strong currents pushed a great many landing craft towards the east. Approaching the coast, the men were reassured after having seen the rockets fired from the LCTs smashing into the coastline. The 1,450

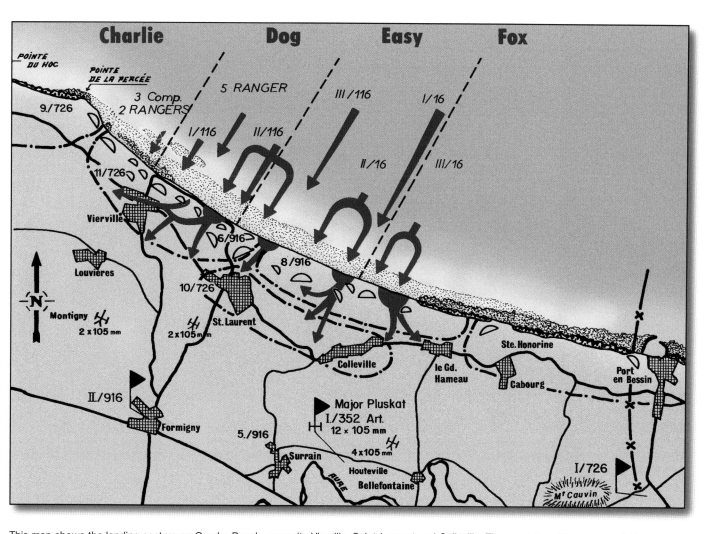

Charlie   Dog   Easy   Fox

POINTE
DU HOC
POINTE
DE LA PERCÉE
9./726
3 Comp.
2 RANGERS
11./726
Vierville
Louvières
Montigny
2 x 105 mm
II./916
Formigny
5./916
Surrain
5 RANGER
I/116   II/116
6/916
8/916
10/726
St. Laurent
2 x 105 mm
Colleville
III /116   I/16
II/16   III/16
Ste. Honorine
le Gd.
Hameau
Cabourg
Port
en Bessin
Major Pluskat
I./352 Art.
12 x 105 mm
4 x 105 mm
Houteville
Bellefontaine
AURE
I/726
Mt Cauvin

This map shows the landing sectors on Omaha Beach, opposite Vierville, Saint-Laurent and Colleville. The coastal positions were held by companies of the 716. Division, whilst Major Pluskat's artillery battalion (I./352) supported this division's artillery. (Heimdal.)

This photo is part of the same set seen on the previous double page. It was taken on a LCVP heading towards the beach. In the middle of the obstacles we can see men of the E/16th and E/116th Companies that are mixed up and pinned down by German fire, especially that of the WN 62 machine-guns on the left. (NA/Coll. Heimdal.)

men of the eight assault companies would receive a warm reception from the German defenders, but they did not yet know it...

At H+6 minutes (6.36 am), the first landing craft hit the beaches. In LCA N°2, Lieutenant Tidrick shouted out: My God, we're in the right spot but look, there is no shelter, no shell holes, nothing! Intense and accurate fire immediately fell on them. A Company of the 116th RCT suffered terrible casualties. One LCA disintegrated under the impact of four mortar projectiles. On the beach, losses were mounting up. Captain Taylor N. Fellers was killed, along with all of the sergeants, also killed or wounded. The survivors could not hold on at the beach and fell back to the water, with some sheltering behind the obstacles. Without their leaders, all movement stopped. The tanks of the B/743rd Tank Battalion, supposed to support them, were hit one after the other with four catching fire within a few minutes. Fifteen minutes after landing, A Company of the 116th RCT (29th Division), was already knocked out of the fight with losses reaching two-thirds of its strength. As well as Captain Fellers, Lieutenant Karfoot was also killed, along with thirty men; only twelve bodies would be found. Two survivors, Pfc Shefer and Lovejoy, joined up with the C Company Rangers who were landing to the right on Charlie Beach, on the far eastern end of the beach. These would be the only two soldiers of the A/116th able to fight on *Omaha Beach!*

On this beach, the Rangers also suffered heavy casualties. LCA N°418 was hit and broke in two before sinking; pulled down by their equipment, the men drowned a few metres from the shoreline. A machine-gun concentrated its fire on LCA N° 1038 and hit 15 Rangers. The survivors crossed the 300 metres to the west. At 7 am, a drifting landing craft carrying men of B/117th RCT,

arrived there, bringing in precious reinforcements. However, it would take another three or four hours of intense fighting before Captain Goranson was able to take, around 11 am, the 'fortified house' (WN 73), the western cornerstone of the German defences on this beach.

To the east, the currents had pushed the landing craft away, leaving two beaches empty, the drifting was everywhere! F and G Companies of the 116th RCT landed towards the draw heading up the valley to Saint-Laurent, opposite WN 66 and 68. Further to the east again, three companies, E/116th (29th Div.) and E and F/16th (the latter from the 1st Division), landed at Easy Red, opposite WN 62. On one of the landing craft there was the famous war correspondent, **Robert Capa**, who would take photos seen all over the world. In his book, Slightly out of Focus, he talks of events at 6.30 am: *"The flat bottom of our barge hit the earth of France. The boatswain lowered the steel-covered barge front, and there, between the grotesque designs of steel obstacles sticking out of the water, was a thin line of land covered with smoke our Europe, the Easy Red beach. My beautiful France looked sordid and uninviting, and a German machine gun, spitting bullets around the barge, fully spoiled my return. The men from my barge waded in the water, waist-deep, with rifles ready to shoot, with the invasion obstacles and the smoking beach in the background this was good enough for the photographer. I paused for a moment on the gangplank to take my first real picture of the invasion. The boatswain, who was in an understandable hurry to get the hell out of there, mistook my picture-taking attitude for explicable hesitation, and helped me make up my mind with a well-aimed kick in the rear. The water was cold, and the beach still more than a hundred yards away. The bullets tore holes in the water around*

Here are three of the saved Robert Capa photos from the 106 which he took at 6.30 am on 6 June. We can see men crawling through the water amidst the beach obstacles. He turned around and saw one of them. The soldiers then advanced towards the beach, hiding behind a few tanks. (Photo National Archives/ Coll.Heimdal.)

me, and I made for the nearest steel obstacle. A soldier got there at the same time, and for a few minutes we shared its cover. He took the water-proofing off his rifle and began to shoot without much-aiming at the smoke-hidden beach. The sound of his rifle gave him enough courage to move forward and he left the obstacle to me. It was a foot larger now, and I felt safe enough to take pictures of the other guys hiding just like I was."

Capa would also take some pictures of a knoc-ked-out tank and, as a veteran of the Spanish Civil War, he wrote: *"It was a new kind of fear shaking my body from toe to hair, and twisting my face."* With great difficulty and with trembling hands, he reloaded his camera. He constantly repeated a sentence he had picked up during the Spanish Civil War: *"Es una cosa muy seria."* (This is a very serious business). He finally took 106 photos. Then, after what seemed a lifetime, he jumped into a LCI to go back to England: *"I knew that I was running away"*. He travelled to London by train and handed in his films for development. However, it was too hot in the dark room and this melted the emulsion leaving only ten pictures which could be

The fourth of the Coast Guards series of photos taken from a LCVP. The beach is approaching, obstacles can be seen above the low tide. The slopes are covered with smoke. On the left, LCVP (PA 26-17) has been hit by a German shell and is smoking badly. (NA/Coll. Heimdal.)

saved! Robert Capa was killed in 1954 whilst reporting for *Life magazine* in Indochina: He stepped on a mine...

Robert Capa landed at the foot of today's American cemetery, on *Easy Red*, to the west of WN 62. It was there that Hein Severloh was waiting with his MG 42. He saw the landing craft as they arrived, at first in the midst of a deathly silence that hung over the entire sector. Indeed, the Germans had been ordered to wait until the Americans had water up to their knees before opening fire. Severloh had run up to a small radio bunker, fifteen metres away, in order to shout to corporals Warnecke and Schulz: *"It's started, they're landing!"* The latter, concentrated on their radio equipment, could not see what was happening outside. Severloh then ran back to his position. He released the safety catch on his MG and started firing. He could see the spray thrown up from his bullets as they hit the water and, when they got closer to the Americans, the latter threw themselves on their stomachs. The calm turned to panic. Some tried to find protection behind the beach obstacles. He fired at the outlines still 300 metres from the top of the beach. He then felt as if he was the only man firing in the entire sector but, in fact, the noise of his MG drowned out the guns of his comrades. He did not even notice the 105 mm shells hitting his own battery. He was so concentrated and in a situation of extreme mental tension, that he did not notice what was happening around him. Things then quietened down. Severloh went to lieutenant Frerking to find out what was going on. He offered his officer, a non-smoker, a cigarette; it was accepted. Their hands were shaking as they lit the cigarettes. Severloh also changed the barrel of his machine-gun, white hot from having just fired thousands of rounds. Severloh counted six assault waves up to midday.

7 am: the second wave

Due to land at **7 am**, B Company of the 116th RCT had not been able to spot its coastal landmarks and the six landing craft would arrive totally scattered along a mile (1,600 metres) of beach overlapping *Dog Green* (to the west of Vierville opposite WN 70 and 71). The three platoons which landed in the centre came under murderous fire, like that experienced by A Company. The survivors of B/116th found themselves mixed up with those of A/116th.

At **7.10 am**, C/116th landed a mile from the Vierville D1 draw, on *Dog White*. German fire there was weak, between two strong-points that were relatively far apart, WN 68 and 70, hidden by a grass fire. This was at last an assembled and virtually intact company, facing a discontinuous German front consisting of isolated strong-points. The company would later go on to achieve success.

D/116th struggled in reaching the shore; a landing craft had been sunk and others were taking on water. As for the three landing craft bringing in the Command Company of the 1st Battalion, of the 116th RCT, they came under fire from German sharpshooters at the top of the cliffs and suffered heavy casualties, almost two-thirds of their strength.

The 3rd Battalion, 116th RCT **(3/116)**, 29th Division, was supposed to land between 7.20 and 7.30 am along a wide sector behind the 2nd Battalion on Dog White, Dog Red and Easy Green. However, here too, the plans went wrong. The Battalion landed ten minutes late... on a front one thousands metres wide, suffering low casualties but with a disorganisation which halted all initiative. The only firing came from a fixed position at the E1 draw (Le Ruquet) and the men had to advan-

LCIs heading to the coast in the Fox Green sector. On the right, one can see the smoke behind WN 62. Hein Severloh was halfway up the slope. Early afternoon, the American soldiers could see the glow of tracer bullets from the training ammunition belts that he now had to use. Upon sighting murderous the glowing bullets, the Americans dubbed it 'The Beast'. (NA/Heimdal.)

ce avoiding this firing. Some companies landed opposite undefended sectors. The first companies, often cut off, were met with heavy fire and suffered terrible losses. But now, the whole beach offered so many confusing targets that the fire was less concentrated and many units were able to slip through the net. It was **a mass effect**, at the cost of heavy casualties, that would win the day; the units which landed eventually overwhelmed the German defenders. It was now 7.30 am and the attacking units were spread out all along the front of the 116th RCT, except for 1/116 at Dog Green, pinned down in front of the D1 Vierville draw after suffering heavy losses. From **7.30 am** onwards, the command units began arriving on the beach. LCVP71 brought in Brigadier-General **Norman Cota** (deputy commander of the 29th Division), Colonel **Charles D.W. Canham** (commander of the 116th Regiment) and Major **Howie**, in all a total of 24 men. But, as it was arriving at Dog White at 7.30 am, the landing craft hit an obstacle and became stuck on a sandbank. The men then had to wade through three feet of water (less than a metre). A DD tank was used as a shelter for these officers who now had to lead the 116th RCT off the beach. They found themselves in the middle of C Company which had been reorganised by Brigadier-General **Cota**.

However, something dramatic happened a few minutes later at **7.35 am**. With the coastline disappearing behind the smoke, **LCI 91** came in, transporting a total of 201 soldiers, including the Alter-

Engineers saving soldiers from drowning. (NA)

nate Command Post Group of the 116th Infantry Regiment and 90 engineers of the B/14th Eng. But on the right, at WN 70, a flak gun was enfilading the beach with its 20 mm shells, guided by tracer rounds. Suddenly, LCI 91 hit an obstacle, Its captain, Lieutenant Vyn, tried to reverse the engines but was unable to shift the boat due to the beach obstacles. The 88 mm gun at WN 72 (Vierville) then opened fire, just as the men were starting to go down the ramps. The whole bow was torn off by

Fox Red, below the hamlet of Cabourg and WN 60. The shelter provided by the cliff has been used to set up an aid post of the 6th Naval Beach Battalion (map page 65).

Above: In this photo taken by the war correspondent, Taylor, wounded men await to be taken away after having received first aid. Three of them have received head wounds. Between 6 and 18 June, 11.25% of wounds were to the head.

Opposite: Here, Taylor has used a close up of a sailor still in a state of shock. Between 6 to 28 June, the US Navy also suffered heavy losses: 12 officers and 95 sailors killed, 204 missing and 313 wounded, most of whom were with the Naval Beach Battalions and the Engineers units who were tasked with clearing the beach obstacles.

A medical captain and his medics transfuse a wounded man who has been covered with a blanket. His head is resting on a rubber life-belt, used here as a pillow. (DAVA/Coll. Heimdal.)

the shot and the ramps were covered with wounded men, 45 for the engineers. As the officers were getting the men off the wreck, a 32 mm incendiary rocket fired from WN 67 (Saint-Laurent) also hit the ship, with the flames covering the decks. With their clothes on fire, the men threw themselves into the water. There were no survivors in compartment N°5 out of the 25 men placed there. Those who managed to get off and reach the shore had to do so with water up to their shoulders and under continuous fire. Most of the equipment was destroyed or abandoned. A few minutes later, another ship, **LCI 92**, arrived in the same sector and suffered almost the same fate when an underwater explosion set the fuel tank on fire. These two ships would burn for hours.

Let us now follow the arrival of the 1st Division's 16th RCT. Its 1st Battalion landed between **7.40**

and 8 am between E1 (Ruquet draw) and E3 (Colleville), mainly facing WN 61 and 62 at Fox Green. Further to the east, the L/16th landed below WN 60 and was protected by the cliffs. After having suffered some casualties, Lieutenant Cutter headed off to the west. The firing from WN 62 had abated a little; it had been hit by allied naval shells after the German fire had been spotted. Now, with the rising tide, the American soldiers had got closer to the top of the beach and within listening distance of the German defenders in the lower part of WN 62. The German fire now fell amidst the shingle covering the top of the beach, throwing shards of pebbles and adding to the wounds of the Americans. Also, in this sector, with the rising tide, two landing craft hit obstacles fitted with mines; the latter being more numerous at the top of the beach (the Germans having planned for landings at high tide); the two ships blew up. By around 8 am, the landings had still not achieved anything. On some beaches it was chaos with mixed up companies, often inexistent communications and partially lost materiel. The units were still stuck at the foot of the shingle bank in what appeared to be hopeless confusion.

The morale of the soldiers was often low. Among the survivors were many young soldiers who had just been through a terrible baptism of fire. The incoming tide brought with it the bodies of their dead comrades and were a reminder of the horror they had just experienced. They were stuck at the foot of the shingle bank or along the waterfront, looking for something to hide behind. In front of them were bullets, minefields, machine-guns and mortars. Any attempt at action seemed to be paralysed. Offshore, **Lieutenant-General Bradley** carefully observed the beach and the smoke-covered chaos there. At **9 am**, he considered **pulling the survivors** off the beach in order to redeploy them at Utah Beach or Gold Beach.

Above: These are lightly wounded men, or shocked after being shipwrecked. On the left is the sailor seen on the previous page.

Opposite: A medic gives first aid to a wounded man whose face is still full of the terror he has just lived through. (DAVA/Coll. Heimdal.)

However, thirty minutes later, good news reached him and the order to evacuate was cancelled.

Attacking the high ground

Indeed, Brigadier-General Cota and Colonel Canham had not remained inactive in their weakly-defended sector between WN 70 and WN 68 at Dog White. Here they had at their disposal mobile forces: C/116th (approximately 120 men) and the 5th Ranger Battalion (450 men). The German strong-points were a few hundred metres away on the flanks. Opposite them, the terrain was flat for 150 metres with marshes and in several places without cover. The ground then rose up fairly steeply, with undulating terrain which afforded cover. The advance of C/116th began at **7.50 am** along the seafront road. On the other side of the wall separating the road from the beach, was a twin row of barbed wire. Pfc. Ingram E. Lambert jumped over the wall, carrying a bangalore, then crossed the road to blow a hole in the barbed wire (a scene which is present in *The Longest Day*). But, when he pulled on the friction fuse, the bangalore did not explode and Lambert was killed by a burst of machine-gun fire. Second-Lieutenant Stanley M. Schwartz also crossed the road and repaired the fuse. The explosion created a wide breach. A man rose and tried to pass through, but he too was killed. But others got through, taking shelter in the trenches beyond the road and were then joined by another group which cut the barbed wire on the left. Five to ten minutes later, whilst other soldiers crossed the road as far as the trenches, they continued towards the slope, the foot of which was covered by smoke that shielded them from the German fire. The advance was only slowed down by fear of mines.

Swinging to the west in order to use a path, the soldiers advanced in single file. At the top of the slope they found the German positions empty. The column continued across the fields on the plateau over approximately 200 metres. After having lost only six men, Captain **Berthier B. Hawks** reached the high ground with his company (C/116th) at around **8.30 am**.

This illustration show us the sectors designated for the 16th RCT of the 1st Infantry Division to the east (here on the left), the beaches of Fox Red, Fox Green and Easy Red and that of the 116th RCT of the 29th Infantry Division and Rangers to the west (here on the right) the beaches of Easy Green, Dog and Charlie. We can see that the companies, designated by letters, drifted. Note the emplacement of WN 60, the first to be captured, WN 62, but also WN 72 whose gun swept the beach. (Heimdal)

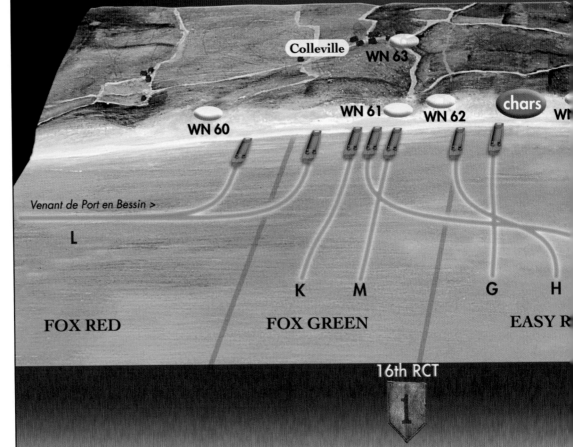

This company was followed by the 5th Ranger Battalion which had reached the seafront wall around 8 am. Lieutenant-Colonel **Schneider** had given his orders for the attack, having sent the "Tallyho" codeword to his officers, for each platoon to cross the road. The latter was crossed at 8.10 am. Four breaches were then opened with

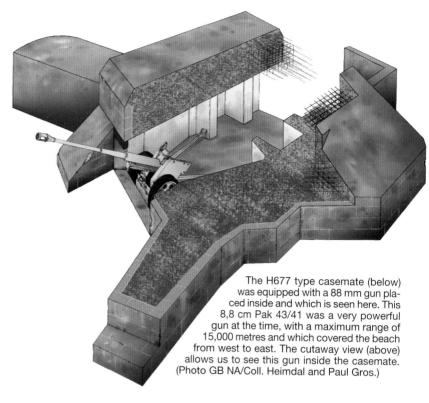

The H677 type casemate (below) was equipped with a 88 mm gun placed inside and which is seen here. This 8,8 cm Pak 43/41 was a very powerful gun at the time, with a maximum range of 15,000 metres and which covered the beach from west to east. The cutaway view (above) allows us to see this gun inside the casemate. (Photo GB NA/Coll. Heimdal and Paul Gros.)

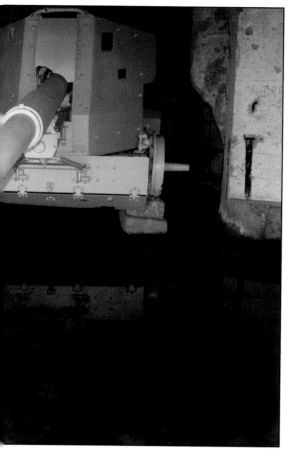

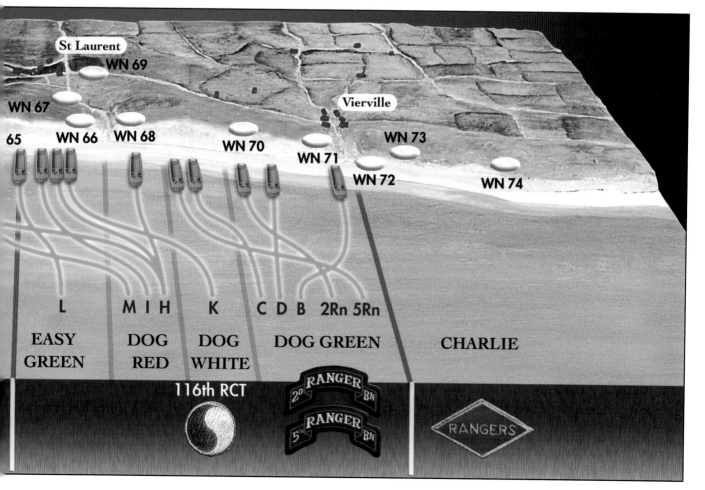

An important advance was made across the plateau from Dog White towards Vierville. Brigadier-General Cota set up his HQ below the crest at 8.30 am. (Heimdal)

Lieutenant-General Omar Bradley commanded the 1st US Army. He paid close attention to the events unfolding at Omaha Beach. At 9 am, he was considering the evacuation of the beach.

Brigadier-General Norman Cota was the deputy commander of the 29th Infantry Division.

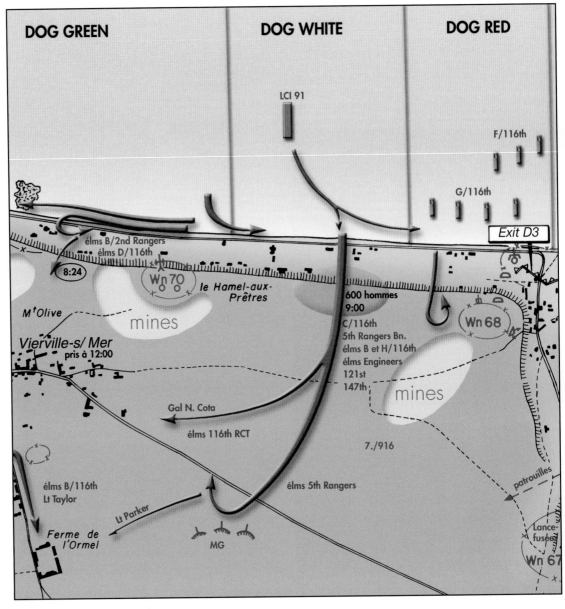

DOG GREEN **DOG WHITE** **DOG RED**

explosives in the barbed wire. The flat terrain was ran across, before climbing up the slope, protected by smoke that was so thick that some men put on their gas masks. Upon reaching the crest, German signs indicated the presence of minefields. The Engineers would remove 150! A platoon from A Company and a few men of F Company headed inland whilst the rest of the unit reorganised at around **8.30 am**. On the left, the Company mopped up the German positions at WN 68.

At the same time, other Rangers, those of the 2nd Battalion, had began to advance at Dog Green! Captain Arnold had gathered together the survivors of H Company (35 men) and B Company (27 men) of the **2nd Ranger Battalion**, telling them that they would only survive if they crossed the road; which they did in one go at around 7.45 am. They were supported by the fire of a few tanks that had landed behind them, knocking out the only machine-gun nest covering the beach from a defilade. Also, the Texas battleship had fired on the positions above the Rangers with its 14-inch guns, with a direct hit having silenced a concrete position. Then, A Company, which was without officers, came under the command of Technical

Sergeant John W. White. During this time, eighteen Rangers from B Company headed off to the right towards D1, the entrance to the draw to Vierville, with the aim of getting to the Pointe du Hoc! But they were halted by firing from the strongly defended WN 72. As for the Rangers of A Company, which had followed those of B Company, they advanced across the plateau attacking light positions along the edge of WN 71, screaming and shouting insults at the Germans that they could see! Crazed with anger at the losses on the beach, they pushed the Germans back. It was 8.24 am when the A Company Rangers mopped-up the German positions. A few minutes later, they spotted their comrades from the 5th Battalion a little further to the east; it was 8.30 am.

It was also **8.30 am** when the last groups of the 116th RCT left the protection of the seawall and took up positions halfway up the slope with Brig.Gen Cota. However, here, the SCR 300 radios were unable to reach the 1st Infantry Division units and the Germans hit the slope with mortars. Two men next to Cota were killed and he and another man were flung to the ground! The command group had to leave this uncomfortable position and set up on the crest. They were joined by other

elements that had landed on Dog White and followed the 'seawall'. Brigadier-General Cota then reorganised all of the elements that had reached the plateau. However, they were still pinned down by sporadic fire and shells that fell around them.

There were other weak spots between the German defensive positions. Thus, the elements that had landed on Dog Red, on the edge of Dog White, would reach the plateau to the west of WN 68 which overlooked the draw at vallée des Moulins (D3 draw) leading to Saint-Laurent. The remains of the first wave's three platoons (F/116th) climbed up the undefended slope, followed closely behind by an isolated platoon of the B/116th. They did not meet with any resistance. It was shortly before 9 am. These elements then headed to the right to join up with the 5th Ranger Battalion. A dozen men of the B/116th went off towards the right and WN 68; they were halted by a machine-gun firing from this position. Second-Lieutenant William B. Williams attacked it alone and was wounded, falling back on Vierville towards the south-west.

On Easy Red, where Robert Capa had landed at the foot of WN 62, there was total chaos. However, between WN 66 and WN 62, there was a wide undefended area along the edge of the plateau (where today's American cemetery is positioned). At the foot of the slope was an area of marshland preceded by a minefield. The summit of the plateau was 130 feet (43 metres) high, preceded by a 200-metre wide slope with thick shrub. A small valley, allowed for an easier access to the summit (where today's paved footpath is below the cemetery's orientation table). Elements that had landed with the first wave (E/116th E/16th) began their advance in the sector at around **8 am**. Lieutenant John M. Spalding, of the 16th RCT (1st Div.) had opened a breach in the barbed wire above

the bank, making his way through and beyond the ruined houses. He was stopped, however, by the marshes and the minefield. They also came under fire from WN 62 on the left. But Spalding's men discovered a small path in the draw and climbed up the slope. Further to the west and not in touch with Spalding's platoon, two E/116th platoons cut through the barbed wire and rushed across the flat terrain, but were halted by the minefields at the foot of the slope. During this time, Captain Dawson's G/116th, having landed at 7 am with the second wave, had reached in good order the foot of the slope. Breaches were opened with bangalores. These men joined those of Spalding. Halfway up the slope, Captain Dawson went around a German machine-gun position which he wiped out with a fragmentation grenade; the way to the top was now open. The 5th Platoon of G/16th was the first to reach the summit at **8.30 am**. There, it destroyed two machine-guns and reorganised on the plateau fifteen minutes later. It continued its advance south at around **9 am**.

Further to the west, Spalding's platoon reached the top of the slope at more or less the same time, assisted by the covering fire provided by G/16th. It now had 23 men, after losing six, and came across German positions before heading west to link up with G/16th. Spalding and his platoon came into contact with WN 64 (the remains of which can be seen north-west of the American cemetery). As the German defences were pointed towards the beach, they were attacked by surprise from the rear. Two hours of confused and close-quarter fighting then followed before Spalding overcame the defenders at around **10 am**, thus clearing, by mid-morning, the entrance to the Ruquet draw (E1).

The gap opened by Captain Dawson's G/16th would allow for a deeper penetration in the Omaha

Beach sector, forming an increasingly wider corner in the German defensive lines, between WN 64 in the west and WN 62 in the east. **Colonel George A. Taylor** (16th RCT) landed at 8.15 am with the second element of the 16th RCT (1st Division) command group. Upon arriving on the beach he realised that he needed to put some order back to all the chaos. He summed up the situation in a sentence which became famous: There are two kinds of people who are staying on this beach: those who are dead and those who are going to die. Now let s get the hell out of here. He reorganised the men regardless of their original unit and sent them beyond the barbed wire and towards the flat terrain. During this time, the Engineers were working flat out to widen the gaps and mark the lanes through the minefields. The advance was made via the small valley used by Captain Dawson.

Whilst these advances were being made to the west and east of the Ruquet draw, opposite the latter, the 1st Battalion of the 16th RCT, which had landed there between 7.30 and 8 am, experienced serious difficulties, particularly A/16th which had come under small arms fire from WN 64, not yet captured by Lieutenant Spalding. It was a massacre, Captain Pence, two other officers and 45 men were killed by fire from WN 64. The survivors took a path heading towards the east.

On Fox Green, at the very eastern side of the Omaha Beach sector, was L/16th led by Second-Lieutenant Cutler. He had left the shelter of the cliffs at around 8 am and advanced towards the west with his company of approximately 120 men, reaching the F1 draw leading from the beach to WN 60 via a small, steep valley. He was joined by two tanks in support. The shrub-covered flanks of the draw were undefended. Cutler led in the attack at around 8.30 am, to the west of WN 60. His 2nd and 3rd Platoons reached the top without signifi-

cant losses, despite crossing a minefield. The 2nd Platoon headed left in order to go around WN 60 from the south.

During this time, Second-Lieutenant Kenneth J. Klenk (1st Platoon of L/16th) had advanced a little further to the west towards Fox Green with a

Dead soldiers along the steps leading to the top of a slope, probably in the Vierville sector, to the east of WN 70. (Coast Guards/ Coll.Heimdal.)

This painting by an American military artist shows soldiers sheltering at the foot of the seawall in the Vierville sector. (US Navy.)

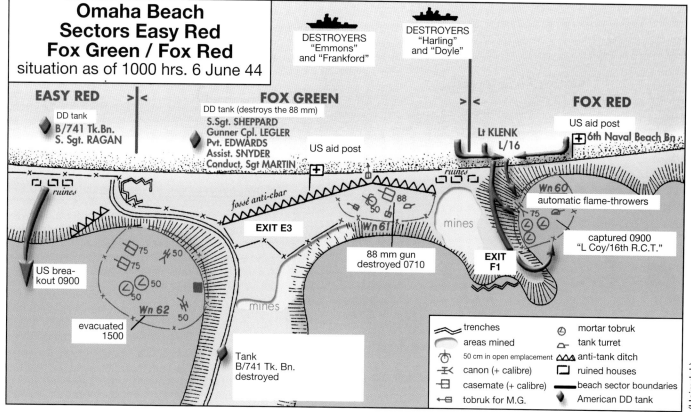

Omaha Beach
Sectors Easy Red
Fox Green / Fox Red
situation as of 1000 hrs. 6 June 44

DESTROYERS "Emmons" and "Frankford"

DESTROYERS "Harling" and "Doyle"

EASY RED > <

DD tank
B/741 Tk.Bn.
S. Sgt. RAGAN

FOX GREEN

DD tank (destroys the 88 mm)
S.Sgt. SHEPPARD
Gunner Cpl. LEGLER
Pvt. EDWARDS
Assist. SNYDER
Conduct. Sgt MARTIN

US aid post

FOX RED

Lt KLENK
L/16

US aid post
6th Naval Beach Bn

ruines

ruines

Wn 60

automatic flame-throwers

fossé anti-char

EXIT E3

Wn 61

88

50

88 mm gun
destroyed 0710

EXIT F1

mines

75

captured 0900
"L Coy/16th R.C.T."

US brea-
kout 0900

75
50
75

50
50
Wn 62
50

evacuated
1500

mines

Tank
B/741 Tk. Bn.
destroyed

trenches	mortar tobruk
areas mined	tank turret
50 cm in open emplacement	anti-tank ditch
canon (+ calibre)	ruined houses
casemate (+ calibre)	beach sector boundaries
tobruk for M.G.	American DD tank

(Heimdal.)

dozen men of his platoon. He headed towards WN 61, but withdrew in the face of fire and went back to the F1 draw. There, with Captain Richmond (I/16th), all the elements of the two companies were reorganised and the advance resumed towards WN 60 to support Lieutenant Cutler. WN 60 then came under fire from a destroyer and that of two tanks. Klenk's men threw explosive charges into the trenches and underground shelters of WN 60. Thus, at **9 am**, the 3rd Battalion, 16th RCT announced the capture of WN 60 along with 31 prisoners (15 of which were wounded). The commander of the position, Unteroffizier Eberhard, had lost an arm and would later die. According to the first-hand account of Franz Gockel, a young girl from the village of Colleville, who came each day with supplies for the position, cried at the loss of a young soldier who she grown fond of and who was killed there. Thus, at 9 am, with Lieutenant-General Bradley considering withdrawal from Omaha Beach, **WN 60** became the **first** strong-point to fall. The eastern pillar of the German defences had just collapsed. From there the whole beach was overlooked and as we have seen, WN 64 would fall an hour later.

A first bridgehead

However, at 9 am, the situation was still worrying. Due to its steep and unusable valley, the F1 draw and WN 60 would not allow vehicles to move off the beach. Even though groups of infantrymen were beginning to spread out inland no usable beach exit was available. Also, on the beach, the few vehicles that had landed were the prey of the German mortars and artillery guided from coastal observation posts, including that of Oberleutnant Frerking and Leutnant Grass, at WN 72, adjusting the firing of the four 10,5 cm howitzers of the 1st battery of AR352. Broken vehicles continued to

burn throughout the day on the beach in the midst of all kinds of debris and hundreds of corpses. Despite the bombardments, the German artillery was intact.

Thus, at around **8.30 am**, the commander of the 7th Naval Beach Battalion ordered over the radio to halt all vehicle landings, including the amphibious DUKWs and Rhino Ferries. The strip of beach was too narrow and, at high tide, the water almost reached the shingle bank. Dozens of DUKWs thus sailed around for hours and they only had enough fuel in their tanks for ten to twelve hours. If the draws could not be opened they would sink!

Two beach exits were priority: E3 was beneath WN 62 and the sector there was very dangerous. However, the deep infantry penetration across the plateau from Easy Red, towards Colleville, would threaten the rear of WN 62. Also, WN 64 on the other end of this plateau, would fall at around 10 am, as we have seen, and it dominated the other essential E1 draw and the Ruquet valley. As for the artillery that was supposed to support the 116th RCT (29th Div.) and the 16th RCT (1st Div.), it experienced total disaster. The **111th Field Artillery Battalion**, was due to land between 8 and 9 am in order to support the 116th, but it suffered terrible losses. Its commander, Lieutenant-Colonel Thornton L. Mullins, was killed. Four 105 mm howitzers, brought in by DUKWs, sank. Most of the other DUKWs could not land and were hit by enemy fire and also ended up at the bottom of the sea. Finally, out of the group's 12 howitzers, only one landed, the eleven others sank. The 105 mm howitzers mounted on an armoured chassis, the M-7 of the **58th Armored Field Artillery Battalion** (29th Div.) were also struck with disaster. After having opened fire from their LCTs, heading towards the coast and firing smoke shells, the LCT

Corporal Franz Gockel was a young soldier in the WN 62 garrison. (Coll. G.B.)

The arrival of reinforcements and the advance inland

With several companies now on the plateau and trying to advance south, reinforcements began to arrive on the beach. The **18th RCT** (1st Division) had been due to arrive on Easy Red from **9.30 am** onwards. It now arrived at a crowded beach with the approaches jammed by ships maneouvering in all directions. Thus, the 2nd Battalion, 18th RCT, landed just after **10 am** to the west of E1 (Ruquet draw), beneath WN 65. As they approached the shore, the men of the battalion were met with a less than cheerful sight: The shingle bank was crowded with tractors, tanks, vehicles, bulldozers and men; the crest was still held by the Germans who pinned down all the men on the beach which itself was still under intense enemy fire from mortars, light weapons and artillery. Also, most of the beach obstacles had not been cleared and, with the rising tide, were particularly dangerous. At this beach, the 18th RCT would lose 22 LCVP, 4 LCT and 2 Lcls (L). They had almost all hit the poles or mines.

At this time, the G/16th found itself on the plateau at around **9.30 am**, where today's American cemetery is situated, its objective being a German bivouac zone 400 metres west of Colleville. However, when approaching this sector and the church, it came under heavy fire from both flanks with mortars and automatic weapons; the fighting would go on until midday and the losses for G/16th were twelve men. But it was joined by elements of F/16th and two E/16th platoons, forming a composite unit of 150 men, thus reaching the first village in the Omaha Beach sector and the coast road. One of the strongest German strong-points in the sector, WN 62 was, therefore, moved around via its west flank and threatened along its southern flank, cutting off its withdrawal route. After the fall of WN 60 at 9 am and that of WN 61 around 10 am, the entire eastern flank of the German defences was now in a very tricky position. Also, a little further to the west, the effort was now being made towards the Ruquet draw. Therefore, in the 1st Infantry Division sector, the German front was starting to collapse and the American beachhead at last strengthening.

The Ruquet - The bunker armed with a 50 mm gun (WN 65) now kept today with its gun as a memorial guarded the entrance to Ruquet draw leading to Saint-Laurent and was still putting up a fight. However, the trap was starting to close around it. To the east, Lieutenant Spalding (E/116th) had knocked-out WN 64 at **10 am**. To the west, the troops were on the plateau and advancing on WN 65. Below, also at 10 am, the engineers of the 3rd Engineer Battalion opened a breach using a bulldozer. The WN 65 bunker had not been knocked-out by a destroyer as its firing slit was invisible from the sea. Indeed, it was facing towards the east in order to cover the beach, as were all the bunkers with artillery pieces. A half-track armed with a 37 mm gun and commanded by Sergeant Hyman Haas of the 467th AAA Weapons Bn. which had landed at 8.30 am, tried to attack the bunker. The unit had already lost 28 of

The LCIs could carry almost 200 men. Some would encounter a dramatic fate, falling victim to German artillery and mines. This was the case of LCI 91 which arrived with the second wave, and LCI (L) 83 which landed at 11.15 am. This illustration (above) shows LCI 93 opposite WN 62, of which the house sheltering the kitchen can be seen. WN 62 is to the right, on the high ground. (US Navy)

Sergeant John Glass in 1944. (Photo J.L.L., Coll. author.)

carrying Sergeant John Glass, was hit by a 88 shell fired from the Vierville bunker (WN 72). It sank along with four vehicles, a half-track and a jeep. Thus, at **10.30 am**, the verdict was clear. As well as the LCT, a second floundered in seven feet of water and a howitzer from the third was pushed overboard in order to keep the LCT afloat. The surviving howitzers were not ready to open fire at the beach until 6.30 pm...

As for the tanks of the two Tank Battalions (741st and 743rd), despite their heavy losses, Major Bingham, commanding the 2nd Battalion, 116th RCT, would say after the battle that: The tanks saved the day. They laid down heavy fire on the Germans, even though they were being heavily fired on themselves. Thus, at 7.10 am, a DD (amphibious) tank landed on Easy Red and scored a direct hit on WN 61. Staff Sergeant Sheppard commanding this DD Sherman tank of the B/743rd Tank Bn. stated that: *"My gunner Corporal Legler started firing immediately at targets I designated (...) there were machine-gun pillboxes and gun emplacements. I spotted a tunnel on my left (in fact ammunition bunkers) and Legler fired two 75 mm armor piercing shells, there was a big explosion..."* It was 7.10 am and, a few minutes later, general Kraiss, commander of the 352.ID and part of the German defences in the sector, received the following message: Gun at WN 61 destroyed. This German position had been silenced. Its commander, Oberfeldwebel Schnön, had been killed. As for the naval gun fire, the destroyer Carmick supported a few tanks in action at Dog Green against the bunkers of WN 72. At the beginning the naval gun support was limited in order to avoid causing losses amongst the first troops to land. However, once targets were better spotted, the naval artillery played an increasingly important role in silencing the German positions. LCT 30 went at full speed through the obstacles, firing with all of

Le Ruquet and the E1 draw:

1. Aerial photo showing the former WN 65 with its casemate for a 50 mm gun, today a memorial, and path made by the American engineers along the side of the plateau. (Photo Roméo-India/Heimdal)

2. The H 667 type casemate which controlled access to the draw. (Heimdal)

its 36 vehicles on the beach. At **10.30 am**, and after having fired ten 37 mm shells, Haas at last knocked-out the 50 mm gun. Twenty prisoners were taken and the engineers immediately set to work, beginning with a road to get off the beach. The vehicles would soon at last be able to make their way up the Ruquet draw and push inland. The battle for the beach was won, but the last positions still needed to be mopped up.

Reinforcements continued to arrive. The 115th RCT also came in at around **10.30 am** and began landing from LCI (L) 142. The units became mixed up and confusion reached its high point, made worse by German fire which continued to sweep the beach. Two battalions of the 18th RCT were not able to land until around 1 pm!

Incomplete reports - despite the first successes, with several breakthroughs and the opening of two exits (Le Ruquet and the Cabourg/WN 60 draws), the command still only had a very confused and worrying idea of what was happening. On board the Ancon (a ship acting as headquarters for the generals commanding V Corps (H. Gerow) and the 1st Infantry Division (Huebner), the messages coming in from the beach were virtually inexistent and the rare information was supplied by the navy ensuring the link with the beach. A less than reassuring message arrived at 11.55 am: *"Situation still critical at the beach exits of Easy, Fox and Dog. 352nd Division identified (the presence of this German division was a bad surprise as it was not known to be in the sector). The 115th RCT was ordered to clear the plateau south-west of Easy Red at 11.31. The 16th RCT and the 116th have both landed, fighting continues on the beaches. Reports state that some Germans have surrendered at Easy Green."*

The E3 (Colleville) draw was still blocked by the resistance of WN 62. There, with the high tide, Hein Severloh had seen the surviving GIs sheltering behind the obstacles or the bodies of their comrades, seeing only their helmets. With each wave he fired at anything that moved, on the beach or at sea. For better accuracy, he also used his

rifle rather than his MG 42, the bursts of which sprayed haphazardly during each big attack. Each American wave placed a hundred men in front of his position. Severloh cut them down with his MG 42 then finished the job off with his rifle, and the 98K was accurate.

From **11 am** onwards, the naval gun support started to swing the balance. Sailing off Easy Red and guided by a radio team on the beach, the destroyer, Emmons, opened fire on the area around Colleville. The ship operated along with the Frankford. Already, before 10 am, one of the two 75 mm guns at the Pointe de la Percée had been destroyed. On Dog White, the breakthrough of the 116th RCT had been supported by the destroyer Carmick. At 11.40 am, a message signalled: *"Troops advancing to the west of E1 thanks to the destroyers".* Most of the heavy weapons had been lost during the landings but now, when contact could be established with the fleet, the fire support of the US Navy was the determining factor in finishing off these last German strong-points.

The only exit that was really open was the E1 (Le Ruquet) draw. However, the engineers still had a lot of work to do before vehicles could make their way up the Ruquet draw: filling in the anti-tank ditch, mine clearing and clearing a path. The engineers of the 16th RCT cleared the draw of mines and the Special Engineer Group worked with bulldozers on the western part of the plateau. This beach exit was not usable until midday. On the beach, Colonel Eugene N. Slappey, commander of the 115th RCT, ordered his battalions which had just landed, to make their way to their assembly points south-east of Saint-Laurent in order to reorganise. There, Slappey met Brigadier-General Wyman, the assistant commander of the 1st Division and they were joined by Brigadier-General Cota, the assistant commander of the 29th Division. The decision was taken to send in the 115th RCT to clear Saint-Laurent. However, there was total confusion inland. Small units were advancing into unknown territory without any coordination between themselves. When Colonel Slappey at

Colonel Eugene N. Slappey, in command of the 116th RCT.

Omaha Beach remained under fire from the 105 mm guns of Artillerie-Regiment 352 until the afternoon, as seen by this Coast Guards photo. The shelling was directed from observation posts.

last left to go inland, at around 4 pm, he had no news from his battalions because the radios were not working!

Thus, at around **11 am**, the penetration inland was still not possible from the beach exits and only the units having climbed up the slopes to the plateau had headed inland. But this advance was still taking place in a confused manner. Units were often mixed up and radio communications virtually non-existent as a lot of equipment had been lost. Often, units did not know where they were. After the open fields along the seafront, they now encountered a dense network of hedgerows that partitioned the countryside. Sometimes, they cleared a sector in which friendly units had operated but where, in the meantime, the Germans had returned. American units crossed paths without actually encountering each other. This mix up remained the norm until the end of the day.

Shortly **after midday** in the **Colleville** sector, a platoon from G/16th entered the western area of the village but was unable to go further than the church. Leutnant Bauch, commanding the German company in the sector, 3./726, on which WN 62 depended, was killed whilst leading a counter-attack against the church and the buildings where the men of G/16th had taken up positions. Unable to go any further, the latter would withdraw to the 'bivouac zone', near the entrance of today's American cemetery. Also, WN 62 was still holding out and constituted, along with WN 63 on the side of

the draw between the coast and Colleville (resisting with mortars and machine-guns), a thorn in the side of the north-east flank of this American penetration. Shortly **before midday** at **WN 62**, Oberfeldwebel Pieh of the 716th division, arrived via a trench that had been partially caved in by shellfire and situated in front of the position. This tall, slim man had blood running from his neck. A bullet had gone through the left-hand side of his neck, but he had continued his dash. Severloh was trying to kick open the breech of his rifle with his boot heel as he could not manage by hand. Seeing this, Pieh said: *"Hey kid, don't bother, your rifle is still too hot"*. When Severloh began firing his MG 42 again, Pieh went to the signals bunker and came back with another rifle: *"They don't need a rifle"*. He said as he held out the rifle. In the meantime, the left-hand side of Pieh's tunic had become stained with blood. At that moment, Severloh looked to his right and saw two of his comrades in a trench, holding their rifles above their heads and shooting without aiming. Pieh ran over to the trench and shouted at them and the two soldiers ran off. Pieh then returned to where Severloh was and pointed out a large pile of pebbles slightly to the left of the position: *"Down there, one of them is running...!"* It was then that Severloh realised that, along a two to three metre -wide strip, where the high tide was lapping, the sand was stained with the blood of hundreds of dead and wounded men. The latter were moving slowly, crawling. Severloh counted between fifty and sixty. He then

On the evening of 6 June, the beach was strewn with all sorts of debris and wrecks landing craft, trucks, jeeps, tanks etc. 79 tanks, 26 artillery guns and more than 50 landing craft were lost on 6 June 1944.

took the rifle that his Oberfeldwebel had given him and began shooting at a GI trying to hide behind the shingle bank. His helmet fell, his chin touched his chest and he collapsed. It was only then that he realised what he had been doing all this time: he had been killing men...

During this time, Pieh had gone but now returned with ammunition for the MG 42; he brought 8,000 rounds. Then he went off again. Suddenly there was a violent shock. Something had flown in front of the barrel of his MG and Severloh's face had been hit like a whiplash, just by his left eye. He then felt great pain all over his face and saw that his fingers were covered with blood. His cheek swelled up. He then saw that the front sight of his rifle had been torn off by a bullet and that the small metal sight had then hit him in the face. Severloh began shouting in anger and went back to shooting at the GIs at the bottom of the beach.

He would find out later that the currents had pushed many landing craft into the sector that was within range of WN 62, from Easy Green to the left, where Robert Capa landed, to Fox Green on the right of this position, where the war correspondent for Collier's, Ernest Hemingway, was approaching without the right to land on that day. The low cliffs were cut by valleys. In one of them was a church tower (Colleville). There was timber which descended to the sea. There was a house to the right of one of the beaches. On all of the headland, the flowering broombush was on fire, but the wind kept the smoke close to the ground (...) And above this house was the crackling machine-gun of Hein Severloh, opposite Ernest Hemingway and Robert Capa...

The Germans also launched counter-attacks. Thus, at **midday**, Leutnant Heinze, who had been flabbergasted at dawn when he saw the allied fleet from his tree-top observation post - *"As if the whole world was against us."* - then realised that he could: *Only hold back this attack for one or two days at most.* (1). He was now called by captain Grimme, commander

of the II./916. This battalion had launched a counter-attack at 10 am in order to push back the Americans near Saint-Laurent. During this attack, almost all of the 7th company men had been killed or wounded. The 5th company had suffered heavy casualties. Oberleutnant Hahn, commanding the 5th company, was wounded. The 3rd platoon, led by Stabsfeldwebel Penningsdorf, had been totally wiped out when it came across a position held by American engineers. After having looked at this less than encouraging situation, captain Grimme handed over command of the 5./916 to Leutnant Heinze. He added that: We have to push back into the sea the enemy which has infiltrated! Hans Heinze then went back to the east of Colleville where the men of his new company only had left two platoons. The latter were very happy to see him; they had known each other since basic training.

They then advanced along the hedgerows, capturing a few exhausted GIs as they went. These were men of the 1st Division, the Big Red One and they did not appear to want to put up a fight. They then arrived at where today's roundabout is, before the path leading to the American cemetery. The unit at last reached the rear of WN 62. Leutnant Heinze and his men leaped forward shouting and throwing grenades. Surprised and terrorised, the Americans fell back and ran down the slope. However, thanks to light radio equipment, the Americans responded immediately and brought down heavy fire on the sector. In order to spare his men the same fate as that of the 7th company, Leutnant Heinze preferred to withdraw and, thanks to the ditch and the hedgerows, the 5./916 managed to escape destruction and were able to withdraw with only a few men being wounded. This unit, which had avoided being wiped out,

(1) This first-hand account was given to the author by Hans Heinze.

The losses suffered on the beaches would fan the desire for vengeance. Up to midday, and the arrival of military police, no prisoners were taken, they were simply shot, a fact stated by, amongst others, the civilian Edmond Scelles. The prisoners seen here were captured later and thus survived. They are bringing a wounded man down the Ruquet draw. (DAVA/ Heimdal.)

received a warm welcome from captain Grimme who, along with Hans Heinze, now set up a hedgehog position to the east of Colleville where it fought off several American attacks.

By **2 pm**, the D1 draw (Vierville in front of WN 72) had been subjected to heavy naval bombardment from midday to 1 pm. The Germans showed white flags at WN 71. The Germans surrendered in this sector but the exit remained blocked by a strong concrete anti-tank wall. Brigadier-General Cota had arrived at this wall at 1.15 pm and ordered it to be broken through with explosives. The exit was at last broken through at 2 pm; it was the third to be cleared but nothing would move further here this day. Le Ruquet remained the only route and would be used by thousands of men and vehicles coming from Omaha Beach. At the end of the day, the beachhead was still very narrow in the **Vierville** sector. As for the **Saint-Laurent** sector, elements of five American battalions were held up in an area of a square mile by a determined German defence which still blocked the coast road. The lack of artillery guns did not allow the Germans to push the Americans out of this pocket.

In the **Colleville** sector, the Germans still held on to the village and the eastern sector at Cabourg. All resistance had ceased at WN 62. At 1 pm, Hein Severloh had seen six American tanks to his left. After having fired thousands of rounds, he only had night fighting ammunition belts left equipped with tracer rounds (one in five bullets), which gave his position away. A shell landed nearby, throwing his MG 42 into the air, and was then followed by another. At **2 pm**, he spotted American soldiers 250 metres to his left, climbing the slope leading to where the American cemetery is today. A shell then hit the overhead shield of Leutnant Frerking's observation bunker. The latter then gave the order: *"Let's get out of here and leave the position"*. Up to that point in time, Severloh had fired a total of

12,000 rounds! The survivors then pulled back across the shell-torn terrain and the Americans seemed to be all around them. Severloh left the trench at **2.30 pm**, running towards the right. He was joined by Kurt Warnecke who told him that Frerking had been hit in the head by a bullet and killed. They were both slightly wounded as they withdrew to WN 63 where Severloh guarded four prisoners. They withdrew again with a small group of Germans. Surrounded, they surrendered at 4 in the morning to the four prisoners and a man of the 16th RCT.

At **3.37 pm**, the Roman tower of the Colleville church was destroyed by the destroyer Emmons, despite not having any Germans in it. This village, which remained occupied by the Germans until the following morning, was now encircled. At **7 pm**, Generals Huebner (1st Infantry Division) and Gerhardt (29th Infantry Division), were on Omaha Beach. They were joined in the fragile beachhead by Major-General Gerow (V Corps) at 8.30 pm.

This sector, unsuitable for a landing and with intact German defences, had cost the determined American soldiers **3,881** casualties, 4,720 if we take into account the naval and air losses. 608 of these casualties can be attributed to the 116th RCT alone; its A Company (of which many soldiers came from the village of Bedford) had been wiped out. Losses were especially heavy for the first wave; 41% or 111 losses out of the first 272 soldiers to land. In the face of all these unfavourable conditions and a terrain which had to be climbed, it was the 'effect of mass' that won the day. The German defences were overwhelmed by wave after wave, a little like the Soviet attacks on the Eastern Front... Also, the 'Atlantic Wall' did not stand up to its name. It was made up of 'resistance nests' (*Widerstandnester*, or WN in abbreviation) that were dispersed and sometimes fairly cut of from one another. After the initial losses,

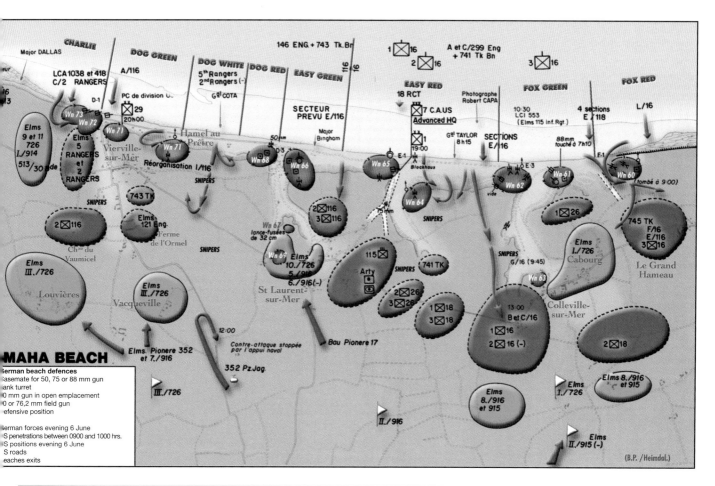

CHARLIE
Major DALLAS
LCA 1038 et 418
C/2 RANGERS
D-1
Wn 73
Wn 72
Elms 9 et 11 726
I./914
513/30 de
Elms 5 RANGERS et 2 RANGERS
Vierville-sur-Mer
SNIPERS
2 ⊠116
Ch^au du Vaumicel
Elms III./726
Louvières

DOG GREEN
A/116
PC de division U...
Wn 71
Wn 71
Réorganisation I/116
SNIPERS
743 TK
Elms 121 Eng.
Ferme de l'Ormel
SNIPERS
Elms III./726
Vacqueville

DOG WHITE DOG RED
5ᵗʰ Rangers
2ⁿᵈ Rangers (-)
Gᵉˡ COTA
Hamel au Prêtre
50 mm
Wn 68
Wn 66
D-3
Wn 67
lance-fusées de 32 cm
Wn 69
Elms 10./726
5./914
6./916(-)
St Laurent-sur-Mer
12:00
Elms. Pionere 352 et 7./916
352 Pz.Jag.
III./726

146 ENG. + 743 Tk.Bn
EASY GREEN
SECTEUR PREVU E/116
Major Bingham
2 ⊠116
3 ⊠116
115 ⊠
Arty
Contre-attaque stoppée par l'appui naval
Bau Pionere 17

1 ⊠16
2 ⊠16
Wn 65
E-1
Blockhaus
Wn 64
SNIPERS
741 TK
SNIPERS
2 ⊠26
3 ⊠26
1 ⊠18
3 ⊠18

A et C/299 Eng + 741 Tk Bn
EASY RED
18 RCT
Photographe Robert CAPA
7 C.A.US
Advanced HQ
1 ⊠
19:00
Gˢᵗ TAYLOR SECTIONS
8 h15 E/16
vide
Wn 62
E-3
Wn 63
SNIPERS 6/16 (9:45)
13:00
8 et C/16
1 ⊠16
2 ⊠16 (-)
Elms 8./916 et 915
II./916

3 ⊠16
FOX GREEN
10:30
LCI 553
(Elms 115 Inf.Rgt.)
Wn 61
88 mm touché 7h10
1 ⊠26
Elms I./726
Cabourg
Colleville-sur-Mer
2 ⊠18
Elms 1./726
Elms 8./916 et 915

FOX RED
L/16
4 sections E / 118
Wn 60
tombé à 9:00
E-1
745 TK
F/16
E/116
3 ⊠16
Le Grand Hameau

(B.P. /Heimdal.)

OMAHA BEACH
German beach defences
Casemate for 50, 75 or 88 mm gun
Tank turret
50 mm gun in open emplacement
70 or 76,2 mm field gun
Defensive position

German forces evening 6 June
US penetrations between 0900 and 1000 hrs.
US positions evening 6 June
US roads
Beaches exits

Above: The beachhead was still fragile on the evening of 6 June. (Heimdal)

Opposite: Only a hundred grateful survivors were gathered up. They are seen here at the Ruquet camp before being shipped back to England on 9 June. (DAVA/Coll. Heimdal.)

some of the troops that landed spotted 'chinks in the armour' and areas that were undefended. If there had been three more WN, the landing troops would never have been able to break through.

Finally, very few German soldiers in the coastal positions survived the D-Day fighting. It had been decided to not become burdened with prisoners in enemy territory in the first hours as long as the beachhead had not been established. The losses on the beach would also increase the desire for vengeance. According to figures, apart from the soldiers killed in combat, there are a missing hundred prisoners. As some civilians remembered, including Edmond Scelles, no prisoners were brought in during the first hours. They were only gathered up when the MPs of the 302nd Military Police Escort Guard arrived. Hein Severloh survived because he held his position for a long time. Omaha Beach would be the worst of all the beach sectors!...

Opposite, right: B-26 Marauder bombers of the 9th US Air Force blast the German positions at the Pointe du Hoc with heavy bombs. The attack by the Rangers would now be able to start. (US Air Force)

Opposite: Lieutenant-Colonel James E. Rudder had taken command of the Provisional Ranger Group made up of 2nd and 5th Battalion men, whose main mission was the attack on the Pointe du Hoc. This photo was taken on 8 June, after the successful outcome of the mission. (Coll. Heimdal)

The casemates were empty at the Pointe du Hoc...

At **5.45 am**, the men of the 2nd Ranger Battalion left two Liberty Ships, HMS Ben Machree and HMS Amsterdam, and boarded twelve small LCA landing craft and four DUKW (amphibious trucks). However, they were still twelve nautical miles (twenty kilometres) from the coast in their small landing craft and already, the choppy sea had swamped one, LCA 914, which sank leaving only one survivor, Pfc John Riley of D Company!

The 225 Rangers led by Lieutenant-Colonel James E. Rudder had already been through an ordeal. They had been loaded on to the two Liberty Ships as early as 2 June and had had to ride out the storm in the hold and the deck spaces, seasick and exhausted, before getting underway during the night of 5 6 June. Lieutenant-Colonel Rudder had taken command of the Provisional Ranger Group made up of men of the 2nd and 5th Battalions, on 9 May. Their main mission was the capture of the Pointe du Hoc where the Germans had installed a powerful battery (2./HKAR 1260). Six concrete emplacements for 155 mm guns had been built in 1942. The position, at the top of twenty metre high cliffs, had been reorganised on 15 December 1943 and, in order to protect it from increasingly heavy aerial bombardment, three concrete casemates were being built. Only two were finished by D-Day. Also, whilst waiting for the construction work to be finished, the guns were placed in a sunken lane, 200 metres south of the position. The guns could not be used but if they had been, they could have threatened the entire Baie de Seine, but no more than those at the Longues battery which were just as powerful, but which did not really constitute a real threat on D-Day! As for those of the Maissy battery...

Despite this, the group of Rangers was tasked with taking the Pointe du Hoc and, between this area and Omaha Beach, the radar position at the Pointe de la Percée (the radars were destroyed before D-Day...) Therefore, the group was split into Force A with D, E and F Companies of the 2nd Battalion for the Pointe du Hoc, and Force C with the 5th Ranger Battalion led by Lieutenant-Colonel Maxwell Schneider, and A and B Companies of the 2nd Battalion in reserve for Dog Green (Omaha), as well as this battalion's C Company engaged towards the Pointe de la Percée. We have followed Force C at Omaha Beach, let us now go back to Rudder''s Force A...

Opposite: Helmet bearing, on the back, the insignia of the 2nd Ranger Battalion. Also seen is a shoulder patch. (Private Collection)

Wilhelm Kirchhoff, the 'Severloh of the Pointe du Hoc.'

Born on 20 May 1925 at Badenthausen, Lower-Saxony, this farmer's son as was Severloh was drafted into the Werfer-Regiment 84 (rocket-launcher regiment) on 25 August 1943. The unit was based at Celle, also in Lower-Saxony, a regiment that was part of Werfer-Brigade 7, sent to the Beauvais sector on 18 May 1944 and which then went to Normandy. Wilhelm Kirchhoff was incorporated into the 2nd battery of WR 84 as a machine-gunner. When the unit was in Rouen, he went to the Pointe du Hoc on 23 May along with a dozen of his comrades. With his tough North German countryside assurance, he wrote to his parents the following: Let them come then with their invasion. We are already here. The war cannot shake us with its bombardments... They made combat positions near the Pointe du Hoc, along with their comrades of the 2./HKAA 1260, making a total of 80 artillerymen and 140 infantry.

Wilhelm Kirchhoff seen here when he met up with Georges Bernage in the Falaise Pocket in 1994. (Coll. G.B.)

1943, Wilhelm Kirchhoff, a new recruit with the 2nd battery of Werfer-Regiment 84, aged 18. (Coll. G.B.)

At 1.40 am on 6 June, 114 bombers hit the area with 637 tonnes of bombs. Wilhelm Kirchhoff remembered: *"Nothing happened to us fifteen men during this bombardment. The explosions had totally caved in many of the trenches and had torn off the camouflage netting all over the place. After, in the darkness, we repaired as much as possible so that we would be able to move around again. We then had something to eat. We were saying to each other, who knows what is going to happen today... Then the Rangers arrived, it was 5.55 am! Sie kommen! When the Americans tried to get out of their landing craft we fired on them, just as they were landing, by firing into their midst from the top of the cliff. They were totally defenceless. I only fired with my MG. I did not take aim, but just fired indiscriminately. The first soldiers out of the landing craft fell over, pushed by their comrades behind them. The dead were floating in the shallow waters and there were wounded men amongst them who I could hear screaming and shouting. More Americans started arriving and grappling hooks were fired at the cliff top. When this began, there were five MG ammunition boxes nearby which were always placed there. I stood up in the trench and put my MG under my arm. I do not know how many belts I fired and I do not know either where everyone went to get the numerous ammunition boxes. We fired a whole box at a boat then, after a brief pause, we started to fire again..."* The attempt to climb the cliff was a failure as the ropes and grappling hook were cut. The position was penetrated at a weak spot, led by Sergeant Lommel. The Werfer unit NCO then gave the order to pull back to the twelve men and they left the position in order to make their way to the Caen sector. They would go through terrible fighting and Wilhelm Kirchhoff, the survivor of the Pointe du Hoc, was eventually taken prisoner in the Falaise Pocket. He was even part of a prisoner exchange... (1)

(1) See article in the No. 322 of *39/45 Magazine.*

73

The coast was still too far away and could not be seen. A second landing craft, LCA 880 also sank (but the twenty men and Captain Slater were taken off in time); the sea was dangerous for these flat-bottomed skiffs. The Rangers were afraid of sinking and used their helmets to bail out the water that was rising in their landing craft. They then got to within three miles of the coast (almost 5 km), but Sergeant Lomell noticed that they were five kilometres too far to the east and found themselves opposite the Pointe de la Percée. He signalled this to Lieutenant-Colonel Rudder (LCA 888) who changed the heading, but a German 20 mm gun on the Pointe de la Percée then opened fire and hit a DUKW wounding or killing five of the nine Rangers it was carrying. Indeed, the landing craft now had to sail parallel to the cliffs in order to reach their objective. Also, at **6.30 am**, the destroyer, HMS Talybont, which had opened fire on the Pointe du Hoc, now ceased its firing; indeed it was H-Hour for the Rangers who were late due to the navigational error. The Germans, therefore, had 30 minutes in which to gather their wits after the heavy calibre shell fire they had just suffered and went to their combat positions. Thus, they met the Rangers with small arms fire.

The 9 LCAs of the attack force then changed heading to approach facing the cliffs, a little to the east of the jutting headland. It was 7.10 am, they were 40 minutes late. The Rangers landed along a 450 metre wide strip of pebbled beach. They came under machine-gun fire from the left, including that of Wilhelm Kirchhof. The USS Satterlee fired on the headland. LCA 888, carrying Lieutenant-Colonel Rudder, his radioman and members of the command company, was the first to come

ashore. Sergeant Domenick B. Boggeto spotted German soldiers at the top of the cliff and shot at them with a burst from his BAR. A German was hit and fell, the others disappeared. Part of the cliff had collapsed due to the bombardments, forming a mound some twelve metres high opposite LCA 888. This was useful for deploying an extension ladder. T5 George J. Putzek was the first to reach the top where he was seriously wounded. Other Rangers fired grappling hooks with attached ropes. The difficult assault succeeded in getting the Rangers to the top. A veritable battle started there in the middle of a landscape cratered by the bombardments, including those of the previous day which had formed wide craters. The advance had to be carried out under enemy fire, moving from one crater to another. The concrete observation post at the tip of the headland was knocked out by throwing three grenades and a shot from a bazooka in the observation slit. But the two gun casemates were empty! Fifty Rangers reached the lane heading south and the coast road was reached around **8 am**. According to a first-hand account by Sergeant Lommel, five 155 mm GPF guns were found in a sunken lane an hour later. Lommel then used thermite charges to destroy their breeches and render them unusable. However, this position was surrounded by the Germans who brought up reinforcements from Grandcamp by truck. The Rangers, spread out over the large position, had to continue fighting against elements of II./914 and 9./726. The fighting there was chaotic. The surviving Rangers found themselves in a critical situation and did not receive any reinforcements until the morning of the 7th and were not relieved until the 8th by troops that came from

Photo, opposite page: An aid post set up by the Rangers near the tip of the headland. Note the presence of a British officer at the bottom right of the photo. This is Lt.Col. Thomas H. Trevor of N°1 Commando. He was the Rangers' instructor in Scotland. A climbing specialist, he followed his pupils on D-Day! He is seen here with a bandaged head after having been wounded by a sniper whilst on the beach as he was encouraging these Rangers as they climbed up the Pointe du Hoc. This photo illustrates another interesting story. One can see the paratrooper Len Goodgal of I/506 (the first man sitting down from the right). His plane was shot down by flak during the night. He managed to jump out in time and landed in the sea off Pointe du Hoc. He got rid of his equipment, except for his rifle, and managed to reach the shore. During the night he tried to climb up the cliff in order to reach his comrades who had landed inland, but did not manage. As day broke, he watched the landing of the Rangers and joined them as they climbed up the Pointe du Hoc. He can be identified, among his new comrades, by his jump boots and reinforced pants typical of those used by paratroopers in Normandy, and also his 101st shoulder patch. (US Army)

Omaha Beach. 77 of the Rangers died and only 120 were still able to fight. Could the five guns, stuck in a sunken lane, have been more dangerous than those of the 352nd division if they had been set up inland? This very costly attack leaves a lot of unanswered questions...

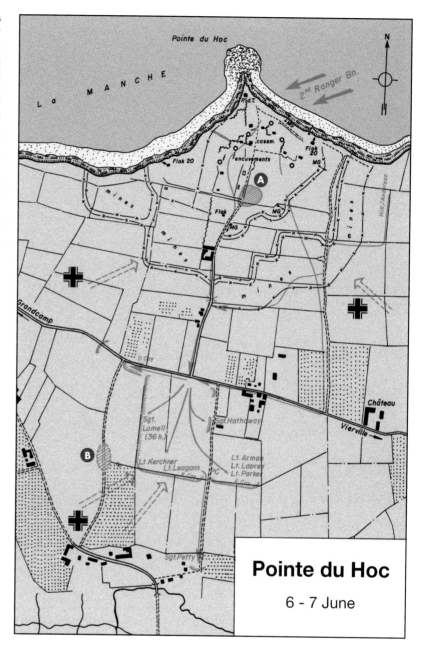

Pointe du Hoc

6 - 7 June

Opposite: A map of the Pointe du Hoc sector with the observation and fire control post to the north, near the tip, the gun emplacements and artillery battery casemates, protected by minefields. However, the casemates had not been finished and the 155 mm GPF guns (captured French guns) were placed in a sunken lane away from the site (marked B on the map). In any case, even if they had been finished, the narrow openings of the casemates pointed north and presented no threat for the troops landing on Utah Beach or Omaha Beach. As for the Rangers, they remained surrounded until the arrival of troops from Omaha Beach. So was this an unnecessary operation? It is increasingly the opinion shared by historians... (Heimdal map)

Opposite: Rangers bringing in their prisoners after the fighting. The flag was used for aerial recognition. The Pointe du Hoc can be seen in the background. (US Army.)

Gold and Juno

Juno Beach - Bernières - Nan White

At **8.05 am**, A and B Companies of the Queen's Own Rifles of Canada, prepared to land on Nan White opposite **Bernières-sur-Mer**. With them was Marcel Ouimet, a French-speaking journalist from Radio Canada. He had already taken part in the Sicily and Italian landings and was there to give a first-hand account over the radio of the events unfolding in front of him: *"We were up very early on the morning of the. At 5am we saw a grey line on the horizon. Yes, this was the French coastline. We were in the Baie de Seine and over there, far away, planes were carrying out their first bomb runs. From time to time, enemy flak filled the sky but squadron after squadron passed over, followed by the dull explosions of our bombs. A little later, the fleet's gunboats were champing at the bit and the battleships and cruisers opened fire. There were no enemy planes in the sky. Everything seemed unreal."* Marcel Ouimet then saw the small landing craft passing by the ship he was on. *"They carried massed assault troops holding their guns, wearing steel helmets and only carrying the essential equipment: their gas masks and 24-hour rations, mess tins, field dressings. Several ships cheered them as they passed and, on another, a Scottish piper played, the same one who had serenaded us the previous day as we left the port in England.*

Plaintive and inspiring sounds came out. The soldiers did not have a bugle to sound the charge."

However, the Queen's Own infantrymen received a tough reception and out of all the Canadian assault units, they suffered the heaviest losses. This was mainly due to the late arrival of the DD tanks; they were put to sea too far from the shore and, because of the swell, did not arrive on time.

Thus, at **8.05 am**, the Queen's Own landed in waist-deep water, using the pointed spire of the Bernières church and the 'Norman house' as landmarks... A Company, led by Major H.E. Dalton, landed on the right, to the west of the station, losing a dozen men and reaching the small railway line where it came under mortar fire. But, further to the east, B Company, led by another Dalton, Major Oscar Dalton, lost a third of its strength crossing the beach: 65 casualties in a few minutes at the foot of the small concrete casemates of a fortified strong point (WN 28), known to the Canadians as the 'Cassine', armed with a 50 mm gun in a casemate. Major Oscar Dalton and Lieutenant MacLean were killed. The position was finally overcome with grenades at 9.30 am. The second wave arrived at **8.45 am** with two reserve companies (C and D). However, with the rising tide, the LCAs were destroyed on the obstacles, damaged by the steel hedgehogs and mines. The men had to swim to the shore.

Opposite page and above: Off Bernières, from where the smoke of fires still rise, the heavy tonnage ships remain offshore whilst the landing craft (LCA 518 above) head towards the beach and the LCLs (here 252, opposite page), prepare to land men and materiel. This is what was seen by Marcel Ouimet. These remarkable colour photos were taken by Ken Bell. (Canadian National Defence Image Library.)

Opposite: This famous photo, taken by Lieutenant Gilbert Milne, shows elements of the Stormont Dundas and Glengarry Highlanders (9th Brigade) landing after 11.40 am. Note the 'big Norman house', one of the two landmarks, along with the church tower of Bernières. (PAC.)

The village of Bernières was finally cleared at 9 am with the arrival of the Fort Garry Horse and, at **9.30 am**, a second echelon landed the French Canadians of the **Régiment de la Chaudière**. Many of the latter lost their equipment and had to swim as four of their five LCAs had been damaged. They were met with amazement in Bernières as they spoke French with the local accent...

Let us now go back to the first-hand account of Marcel Ouimet: *"The first French people that I saw in France were those of Bernières, mostly Normans but also a few Parisians who had come to seaside for the holidays. It was these people, their wives and daughters who threw flowers to our troops as they marched through the streets. Yet, during the night they had not slept much and for some, the landings signified the loss of their property."* However, the Canadians believed that there were a lot of collaborators in the population and initially decided to group these people together, as a precaution, in front the 'Norman house'!

There then followed a huge traffic jam as the vehicles tried to get through the small streets of Bernières before heading inland.

Thus, the **8th Brigade** commanded by Brigadier K.G. Blackadder, had landed on Nan White (BerniËres) with the Queen's Own and Chaudières, but also on Nan Red (Saint-Aubin-sur-mer) with the North Shores and the British 45th Royal Marines Commando. The Brigade was one of three of the 3rd Canadian Infantry Division, commanded by Major-General Keller who had the landing sector with the codename of Juno Beach. Further west,

Brigadier Harry W. Foster's **7th Brigade** landed at the Seulles estuary, at Courseulles and Graye-sur-mer. This Division's third brigade, the 9th Brigade, led by Brigadier D.G. Cunningham, known as the 'Scottish Brigade', was in reserve. Also, this completely mechanised Canadian division with a strength of 18,000 men, was supported by four artillery groups (12th, 13th, 14th and 19th), a reconnaissance group, machine units supporting the infantry, four engineers companies (5th, 6th, 16th and 18th) and the 3rd Antitank Regiment. But the division was also strengthened by an armoured brigade (3,500 extra men), the **2nd Armoured brigade** led by Brigadier R.A. Wyman, with three tank regiments, the 1st Hussars (6th Tank Regiment), attached to the 7th Brigade, the Fort Garry Horse (10th Regiment) attached to the 8th Brigade, and the Sherbrooke Fusiliers (27th Regiment) attached to the 9th Brigade. With such a strength and means, this reinforced division constituted a strike force that was greatly superior to a German Panzer-Division!

Marcel Ouimet, a journalist for Radio Canada, followed the landing operations on Nan White and broadcast from BerniËres, but his broadcasting equipment was basic and he had to engrave his reports onto discs which were then sent to London. (Radio Canada)

Above: Fearing acts of sabotage or francs tireurs by the French, it was decided to gather the civilian population in front of the 'Norman house'. (PAC)

Below: On the beach at Bernières, a little to the west of the 'Norman house', a MP of the Beach Groups, searches a German prisoner. A soldier of the Régiment de la Chaudière has his back to the camera. (PAC)

Opposite: The beach is strewn with the wrecks of landing craft and armoured vehicles destroyed at high tide during the assault. They were rapidly towed away by bulldozers. Wire and wood mats have been placed on the ground to make it easier for men and materiel to move over the soft sand. (Ken Bell/National Defence Images Library.)

Above: A group of soldiers from the 8th Beach Group, a regiment formed from the Royal Berkshire Regiment (identifiable by white strip on their helmets), sit in a DUKW next to the 'Bernières house'. (PAC)

A soldier of the Régiment de la Chaudière plays with a young Norman boy. The Norman civilians were surprised to hear 'Tommies' speaking French, sometimes even with the old Normandy dialect. (PAC)

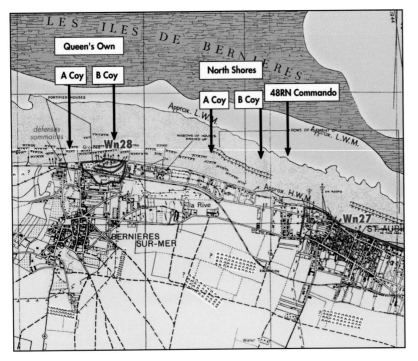

Saint-Aubin - Nan Red

Let us now go back to the rest of the 8th Brigade and the Royal Marines at Nan Red. The North Shore Regiment landed at **7.55 am** in the sector west of **Saint-Aubin**, where WN 27 was situated, a resistance point with only a few defensive points, including a small casemate armed with a 5 cm gun on the seafront (the casemate is still there today), and the village was only defended by soldiers of the 5./736 under the command of lieutenant Gustav Pfloksch.

To the west, A Company, supported by the amphibious tanks of the Fort Garry Horse, encountered little opposition and reached the first objective line at 9.50 am with only nine dead and 25 wounded. But further to the east, B Company led by Major Bob Forbes, landed under fire from WN 27 and suffered heavy casualties opposite the 'strongpoint' and the combined fire from small arms, mortars and guns of the Germans. The infantry landed at **8 am** but found itself pinned down beneath the seawall; the Fort Garry Horse DD tanks did not arrive until around **10 am**. The 5 cm gun in the casemate swept the beach. By the time the tanks turned up there were already seventeen dead and wounded. Captain Canet went via the village in order to knock the gun out but he could not get through due to a log road block barring the way. The fighting went on for two hours at the end of which the Germans showed a white flag, before continuing the fight; the Canadians did not take any prisoners with these: fifty Germans were killed or wounded and 79 prisoners taken, including four officers. However, it took another 24 hours before the area was cleared.

C Company landed with Tailleville as their objective where the headquarters of a German battalion was based, II./736; the time was **2.30 pm**. However, the HQ was in a ch,teau north of the village and its perimeter wall had been fortified. It was not until 6 pm that the attack could go in, supported by thirteen Fort Garry Horse tanks. Fifty prisoners were taken but hidden snipers continued to shoot until nightfall when they were cleared out with flame throwers. But the North Shore's second mission, the capture of the **Douvres radar station**, failed. This entrenched position would hold out for **eleven days** in the middle of the allied lines, a cut-off defensive island which informed by radio the German command on allied movement in the sector!

Bernières

Above: This small casemate, part of WN 28 defended by 5./736, held a 5 cm KwK gun which caused a lot of problems for the Queen's Own Rifles who lost 65 men on this beach. (PAC) The casemate is still there (below) and there are two memorials nearby, one of which is to the Queen's and the other to the Fort Garry Horse. A little further on, near a Tobruck bunker, is another memorial to the Régiment de la Chaudière. (EG/Heimdal.)

Opposite, right: Another photo taken at the same place on the same day, showing a lance-corporal of the Régiment de la Chaudière guarding German prisoners. (PAC)

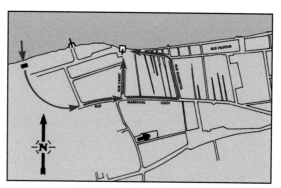

The advance of the North Shores in Saint-Aubin, from the west of the beach to the casemate with the 5 cm gun, neutralised from the centre of the village, principally in rue Canet. The second map shows the advance inland, as far as Tailleville where the grounds of a ch,teau were a veritable defensive redoubt.

On the other hand, the Douvres radar station remained a redoubt in the middle of the Canadian lines for several days... (Heimdal maps)

1 and 2. This 50 cm KwK gun in the heart of WN 27 caused heavy casualties to the North Shores who had to advance through the village of Saint-Aubin in order to knock it out. (EG/Heimdal.)

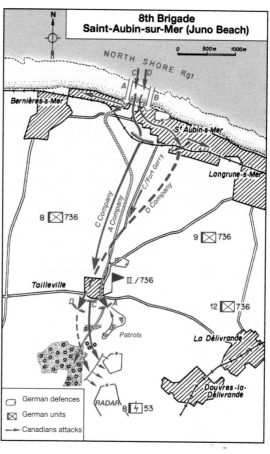

**8th Brigade
Saint-Aubin-sur-Mer (Juno Beach)**

0   500m   1000m

NORTH SHORE Rgt

Bernières-s-Mer

St Aubin-s-Mer

Langrune-s-Mer

8 ⊠ 736

C Company

A Company

C/Fort Garry

D Company

9 ⊠ 736

Tailleville

II. / 736

12 ⊠ 736

D   C   A

Patrols

La Délivrande

RADAR 8 ⚡ 53

Douvres-la-
Délivrande

⊏⊐ German defences
⊠ German units
→ Canadians attacks

3 and 4. Nan-Red Saint-Aubin.

When the Royal Marines landed to the west of Saint-Aubin at 8.43 am, the tide was rising and two LCI (S) hit mines placed on obstacles and sank. They also came under fire from the 50 mm gun that had not yet been knocked out. (IWM)

And today. (Heimdal)

Above and below: The 48 RM Commando landed at 8.43 am on the eastern edge of Nan Red, next to Oboe Beach and the outskirts of Saint-Aubin and the threat of the 5 cm gun installed there. The landing was made at high tide and on the obstacles. The unit suffered 50% casualties, three quarters of which were on the beach. Seen here is the landing of the headquarters of the 4th S.S. Brigade at 9 am. The ramps were steep and bobbed up and down with the waves, some heavily loaded Royal Marines slipped off. (IWM)

The Royal Marines

The **48th Royal Marine Commando** was supposed to land behind the North Shores then head off to the east and capture Langrune, defended by WN 26, then continue towards the east and Luc to link up with the 41st Royal Marine Commando in action at Lion. However, the 48 RM Commando suffered from several handicaps. It was a recently formed unit and had not yet seen action. Also, it only had light weapons. The only tanks available in the Nan Red sector were those of C Squadron, Fort Garry Horse (which were sent to Tailleville), the 'Funnies' of B Squadron, 22nd Dragoons, AVREs of the 80th Assault Squadron and six Centaur tanks of the 2nd Armoured (Royal Marine) Support Regiment. Only two Centaur tanks assisted the Royal Marines in their advance to Langrune.

The 48 RM Commando was transported on six LCI(S) that departed from the river Hamble. They were facing Nan Red at **8.43 am** and two of them sank after hitting mines, taking many heavily loaded commandos with them beneath the waves. The LCI carrying Lieutenant-Colonel Moulton, hit an obstacle and Captain Flunder, who was on board, was thrown into the sea as he prepared to lead his men down the ramps of this LCI. The landing craft bringing in Y Troop was halted 135 metres from the shore. The Commandos of Z Troop came under fire from the 5 cm gun situated in the small casemate at the end of rue Canet. Small arms fire pinned them down along the foot of the seawall. When the situation improved, the Royal Marines advanced along the coast road towards Langrune. There, they came under mortar fire and were forced to take cover, before continuing their advance and reaching WN 26, a strong point established in Langrune. B Troop attacked it with the support of two Centaur tanks.

This position proved to be a tough nut to crack. The first of the two Centaur tanks hit a mine and the second could not do much with its gun against concrete bunkers, what was needed was an AVRE tank with its formidable Petard rounds. The Royal Marines were unable to take WN 26 on this day. They suffered 50% casualties for little gain. Opposite the breach still open between Juno Beach and Sword Beach sectors, the Nan Red sub-sector had the smallest advance in the Juno sector on 6 June.

The beach at Saint-Aubin seen from the small casemate with its 5 cm gun visible in the foreground and which enfiladed the Royal Marines to the east. The seafront is almost undamaged. (Heimdal.)

A little further on, in Langrune, civilians provide information to Captain Wilmot, one of the intelligence officers of the 4th Special Service Brigade. This unit was tasked with taking Langrune and continuing eastwards. (IWM)

1, 2 and 3. The II battalion of Grenadier-Regiment 736 had its HQ in the ch‚teau at Tailleville and the wall surrounding the grounds had been fortified, as we can see in these three photos. The wall, pierced with firing slits, was strengthened with concrete machine-gun pillboxes. Also (still visible, third photo) an observation post was built in a tree. (E.G./Heimdal.)

The tanks of the Fort Garry Horse in Bernières and Saint-Aubin

Opposite: Tanks of the Fort Garry Horse (10th Canadian Armoured Regiment) landed at Bernières (With A and B Squadrons) to support the Queen's Own, and at Saint-Aubin (with C Squadron) to support the North Shores. Here are some pictures of these DD tanks going through Bernières-sur-mer. This one, a Sherman M4 of B Squadron, is entering the church square, its flotation skirts have been raised.

The fighting is over and the tank men are partially out of their tank. Note the number '176' painted on the left-hand side running gear support.
(Coll. Heimdal.)

Opposite. This tank is from an unidentified squadron but bears an interesting marking painted by the crew on the left flank of the Sherman: 'Death takes a holiday', accompanied by a skull and crossbones. This inscription is a reminder of a 1934 film in which death takes a rest to come and live with humans to find out how they hold on to life.

(Photo coll. Heimdal and profile by Thierry Vallet/Heimdal.)

© Thierry Vallet / 2012

Inspired by a photo from the same set, here is another Sherman of the Fort Garry Horse bearing a square on its turret signifying that it belongs to B Squadron. The square is black with a yellow border. (Profile by Thierry Vallet/Heimdal.)

This other Sherman DD is parked on the church square. It belongs to the 3rd Troop, B Squadron. Despite its flotation screen, this Duplex Drive did not take to sea but landed on the beach, as did all the B Squadron tanks. Note here the different marking on the cover placed along the side of the turret. (Photo Coll. Heimdal and profile by Thierry Vallet/ Heimdal.)

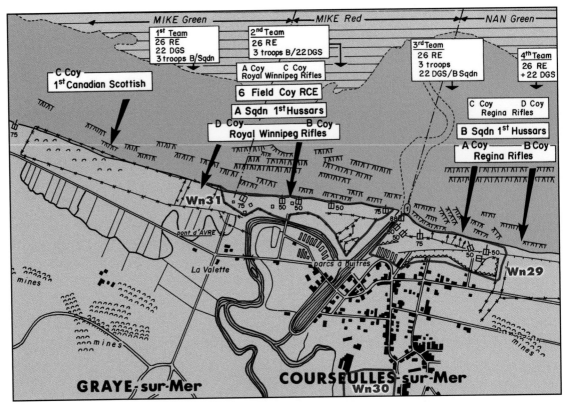

Nan Green, the Courseulles beach, to the east, and Mike Beach, to the west of the river Seulles, were the best defended beaches and caused heavy losses to the 7th Canadian Brigade. (Heimdal map)

Map labels:
MIKE Green — MIKE Red — NAN Green

1st Team
26 RE
22 DGS
3 troops B/Sqdn

2nd Team
26 RE
3 troops B/22 DGS

3rd Team
26 RE
3 troops
22 DGS/B Sqdn

4th Team
26 RE
+ 22 DGS

C Coy
1st Canadian Scottish

A Coy   C Coy
Royal Winnipeg Rifles

6 Field Coy RCE

A Sqdn 1st Hussars

D Coy — B Coy
Royal Winnipeg Rifles

C Coy   D Coy
Regina Rifles

B Sqdn 1st Hussars

A Coy — B Coy
Regina Rifles

Wn31
pont d'AVRE
La Valette
mines
parcs à huitres
Wn29
mines

GRAYE-sur-Mer   COURSEULLES-sur-Mer
Wn30

Courseulles: Nan Green

The other wave of the Canadian assault, the **7th Brigade**, commanded by Brigadier **H.W. Foster**, landed on the other side of the Seulles estuary, in front of solid German positions formed by three 'resistance nests': WN 29, defending the beach at Courseulles, WN 31 of Graye, to the west of the river Seulles, and WN 30, to the rear of the village of Courceulles.

Nan Green, facing Courseulles and WN 29, was the landing area of the **Regina Rifle Regiment** commanded by Lieutenant-Colonel Foster M. Matheson, nicknamed 'Matt' by his men. This regiment sent in two of its companies (see map), with A to the west and B to the east. They had support from the DD tanks of B Squadron, 1st Hussars (Major Duncan), but also special tanks of the 4th Team and AVREs and tanks of B Squadron, 22nd Dragoons, shared out between the three brigade assault companies. They had to take on a 8,8 cm gun in a casemate (see photo), but also three 7,5 cm guns, three 5 cm guns, twelve machine-gun pillboxes and two mortar positions. They would be encountering hell!

Therefore, shortly after **8 am**, the two Regina Rifles assault companies arrived off the beach in their LCAs. However, **A Company** did not have the support it expected: all of the DD tanks had sunk. 19 DD tanks had been put into the rough sea 3,600 metres (4,000 yards) from the shore. Major Duncan's tank sank immediately. Those that did not sink arrived too far to the east and could not support Major Grosch's A Company faced with a 8,8 cm gun in a casemate and another with a 7,5 gun.

On the left, **B Company**, led by Major Peters, did not experience the same problems; opposition was weak to the east of the resistance nest, especially as the DD and special tanks were already on the beach. Courseulles was divided up into twelve blocks by this company. It cleared Block

Lieutenant-Colonel Foster M. Matheson, commander of the Regina Rifles. He was a professional soldier and an excellent leader. He took command of the 1st Battalion, Regina Rifles in April 1942 before taking command of the regiment in March 1943 and leading its training. He was nicknamed 'Matt' by his men, due to his black hair and eyes, and soon after, his thin moustache. He is seen here watching his men training in England. (PAC)

2, then continued on to Block 3, whilst the AVRE tanks opened breaches along the seafront, through which the DD tanks sped through, including Sergeant Leo Gariepy's 'Bucéphale' and several Centaur tanks, supporting the mopping up of the various blocks of housing into the heart of the village, where B Company was clearing Block 8. On the right, A Company only overcame the casemates at **9.30 am** (Block 1) after suffering heavy casualties and thanks to the arrival of Centaur and Churchill tanks with their Petard rounds. A tunnel network helped the Germans to reoccupy their positions and cause problems to the rear of the Canadians.

The reinforcement companies then arrived (C and D Company). However, the tide was rising and the landing craft suffered heavy losses on the beach obstacles. Five of the D Company (Major Love) LCAs hit mined obstacles and there were more than sixty casualties on the beach. Major Love was killed and only 49 survivors from this company were able to carry on fighting.

C Company soon arrived in the centre of Courseulles and cleared Block 9, 10 and 11. The battalion HQ was then set up in the centre of the village. WN 30 was behind the ch,teau and was defended by mortars and machine-guns; it was silenced by tanks. The next objective was the village of Reviers. The time was **10.30 am**. However, in the meantime, A Company was still held up on the beach close to its initial objective, Block 1, where fighting regularly started again due to a tunnel network which allowed the German resistance to hold on. It took the support of tanks and flame throwers to overcome it as late as approximately 1 pm!

80 Germans were taken prisoner in Courseulles and many more were killed or wounded; others

This H677 type casemate was to the west of WN 29, the position defending the beach at Courseulles and here, the entrance to the port. It held a formidable 8,8 cm Pak 43:41. This photo was taken a few days after the landings and the Canadians have, in the meantime, set up an anti-aircraft gun on top. (PAC)

Courseulles

1. The mouth of the river Seulles in front of the port, seen here after the Canadian landings. The Reginas landed on the right (to the east) and the Winnipegs on the left of this estuary. (PAC)

2. In the same area, but a little more to the rear, can still be found the 5 cm gun guarding the entrance to the port. Its steel shield has been hit several times. Originally, this gun was in a bunker. (EG/Heimdal)

3. Aerial photo showing the landing sector of the Royal Winnipeg Rifles at Graye-sur-Mer (Mike Beach). The bend of the river Seulles can be clearly seen before arriving in the port of Courseulles. (IWM)

withdrew to the south. At around **11 am**, the two reinforcement companies, C and D, landed at **Reviers**, followed by the battalion headquarters. During this time, B Company finished mopping up Courseulles, flushing out snipers, even as far as the church tower, before also heading to Reviers at approximately 3 pm. A Company only reached Reviers three hours later.

Mike Beach: Graye-sur-mer

Mike Red was to the west of the Seulles estuary and was overlooked by dunes defended by WN 31, placed between the bend of the river Seulles and the sea. This was where B Company of the Winnipegs was due to land. Further west, beyond the formidable WN 31 at Mike Green Beach, were more dunes, barbed wire, an area of marshland, then the village of Graye-sur-mer behind minefields. This was the landing zone for D Company of the Winnipegs. It was supported on its right by C Company of the 1st Canadian Scottish. These three assault companies would be supported by DD tanks of the 1st Hussars, the 6th Field Company RCE and 2nd Team special tanks on Mike Red and the 1st Team on Mike Green.

At 7.49 am, the two assault companies of the **Royal Winnipeg Rifles**, the Little Black Devils, led by Lieutenant-Colonel Meldrem, leapt from their LCAs into a metre of water. But they were alone. A navigational error meant that they had no tanks with them. Changes to the plans held up the arrival of the DD tanks. Navigational errors held up the LCTs bringing the special tanks; they would arrive thirty minutes later. On the left, near the estuary, B Company landed directly in front of WN 31 and a salvo of mortar projectiles rained down on the LCAs with twenty men lost before they even set foot on the beach. On the beach the men had

to advance under a hail of fire as far as the concrete positions. The Black Devils attacked them with grenades and Sten guns in tough close-quarter fighting against a determined enemy. Then, six DD Shermans at last emerged from the water, fired on by two 7,5 cm and 8,8 cm guns in casemates. Casualties were heavy: 48 dead and 85 wounded out of an initial strength of 160 men. Finally, at **11 am**, the bulk of the A Squadron's DD tanks landed directly on the beach from LCTs. B Company suffered the heaviest losses and only its leader, Captain Gower, and 26 men were still combat fit at the end of D-Day. For now, the survivors left the dunes and crossed the steel bridge over the Seulles, mopping up the La Valette hamlet.

D Company had fewer problems. It landed to the west of WN 31 and quickly crossed the beach, opening up a path through the minefields at La Valette and clearing Graye-sur-mer. This rapid advance allowed the reinforcement A and B Companies to reach their first objectives. **A Company** was commanded by Major Fred Hodge who reorganised his unit in the dunes opposite the barbed wire and a minefield, through which he led his men with worry. They then went beyond D Company. C Company went to **Banville**. A Company advanced to **Sainte-Croix-sur-mer** at **9 am** where it

A Churchill AVRE tank which took part in the landings on Juno Beach. It was recovered and is now displayed at Graye-sur-mer. (E.G./Heimdal)

encountered stiff resistance. It was pinned down there by six or eight machine-guns then headed to Banville.

Further west, **C Company** of the **1st Canadian Scottish**, was attached to the Winnipegs in order to knock out a casemate housing a 7,5 cm threatening Mike Beach. However, the navy had already dealt with this gun when the Cannucks (1st Canadian Scottish) landed and they were able, therefore, to continue on to their second objective, the Vaux ch,teau defended by the Russians of Ost-Bataillon 441. The Canadians found themselves confronted by an unexpected enemy! The fighting with sub machine-guns and grenades caused a dozen losses in the ranks of the Cannucks. At around **9.30 am**, the rest of the 1st Canadian Scottish Regiment, with its commander, Lieutenant-Colonel Fred Cabeldu, also landed and followed the path taken by the C Company of the Winnipegs. Once out of the dunes, they had to cross a marshy area before reaching the hamlet of La Valette. A 1st Team AVRE tank had sunk there and fascines were placed on it to make a crossing point; this tank remained buried under the road until 1976. It was removed by the a British REME unit, restored and displayed to bear witness to the events of this historic day and the role it played. At La Valette, the Cannucks established contact with the B Company Winnipegs. Their objective now was **Sainte-Croix** which they finished clearing it with C Company of the Winnipegs who were in action there, as we have already seen.

Towards the D-Day objectives

At **12 pm**, Brigadier Harry Foster, commanding the 7th Brigade, signalled to the command ship, HMS Hilary, that the Mike-Nan Beach sector was now totally cleared. His brigade would continue its advance in the afternoon. After Sainte-Croix-sur-mer, the 1st Canadian Scottish continued on to **Creully** and **Colombiers-sur-Seulles** (brigade HQ was set up there), also reached, via Banville, by the Winnipegs. Together, the Cannucks and Winnipegs continued to **Pierrepont,** thus reaching the first line of the D-Day objective, the Elm Line. This line was passed as far as the outskirts of

Camilly. However, the Oak Line second objective along the Bayeaux-Caen railway line south of the RN 13 road, would not be reached on this day by the units of the Second British Army. The Reginas arrived at Perriers and advanced as far as **Fontaine-Henry** where they spent the night. However, the tanks engaged on the plateau to the west of this this village, were confronted by 8,8 cm guns and six Shermans were destroyed.

To the east and in the **8th** and **9th Brigade** sector, the Chaudières reached **Bény-sur-mer** and **Basly**. As for the Queen's, as we have seen, they reached Anguerny and 9th Brigade elements arrived at **Anisy** and **Villons-les-Buissons**, a deep

The advance inland by the 7th and 8th Canadian Brigades on 6 June. (Heimdal map)

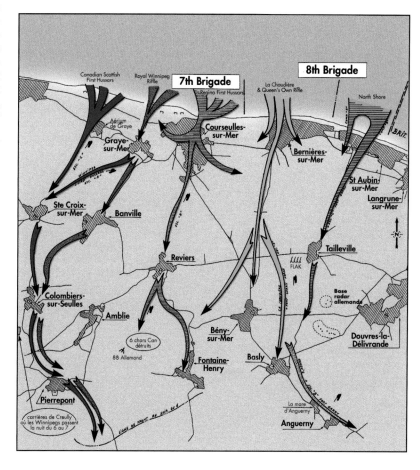

advance towards Caen. An even deeper advance was made from Camilly in the 7th Brigade sector; Lieutenant Mc Cormick of the 1st Hussars, reached the RN 13 road unopposed in a deep reconnaissance. The front had broken up and there was barely any enemy left in the sector before German reinforcements began arriving. He saw the hangers at Carpiquet. He turned back in Secqueville, coming across a few surprised Germans. It took a month of hard fighting to get to Carpiquet when, on 6 June, this objective was within firing distance. The determined German resistance in the coastal positions and the awful traffic jams coming off the beaches set back the timetable and despite the fact that the Canadians advanced further than the British in the Sword sector, the entire advance stopped at the end of day and did not start again until the following morning with German armour making its way into the sector.

Losses to the units of the 3rd Canadian Infantry Division on 6 June 1944 were **961 men**, of which 319 were killed. The heaviest losses were suffered by the Queen's Own Rifles of Canada, with 143 casualties, of which 61 were killed. They were followed by those of the Royal Winnipeg Rifles with 55 dead out of their 128 casualties. The North Shore Regiment lost 125 men with 33 killed, the Regina Regiment 108 losses with 42 dead and the Régiment de la Chaudière, 105 casualties of which 16 were killed.

Gold Beach

The Gold Beach sector was spread out over ten miles (16 kilometres), but its western side consisted of cliffs overlooking the sea. However, this sector had a bay in which a Mulberry artificial harbour would be set up, and the Port-en-Bessin disembarkation port. These were, therefore, essential objectives which would be captured from the only available beaches at Asnelles (Jig Beach) and Ver-sur-mer (King Beach), the main objective for the evening of D-Day being the town of Bayeux, an important road junction. The landings were made with the considerably strengthened 50th Northumbrian Division led by Major-General Graham. Thus, by the evening of D-Day, 25,000 men would have landed on these two beaches.

The initial assault was made with two infantry brigades (the Division exceptionally had four brigades

for D-Day). To the east, on King Beach, the 69th Infantry Brigade engaged the 6th Green Howards and the 5th East Yorkshires. To the west, on Jig Green (east of Asnelles), the 231st Infantry Brigade engaged the 1st Hampshires, near Roquettes (attacked by the 1st Dorsets) in order to capture WN 36, then head towards Le Hamel and WN 37 positioned in the seaside part of Asnelles.

Artillery duel with the Longues battery

As Force G approached the coast, to the west of the sector at **6.05 am**, the Longues battery (Wn 48, 4./HKAA 1260) opened fire on the allied fleet. It had been under fire from the French cruiser Georges Leygues as early as 5.37 am and also that of USS Arkansas. The battery had fired back at the destroyer USS Emmons, then the French cruiser Montcalm. It was now Force G that offered the most targets and it caused problems for the command ship HMS Bulolo which had to weigh anchor and withdraw. HMS Ajax then attacked the battery and a duel began over a range of 11,000 metres, forcing the battery to cease firing at 6.20 am. However, the battery began firing again at **7 am**, this time against the Americans landing at Omaha Beach. HMS Ajax and HMS Argonaut then joined forces to silence the battery and three of the four 15,2 cm guns were silenced. The last gun continued firing until 5 pm at the ships and landing beaches.

King Beach: Ver-sur-mer

The **69th Brigade** (Brigadier Knox) approached with two battalions next to each other: the **5th East Yorkshires** to the left (east) facing La Rivière (the seaside part of Ver) and the **6th Green Howards** to the right (west) facing Hable de Heurtot (WN 35). The DD tanks of the **4th/7th Dragoon Guards** supported this attack, C Squadron for the East Yorks and B Squadron for the Green Howards. The follow-up battalion of the **7th Green Howards** came in next and was supported by A Squadron of the Dragoon Guards. The DD tanks were supposed to enter the sea from their LCTs at H+50 but, due to the sea conditions, the LCTs brought them right up to the shore, adding to the jam on the beaches. Special tanks also came in,

Aerial view of King Beach with the anti-tank ditch clearly visible, dug along the foot of the Mont Fleury battery where CSM Hollis was in action. Note the already busy road which crosses the ditch, then goes along the battery. (IWM)

Below: One of the naval 15 cm TBtsK C/36 guns of the naval battery attached to the army, 4./HKAA 1260, shortly after the landings. The aerial bombing and naval bombardments destroyed one of these casemates and churned up the surrounding ground, as we can see in this photo. However, three of the M 272 type casemates remained intact. (IWM)

Flail tanks of C Squadron, Westminster Dragoons for mine clearing and AVREs of the 81st Squadron, 6th Assault Regiment R.E.

The landings at Rivière began well but, shortly after the tanks arrived, a 8,8 mm gun in a H 677 casemate in **WN 33**, enfiladed the beach and two special tanks were immediately destroyed. It was chaos. However, a Flail tank of the Westminster Dragoons closed in on the casemate and succeeded in firing three shells into the embrasure, thus silencing the gun. Naval gunfire support to the rear of WN 33 kept the defenders' heads down and allowed the East Yorks to cross the beach front and enter into the defensive positions and clear them one by one. WN 33 was captured at **8.30 am** and 45 prisoners taken, but the attack had cost the East Yorks 90 men killed or wounded, including 6 officers. A company from this battalion had gone around WN 33 and made its way to the high ground where it captured WN 34, the small position around the Mont Fleury lighthouse; thirty prisoners were taken there.

To the west, the **6th Green Howards** (Lieutenant-Colonel Robin Hastings) landed at Hable de Heurtot where it was met by fire coming from **WN 35**, defended by a company of Russian volunteers; 3./441. However, the arrival of tanks silenced this position and the Russians were perhaps not quite as motivated as the Germans. Three AVREs led by Captain King, assisted by **A Company** infantry, overcame these concrete positions. Under the command of Major Lofthouse, **D Company**, Green Howards, then crossed the marshes via the only road, avoiding the anti-tank ditch on its right and moving up in a straight line to the high ground as far as the 'Mont Fleury' battery (3./HKAA 1260). It was here that one of the company's leaders, CSM CSM Stan Hollis, first came to the fore, later being awarded the prestigious Victoria Cross for his bravery. This position was rapidly mopped-up; the gunners were still stunned by the bombardment

Seen here is the remarkable two-level M 262a type fire control position which is undamaged and on the edge of the clay cliff. It was made famous when used in scenes in 'The Longest Day' film, as well as the battery's casemates. (E.G./Heimdal.)

they had suffered. Twelve hits from HMS Orion were counted on the casemates. Now, the two other battalion companies, **B** and **C Companies** also landed and were able to quickly advance inland following the rapid clearing of the beach exits. B Company advanced towards the southwest to clear the small concrete positions which ran along the Meuvaines crest and some fighting took place there. C Company occupied high

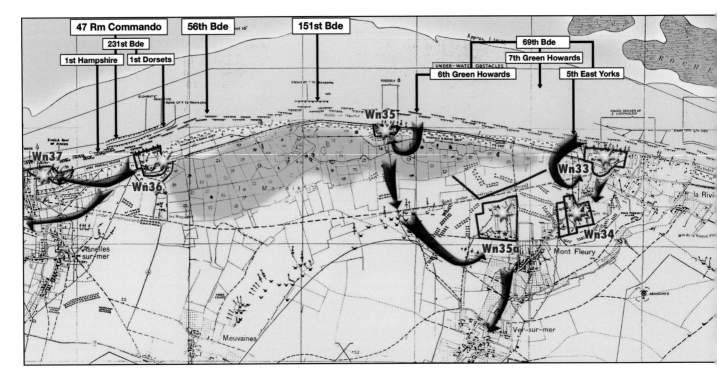

231st Bde | 7th Green Howards

1st Hampshire | 1st Dorsets | 6th Green Howards | 5th East Yorks

Wn37 | Wn36 | Wn35 | Wn35a | Wn33 | Wn34

Opposite: Asnelles (Wn 37), this H 612 type casemate housed the only 7,5 cm FK gun. We see here the now closed-up embrasure of this casemate. Note the strong concrete shoulders designed to protect the embrasure and rear from direct fire. (E.G./Heimdal.)

Opposite, below: A 2 cm flak gun positioned in a concrete bunker on the Meuvaines plateau, between Asnelles (left) and Ver-sur-mer (right). This photo was taken by RAF personnel who were interested in how this anti-aircraft gun worked. (IWM)

ground (Hill 52) west of Ver and the advance continued towards **Crépon**. The village was reached but a German HQ was there and, above all, southwest of the village, an artillery battery 5./1716, with four Czech-made 10 cm guns. Upon reaching Crepon, Lieutenant-Colonel Hastings was keen to get to Saint-Léger on the RN 13 road. He wanted to avoid costly street fighting in the village so B and C Companies went around it with Major Lofthouse remaining behind with D Company to clear it. The Major issued his orders to the platoon commanders: Just do the minimum necessary to open the road for us to use. Company Sergeant Major **Hollis** was tasked with taking the farm at the south-west exit of the village. It was empty, except for a young boy who would act as a guide. He came out of the garden facing a field of rhubarb; there were Germans from the 5./1716 with their four 10 cm guns. He took a PIAT and led seven or eight men into the rhubarb field, crawling towards the battery. All of the men were hit. The PIAT did not work and the guns opened up on the farm buildings forcing a withdrawal, but he ended up knocking out all of the guns and would later be awarded the Victoria Cross.

The **7th Green Howards** had, in the meantime, landed at **8.20 am**. They went through Ver-sur-mer, abandoned by the Germans and reached the battery at Mare Fontaine (6./1716) to the southeast sud-est of the village. The German gunners had been demoralised by the bombardment and surrendered. Eighty-seven shell cases for the 10 cm Czech guns were counted around the battery. On the beach, the self-propelled guns of the 124th Field Artillery Regiment were now ready to support the advance of the 69th Brigade inland.

This advance went via Crepon, but also **Creully** where four Dragoon Guards' tanks were lost crossing the river Seulles. At around **4 pm**, the Germans launched a counter-attack with ten assault guns of the 1352. Panzerjäger-Kompanie, plus elements of Füsilier-Bataillon 352 and I./915. The British buckled under the attack between Bazenville and Villiers-le-Sec, but the Germans were in turn forced to withdraw back to Saint-Gabriel (south-west of Creully), at 9.35 pm. Regrouped around Ducy-Sainte-Marguerite at 10.35 pm, these German forces now only had six assault guns and ninety men, but they had slowed down the 69th Brigade advance. South-east of Tierceville, the 7th Green Howards had linked up with the Canadians of the Royal Winnipeg Rifles.

Jig Beach: Asnelles

To the west, the **231st Brigade** also landed with two battalions side-by-side. However, with the **1st Hampshires** due to land near Hamel (Asnelles) and capture WN 37 to the west, and the **1st Dorsets** to the east to take **WN 36** ('La cabane des Douanes' at the Roquettes hamlet), they in fact landed side-by-side in the Roquettes sector. More seriously, the tanks did not turn up. Only two of the sixteen LCTs carrying Centaur tanks arrived on time.

A and **B Companies** of the **1st Dorsets** landed near **Roquettes** at **7.30 am** and had to advance along the beach in order to reach WN 36, coming under fire from the 7,5 cm gun in the H 612 type casemate of WN 37 at Hamel. C Squadron of the Sherwood Rangers, supporting this battalion, had lost seven tanks. The special tanks also had problems: A Flail tank of the Westminster Dragoons (6th Assault Regt. R.E.) struck a mine that its flail had not set off. The AVRE tank following behind was stuck in the beach exit, another Flail tank became bogged down and the AVRE behind was destroyed by a shell. WN 36 was finally taken and mopped-up by **C Company** which came in with the second wave. B Company set up a defensive curtain around the captured ground, whilst A and D Companies advanced inland. They at first advanced towards the south and were at **Meuvaines** at **9.30 am**, then headed towards the west, passing south of Asnelles via the German positions at Petit-Fontaine and Puits Hérode, partially abandoned and held by the Germans of I./196. These two companies then arrived south of **Arromanches**, supported by the armour of the Nottingham Yeomanry. Losses on this day for the Battalion were 128 killed, including 4 officers.

To the west, the **1st Hampshires** encountered serious difficulties. **A** and **D Companies** landed at 7.35 am to the west of Roquettes and headed west towards **WN 37** (Le Hamel) but they were pinned down by heavy fire coming from this position that remained intact despite the air and naval bombardments. Much of the fire came from the sanitarium, a huge building in the middle of the position and a H 612 casemate armed with a 7,5 cm gun, as well as various Tobruks armed with machine-guns. Lieutenant-Colonel Smith, commanding the 1st Hampshires, was wounded twice near the beach and was evacuated. Artillery observers were also hit and the radio equipment destroyed. Twenty minutes later, the reinforcement companies (**C** and **D**) also landed and came under

Company Sergeant Major Stanley Hollis who was awarded the Victoria Cross, the highest British medal for bravery.

A Westminster Dragoons Flail tank knocked-out on Gold Beach. The special tanks suffered heavy losses in the sector. On Jig Beach, a Flail tank struck a mine that its flail had not set off. (IWM)

Royal Marines of 47th RM Commando land their LCAs on Jig Beach which is jammed with the LCTs which have brought in the special tanks. On the left, a bulldozer pushes a cart loaded with fascines. (IWM)

Lieutenant-Colonel Phillips, commanding officer of 47th RM Commando.

fire. It was total chaos. The 7,5 cm gun had already knocked-out two Flail tanks; B Squadron of the Sherwood Rangers had lost four tanks and three others had become bogged down. One B Squadron, Westminster Dragoons, Flail tank (Sergeant Lindsay) was knocked-out out after having cleared a way through the dunes. The Battalion's second in command, Major Martin, had taken over command but was also wounded and replaced by Major Warren (who was killed by a sniper two hours later). The attack started again at **1.45 pm**. B Company went around Asnelles via the south and took the position from the west at only **4 pm** following tough fighting. At the same time, D Company had gone around Asnelles, cleared WN 38 at Saint-Côme-de-Fresné, then the radar station and at the end of the day, had reached the eastern edge of Arromanches which it entered with little resistance that evening. In the evening, the 1st Hampshire held a roll call: there were 182 killed and many wounded. Also, the Brigade's third battalion, the **2nd Devons**, landed at **8.15 am**. One of its companies reinforced the Hampshires for their attack on Le Hamel and the rest of the Battalion advanced as far as Ryes on the Bayeux road. C Company entered La Rosière (the road from Arromanches to Bayeux).

The Commandos

The **47th RM Commando** led by Lieutenant-Colonel Phillips, landed at H+90 to the east of the 231st Brigade sector but four of its fourteen LCAs were lost (including that of Captain Wood), three due to mines and one from shell fire. When the Royal Marines regrouped to the rear of Roquettes, 4 officers and 68 other ranks were missing (out of 445) and most of the heavy weapons had been lost. Lieutenant-Colonel Phillips was also missing and Major Donnel took over command and headed towards the church of Asnelles through a massive jam, but the bulk of the Royal Marines did not arrive until **1.50 pm**. The 47th RM Commando then set off towards its objective of Port-en-Bessin. However due to the delays, it only got to Hill 72 by the end of the day, near the road leading from Bayeux to Longues, after having passed through La Rosière and avoiding coming into contact with the enemy. Lieutenant-Colonel Phillips would only rejoin his unit the following morning and the attack on the positions at Port-en-Bessin was launched on the evening of the 7th and they were not captured until the morning of the 8th.

The other brigades

The Division's two other brigades landed at **11 am** on King Beach, which was the also the best cleared. By midday, the entire division had been landed. The **151st Brigade** (Brigadier Senior), supported by the 90th Field Artillery, advanced in two groups which both had the objective of the RN 13 road. To the east, the 6th Durham Light Infantry and a squadron of the 4th/7th Dragoon Guards, advanced on Crépon, Villiers-le-Sec, as far as **Esquay-sur-Seulles**, near the RN 13. To the west, the 9th Durham Light Infantry, as well as the 8th D.L.I., advanced along the Crepon to Bayeux road as far as **Sommervieu**, from where they could see the spires of Bayeux cathedral; the town was now close. Further west, the **56th Brigade** (Brigadier Pepper) advanced to the north-west of Bayeux. The 2nd Essex marched to the right of the 9th D.L.I. The 2nd Glosters halted at **Magny** for the night, sending out patrols as far as Saint-Vigor, a suburb of Bayeux. The 2nd South Wales Borderers found the radio station at Pouligny had been set on fire by the Germans, then took the bridge at **Vaux-sur-Aure**, near Bayeux, at 11.50 pm. Thus, on the evening of 6 June, almost all of the objectives in this sector had been taken. The troops entered Bayeux at dawn the next day.

This photo was taken on 6 June by Sergeant Parkinson at the exit of Ver-sur-Mer leading to Crépon. This road was taken by the 6th Green Howards and CSM Hollis (IWM)
The area is still recognisable today.
(EG/Heimdal.)

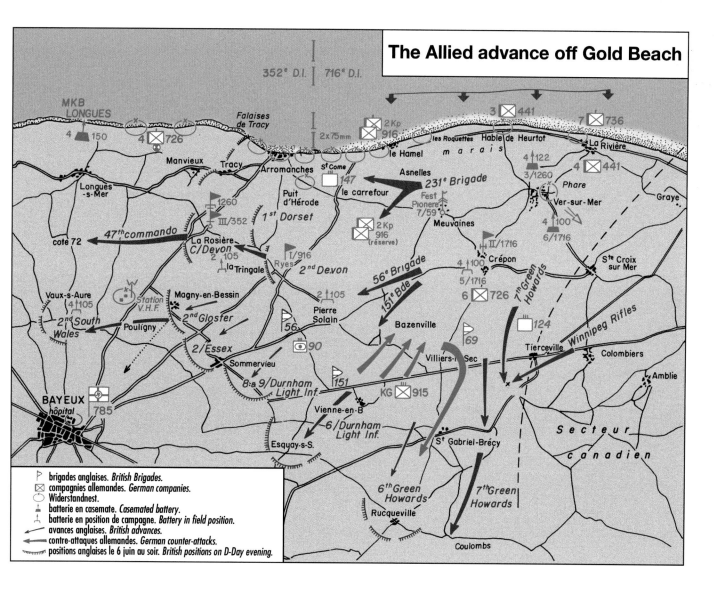

The Allied advance off Gold Beach

95

7

Sword Beach:
Failure opposite Caen!

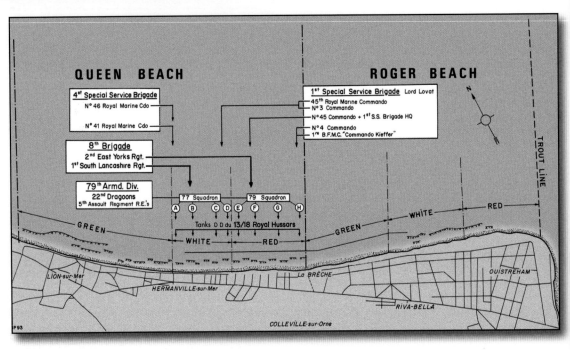

Above: The remarkable fire control post at Riva Bella is a one-off type which overlooked the 1./HKAA 1260 sector, directing the fire of this artillery battery. It has been preserved and houses a remarkable museum on the Atlantic Wall. (A.D.)

Opposite: The Sword Beach landing sector was spread out between Queen Beach and Roger Beach. Each beach sector was split into sub-sectors. We see here that the troops landed on Queen White and Queen Red. (Heimdal)

Sailing off Queen Beach at around **6 am**, eight LCTs (LCT 101 to 108), transporting DD tanks of the 13th/18th Hussars, were in the vanguard heading towards this western sector of Sword Beach. They would be taking on a defensive sector held by elements of the 716.Infanterie-Division, a company of Russian volunteers (from an Ost battalion stationed east of the Orne), the 3./642 defending Hermanville and its WN 18, the 2./736 defending the powerful St.tzpunkt Riva Bella (Stp 08) flanked to the west by WN 10. To the rear, the German artillery was in positions at WN16 (2./AR 1716, 100 mm guns), to the west of Colleville, in WN 12 (4./AR 1716, with four 155 mm howitzers, of which three were in casemates south of Ouistreham. The Riva Bella strong-point had six 155 mm guns with a remarkable five-floor concrete observation post (today it houses the 'Grand Bunker' museum), but whose guns were in field positions to the east of Saint-Aubin-d Arquenay (south of Ouistreham) as they waited for their casemates to be built. In this sector the coastline was low, forming a coastal strip with the three seaside localities of Brèche d Hermanville, Colleville-plage and Ouistreham/Riva Bella from west to east. Behind this coastal strip was a low-lying and poorly-drained area which was relatively marshy and crossed by a few roads linking the inland region with the sea. Behind this wet zone, a plateau quickly climbed up to 50 metres above sea level, two kilomteres from the coast. Between this crest and the wet zone, there were several villages spread out along the side of the plateau. On good farmland behind La Brèche, was the old village of Hermanville, to the rear of Colleville-plage. Spread out from north to south was the old village of Colleville and, to the east,

overlooking the Orne estuary was the old village of Ouistreham which in the old days had been lightly fortified and which was dominated by its Roman church. The assault on Hermanville and Colleville had two objectives: that of clearing Ouistreham and the Orne Estuary with French commandos who would then make their way to the bridges held by Major Howard in the airborne bridgehead, then reach and take the town of Caen.

At **5.47 am**, HMS Frobisher opened fire on Ouistreham beach. Destroyers then joined in between 6.22 and 7.05 am, but they fired blindly. Armed with rockets, the LCT, LCG and LCS carried out more accurate fire. These salvos, screeching overhead, reassured the infantrymen who had been crammed into the LCAs since 5.30 am and who were suffering from seasickness. 18 LCTs were carrying the self-propelled guns of the 7th, 76th (Highland) and 33rd Field Regiments which fired shells towards the coast. The first salvo was fired from LCT 331 at **6.44 am** and the third salvo hit the coast. The seventy-two 105 mm guns were now bombarding the defences on Queen Beach at a rate of fire of 200 rounds per minute! 6,500 rounds were fired by the end of this bombardment. However, the Germans soon returned fire.

Finally, the DD tanks (which were amphibious thanks to their canvas skirts) could not take to sea due to the rough conditions. At **7.20 am** dawn was breaking under a grey sky and there was daylight. The landings on Sword Beach were held back by almost an hour and a half in the other beach sectors. The German defenders had pulled themselves together following the hail of fire. The Flail tanks of the 22nd Dragoons, with their chain flails desi-

gned to clear minefields, were the first to reach the beach with the Royal Engineers teams. The first of the special bunker-busting AVRE tanks arrived at **7.25 am**. These powerful tanks attacked the German positions. The 31 amphibious tanks of the 13th/18th Hussars then came in, silencing the 50 and 75 mm guns; the Engineers tanks had done a good job. At **7.30 am**, twenty LCAs brought in the assault companies with, to the west, on Queen White, A and C Companies, 1st South Lancashires and to the east, on Queen Red, A and C Companies, 2nd East Yorkshires. However, they were all pinned down along the anti-tank wall at the top of the beach. Major Harwood, commanding A Company of the South Lancs was killed on Queen Beach, along with one his junior officers as they crossed the beach. Lieutenant Pierce then took over command of the Company, leading it to the right in order to clear the fortified houses towards the seaside resort of Hermanville. C Company was luckier and crossed the beach with relatively few casualties. However, the reinforcement B Company drifted too far to the east and suffered heavy losses, with Major Harrison being killed straight away. Lieutenant Bob Bell-Walker then took over command and led a platoon to the left to capture a concrete casemate that was laying down devastating fire all along the right-hand beach (towards the west). Bell-Walker then led a textbook attack, crawling up to the rear of the casemate and threw a grenade into the embra-

Above: The Queen Red sector at around 8 am. The special and DD tanks arrived with the first wave. One of them is seen burning here. (IWM)

Opposite: The 3rd Infantry Division shoulder patch.

Below: This photo was taken by the war correspondent Sergeant Mapham. It probably shows men of the East Lancs amidst the chaos of vehicles on the beach. The jeep is equipped with a special system protecting its exhaust pipe when landing. A special AVRE tank can be seen on the right armed with a Petard round. (IWM)

This well-known photo was taken by Sergeant Mapham at around 8.45 am on White Beach (looking towards Red Beach) and shows men of N°8 Field Company Royal Engineers) who bear the shoulder insignia of the Beach Groups with the anchor. A man from this unit can be seen on the right, Fred Sadler, who was accompanied by Cyril Hawkins and Jimmy Leask for mine clearing. In the background are heavily-loaded medics of the 8th Field Ambulance who were part of 8th Brigade. On the right is a 2nd Middlesex Carrier.

sure in order to rake the inside with his Sten gun. However, he was immediately killed by a machine-gun firing from the strong-point on the left. But this action did open up a way through and allowed B Company, South Lancs to get off the beach. In the meantime, the Battalion's C.O., Lieutenant-Colonel Richard Burbury, had also landed. He had planned to guide the movement of the South Lancs on the beach with small flags, but he was killed by a sniper as he got to the barbed wire. The Second-in-Command of the South Lancs, Major Jack Stone, took over. The fighting was then confused but, thanks to the capture of the casemate to the west by Lieutenant Bell-Walker, the South Lancs were able to take the position from the rear and thus ease the situation for the East Yorks who had landed on their left flank and thus establish a link-up between the two beaches at around **8.45 am**.

Indeed, on the left (further to the east), at Queen Red, the 2nd East Yorkshire Regiment had landed facing the fortified position at Hermanville, named Cod by the British and WN 18 by the Germans. Here there were several casemates armed with 47 and 50 mm guns and machine-gun positions. The positions were almost undamaged and the men arriving in the landing craft were met with a hell of small arms fire. Added to this was the fire from a 88 mm gun enfilading the beach. Despite the return fire from the DD tanks of the 13th/18th Hussars and the special tanks of the 22nd Dragoons, the East Yorks lost 200 men on the beach within a few minutes! There was not much cover afforded amongst the obstacles and barbed wire. The bypassing manoeuvre of the position by the South Lancs allowed them to escape from this hell...

The Commandos

After the tanks, then the 8th Brigade infantrymen who took the first brunt, would now land the commandos. To the west, behind the South Lancs, came the **4th Special Service Commando** (Brigadier B.W. Leicester) regrouping N°41 Royal Marine Commando and N°46 Royal Marine Commando. They suffered casualties on the beach before heading towards the west in order to take the position of Lion-sur-Mer (codenamed 'Trout' by the British). The Germans were waiting for them and, displaying great discipline, only opened fire at point blank range, at less than one hundred metres. The three Centaur support tanks were destroyed and mortar fire caused heavy casualties within the ranks of the Royal Marines. Added to this, the Germans launched a counter-attack at around 1 pm with sixty infantrymen and a self-propelled gun. Lieutenant-Colonel Gray (commanding the 41st Royal Marines) was forced to withdraw. These Royal Marines would fail in their attempt to link-up with the Royal Marines which had landed at Langrune to the east of Juno Beach!

In the east at the Queen Red sector, Lord Lovat's **1st Special Service Brigade** landed, with its N∞4 Commando led by Lieutenant-Colonel Dawson allowing the French of the 1er BFMC the honour of being the first to land. The 1er Bataillon de Fusilier-Marins Commandos led by Commandant Philippe Kieffer, known by the British as N°10 (Interlallied) Commando, arrived on board two LCIs, LCI 523 and 527. They landed at **7.21 am** just as a German shell struck the forward starboard side of LCI 527, wounding some of the commandos; one of whom, Jean Pinelli, had his legs riddled with shell splinters. The French commandos then continued towards the dune where Second-maître

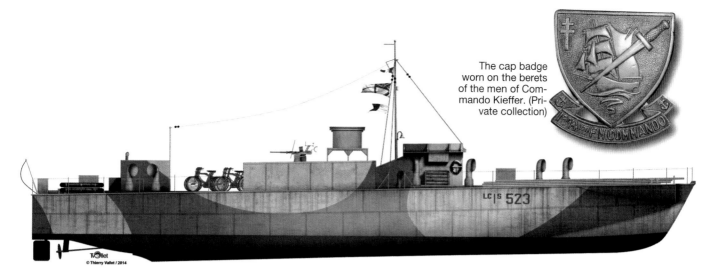

LCI 523 which carried Troop 8 led by Lieutenant Lofi (71 men), as well as half of the K-Gun platoon led by Lieutenant Pierre Amaury (12 men. (Illustration by Thierry Vallet.)

Above: Capitaine de corvette Philippe Kieffer. (IWM.)

Opposite: Commandos advancing towards Ouistreham, supported here by DD tanks. Note the local narrow-gauge railway lines.

(second master) Thubé opened up a breach in the barbed wire with wire cutters. Commandant Kieffer was wounded on the beach but was quickly bandaged up and remained in contact with his men and the British officers. Along with him and the 177 French commandos, 40 did not get off the beach either wounded or killed. They were split into three groups: Troop 1 (Guy Vourch),Troop 8 (Lofi) and the K-Gun Troop with light machine-guns (Lieutenant Amaury). However, they first had to clear a small network of bunkers towards the Riva Bella strong-point, a task given to Lofi's 8 Troop 8. At the same time, Troop 1 advanced towards Ouistreham. Its leader, Guy Vourch was one of the first to be wounded and was replaced by Premier-maître Hubert Faure. This troop followed the narrow-gauge railway and the main road leading into Riva Bella, to the north of the old Ouistreham village. The French picked up a British

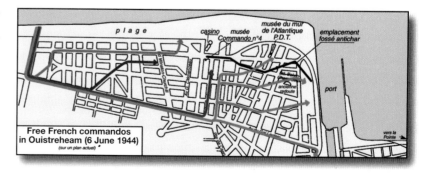

Free French commandos in Ouistreheam (6 June 1944)
(sur un plan actuel)

troop which had lost its officer. Lofi's Troop 8 went along boulevard Maréchal Joffre. Faure's Troop 1, with Amaury's K-Guns and the British troop, advanced along the Lion road following the railway line and arrived at the corner of rue Pasteur, next to the Chateaubriand restaurant. These two

The advance of the commandos in Ouistreham. (Heimdal.)

These smiling French commandos of the K-Gun platoon (Amaury) lead the DD tanks into Ouistreham. The first, from the left, is Yvan Monceau, the second Ravel and the third Francis Guezennec. (Coll. MusÉe du Grand Bunker, Ouistreham.)

Lieutenant-Colonel R.W.E Dawson, N°4 Commando.

The French commandos were followed by N°4 Commando led by Lieutenant-Colonel Dawson. They had reached the port of Ouistreham at around 10 am. German resistance stiffened there by the locks. It was not until 3.30 pm and the arrival of an AVRE tank before this was dealt with. Other elements of this commando unit (Troops D,E,F) mopped up the Riva Bella strong-point, noting the absence of 155 mm guns but not inspecting the concrete tower of the fire control post; 53 Germans would remain inside, unknown to all, until the evening of 9 June!... However, let us return to the beach and follow the landing and advance of the rest of the 1st S.S. Brigade.

The advance of the 1st S.S. Brigade - The landing of this brigade had been planned to be on the far left (east) of the Sword Beach sector, to the east of WN 18 (Cod), in front of the children's holiday camp for the French (the first to land at H+30) who immediately headed off towards Ouistreham, followed by N°4 Commando. The rest of the Brigade landed thirty minutes later. Its HQ landed at **8.40** am with Lord Lovat, followed by N°6 and N°3 Commando at H+90, then N°45 (RM) Commando.

The LCIs bringing in the second wave of the commandos advanced in arrowhead formation towards the beach. The Brigade's HQ was on LCI 519. Lord Lovat and Bill Millin were on LCI 502, accompanied by five LCIs transporting N°3 Commando, followed by those of 45 (RM) Commando. On LCI 519, Bill Millin joined the commandos at the front of the landing craft. German fire sent up spray. A landing craft received a direct hit starboard and fire broke out with men jumping over the side. However, despite this firing, all eyes were fixed on the coast. Two tanks were burning on the beach, letting off a thick black smoke. The beach was now only one-hundred metres away. The wooden ramps were slowly lowered and 'Shimi' Lovat was already pushing his through the waist-deep water. Bill Millin followed behind, almost falling over due to his heavy haversack. Then, with the water now only up to his knees, he began playing Highland Laddie. Lord Lovat turned and smiled at him. The noise was terrible as they arrived on the beach. N°4 Commando had pushed its way through there but not all of the German positions had been annihilated and men were falling. Bill Millin then saw two corpses; one of them with half its face torn off. They had to make their way as quickly as possible to the top of the beach. Lord Lovat was talking with someone at the top of the dunes. It was then that Bill Millin spotted eight or nine wounded men and, a few moments later, a Flail tank coming along clearing mines; it did not see the wounded men and its flails left behind nothing but shredded bodies... The Germans surrendered, holding their hands up and shouting *"Engeland, Engeland!"* Then Bill Millin joined Lord Lovat just as the Brigadier informed his commander that a message had arrived saying that the bridges over the Orne and the canal had been captured by the airborne troops. The Brigadier then turned to Bill Millin and asked him to play something; it would be *'The Road to the Isles'*. Lord Lovat's piper then began playing the pipes along the beach, cursed by a sergeant who worried that: *"As well as the bloody mess on the beach, his pipes alerted the fucking Germans!"* Shells continued to fall and

roads were parallel to the seafront and the casemates and machine-gun nests were cleared from the rear, often with flame-throwers. German snipers continued causing casualties among the commandos.

The foundations of the former casino now had to be taken; it had been turned into a fortified strongpoint by the Germans. The time was **9 am**, and rue Pasteur, parallel to the sea, led to the **Casino**. Second maître de Montlaur prepared to take it from the rear by using this road. However, the end of the road had a chicane concrete wall road block. Matelot Paul Rollin (Troop 1) moved to the other side of this wall and fell, hit by a bullet from a hidden German. Helped by the medical officer Lion, Bolloré pulled the wounded sailor back to the other side of the wall; the medical officer was the hit in the heart by a bullet and Bolloré wounded. Montlaur pulled in Rollin who would later die. The casino was defended by a 20 mm gun which Montlaur succeeded in knocking out with two PIAT rocket-launchers. The two first projectiles hit the base of the casino, as did the two next ones but the gun appeared to have been neutralised. However, the Germans in the concrete flak emplacement situated on the right (which is still there), saw where the PIAT fire was coming from and fired at it. Montlaur and Lardenois had just enough time to leap into the road but Matelot Renault was killed. The advance of Troop 1 to the casino was halted. However, at the same time, Lofi's Troop 8 had continued clearing the fortified positions along the beach. Commandant Kieffer also arrived and climbed up onto a 13th/18th Hussars DD tank. He ordered Matelot Morel to go back to the beach and bring back Troop 8; it was **9.30 am**. The tank definitively silenced the casino position and the commandos advanced in two columns towards the flak emplacement where twenty German soldiers then surrendered. Commandant Kieffer was wounded for a second time and the French commandos, with their mission accomplished in Ouistreham, went back to the resort after an hour and a half to pick up their haversacks and advance, at around 1 pm, behind the British commandos in order to join Major Howard on the right bank of the Orne.

gunfire rang out. Along the road, Bill spotted a wounded commando; he had seen him on the ship reading a cowboy book. Then, without N°4 Commando and the French commandos who would come up later, the 1st S.S. Brigade headed southeast, passing through Colleville, then Saint-Aubin-d'Arquenay where Bill played *Rawentree* (a tune about holly, a sacred tree for the Scottish, which chases away evil spirits), applauded by the local inhabitants. They were now in the fields where the gliders of the 6th Airlanding Brigade would land that afternoon. The commandos marched in two columns. Bill followed Lord Lovat in front. Exiting the village, he played *Highland Laddie* again; two shots rang out, a German was hidden in a tree and then ran off into a field of wheat. As they approached Bénouville, Lord Lovat asked his piper to continue playing so that Major Howard and the paras defending the bridge would hear them. He played the well-known tune of Lochan Side. Since the First World War, pipers had been forbidden to play in the front line due to heavy losses. But, with his Lovat's Scouts, Lord Lovat had a sort of private army and the special commando spirit had allowed him to do things differently compared to others. He had, therefore, decided to land with his personal piper, the only one to do so on D-Day and during the Battle of Normandy and get him to play the pipes at the front of his men. He played his bagpipes almost non-stop from Colleville to Bénouville. Lord Lovat and Bill Millin had just become the stuff of legend.

Nearing Bénouville they sped up their march, hearing the sound of artillery. They passed a group of terrorised German prisoners. The road headed to the right in the village, leading to the church. The column found itself halted by automatic weapons

Above: The 1st Special Service Brigade landed at 'La Brèche' at Hermanville, approximately an hour after the first attack wave. Lord Lovat wades through the water to the right of his men and we can see Bill Millin, to the right, with his bagpipes. (IWM)

Opposite: Lord Lovat, Commanding Officer of the commandos of the 1st S.S. Brigade.

Below: Commandos of the 1st S.S. Brigade in the ruins of the children's holiday camp where they picked up their haversacks before advancing inland. (IWM)

fire. Bill stopped playing, men were wounded. A light tank turned up and Mills Roberts, leader of N°6 Commando, ordered the piper to follow it. Bill Millins then played *Blue Bonnets over the Border* (a Jacobite tune). The tank opened fire on the church tower from where the Germans had fired. The shot hit the bell chamber, killing the Germans. The piper stopped playing and contact was made with the first paras who seemed to be as stunned as the civilians in the midst of a surreal atmosphere where the air was laden with dust. Lord Lovat asked Bill to play his bagpipes so that they would be heard by the men holding the bridge and he struck up Blue Bonnets again. They rounded a bend then saw the road to the bridge on the left with the structure itself two-hundred metres away, covered in a shroud of black smoke. Lord Lovat greeted Major Howard, the link-up was made and a page in history had been written! The column then continued its advance with Bill at the front. Bullets were hitting the metal framework of the bridge. It was **midday**. Bill Millin was ordered to cease playing and did so as they left the bridge. The column bent down behind the rail of the bridge, sheltering from the shots coming from the south-west and the Bénouville ch,teau, where elements of the 21.Panzer-Division were positioned. They then crossed the lifting bridge which entered into posterity under the name of Pegasus Bridge. Upon reaching the other side, between the canal and the Orne river, Lord Lovat spoke with an officer holding the position. He then turned around impatiently: *"Come on piper, carry on playing along the road and across the next bridge."* Bill now played March of the Cameron Men.

Above and bottom left: Commandos now passing through Colleville in front of the church. (IWM) Nothing has changed today. (G.B.)

Bill Millin, Lord Lovat's piper. (Coll. author.)

Opposite: Bill Millin seen here in 1994, crossing the Ranville bridge once more. (Heimdal.)

The commandos of the 1st S.S. Brigade crossing the fields as they make their way to link-up with Major Howard's men at Bénouville. (IWM)

However, when they reached the second bridge, the paras signalled to them to halt as it was still under sniper fire. But Bill played *Blue Bonnets* once more and Lord Lovat, at the front and as cool as a cucumber, signalled his men to advance. Suddenly a para appeared and held out his hand, exclaiming

"We are very pleased to see you, old boy." And Lovat said, *"Aye, we are very pleased to see you, old boy! Sorry, we are two and a half minutes late."* The column was now on the right bank along the tree-lined main road. They quickly left the road and took a path to the left. They passed through the buildings of the Ecarde farm where a little red-haired girl, in fact Josette Lemanissier, shouted *"Music, music...!"* to Bill. He played her *the Nut Brown Maiden*. This small girl reminded him of the little girls of Scotland and she was a ray of sunshine for Bill. Every year he returned there hoping to see her until our investigations allowed for a moving reunion in 1994. The commandos of the 1st S.S. Brigade would now take up positions to the east of the Orne in order to strengthen the airborne bridgehead. They would fight alongside the paras in its defence.

Above: Lieutenant-General John T. Crocker took command of I Corps in August 1943.

Opposite: Major-General Tom G.Rennie, commanding 3rd Division. (IWM)

The 8th Infantry Brigade advances inland

With the 1st S.S. Brigade accomplishing its missions, the seaborne element of the 3rd British Infantry Division, the 8th Infantry Brigade, began to push inland after breaking through the coastal defences. They had to first cross the low-lying and slightly wet zone behind the coastal strip. To the west, the *1st South Lancashire Regiment* moved off from Queen White via the three breaches on the beach at La Brèche d Hermanville.

Its A Company turned west towards Lion-sur-Mer in order to lend support to the Royal Marines but, as we have seen, without success. B, C, D Companies and the Brigade HQ advanced on the village of Hermanville which was only accessible via a single road. The spearhead elements came under fire from the church tower; this was quickly dealt with and at **9.30 am**, the village was held by the South Lancs. Joined by tanks from A Squadron,13th/18th Hussars, they were tasked with marching on Biéville, then Caen. However, at 9.45 am, a RAF reconnaissance sortie signalled the presence of German armour north of Caen. But this was only the armoured vehicles of two mecha-

nised infantry companies from the 21.Panzer-Division, the 7./192 and 8./192 that had been ordered at 9.16 am to set up defensive positions between Périers-sur-le-Dan and Saint-Aubin d Arquenay. But these were just two companies facing a landing division and behind them was virtually nothing as the 21.Panzer-Division had not yet made its way to the front line. However, these two companies would be enough to halt the attack that was supposed to capture Caen on this day!

Indeed, the attack would become bogged-down before it had barely begun. The 'Intermediate Brigade', the **185th Brigade** led by Brigadier K.P. Smith, landed at H+150 and H+250. The three battalions were in place north of Hermanville at **11 am** with orders to speed towards Caen behind the 8th Brigade which had landed but which was commanded by Brigadier Cass who would be deemed as having been too 'stolid'. The latter had still not taken the 'Hillman' position on the Périers crest and finally, nothing was happening. The 185th Brigade was halted and the beach jammed. At **11.45 am**, Lieutenant-Colonel Maurice, commanding the 2nd K.S.L.I, one of the battalions of this brigade and due to be in the vanguard of this attack, took a bicycle and rode down to the beach to see what

Above: This photo, also taken by Sergeant Mapham, was taken as he reached the square in La Brèche d Hermanville, seen here to the west. The sign marked '94' indicates the direction of the 185th Brigade HQ.
Above, Centre: By turning around, he shows us the front of a seaside villa in front of which is parked a Petard AVRE of the 77th Assault Squadron, bearing the name 'Bulldog'. **Right:** 2nd Middlesex carriers (number '64'), the machine-gun battalion. (IWM)

Captain Eric T. Lummis, 1st Suffolk,1945, seen here in front of Hillman in 1991. (Heimdal)

was going on. The tanks of the Staffordshire Yeomanry were on the beach with their engines turning over stuck in the jam. The operational planners had thought that the high tide would leave enough of a beach sector, but strong winds pushed the sea up to ten metres from the dunes and the vehicles were crammed together in an incredible shambles that the Beach Masters were trying to deal with. Lieutenant-Colonel Maurice then turned back to find Brigadier Cass. Despite the absence of tanks and the failure of the 8th Brigade, the Brigadier gave the order to attack at **11.30 am**.

At the end of the morning, a meeting was held in an orchard near Hermanville between the I Corps leader, Lieutenant-General John T. Crocker and that of the 3rd Division, Major-General Tom G. Rennie, both of whom were preoccupied by the situation. To the west, the Royal Marines had failed in taking the Lion-sur-mer position. To the south, 8th Brigade was halted and inactive in front of Caen. To the east, the 6th Airborne Division had already come under counter-attack from Kampfgruppe Luck (a strengthened regiment of the 21.Panzer-Division commanded by Major von Luck). Crocker suggested being prudent! But at the same time the Reserve Brigade, **9th Brigade**, led by Brigadier J.C. Cunningham arrived, also with three infantry battalions and a tank battalion. The latter presented himself to the two generals in order to receive his orders. He was tasked with advancing to the west, on the right flank of the 185th Brigade and try to link-up with the Canadian forces that had landed at Juno Beach. However, due to the failure of the Royal Marines, this order was cancelled by Crocker, to the great disappointment of Cunningham who then saw his brigade dispersed to strengthen the bridgehead. Something dramatic then took place which was told to me by Captain Eric T. Lummis, 1st Suffolk

(8th Brigade): *"We had just finished our trenches south-east of the beach at Hermanville when we saw other troops coming. At first there were a few men from the Beach Groups, followed by 9th Brigade Headquarters vehicles with the C.O. of this unit (Cunningham) in a carrier. They carried on their way. A few minutes later we heard three explosions near our positions. Mortar shells had hit the HQ vehicles that we had seen pass by, wounding Brigadier Cunningham who we had spotted earlier, plus his intelligence officer, and killing three other officers, one of whom was a Canadian liaison officer from the brigade to our right."* Brigadier Cunningham was unconscious and no longer able to give his orders. Colonel Denis Orr, the man who could have replaced him, was at Bénouville. The Brigade was without a leader and paralysed during these decisive hours.

The 21.Panzer-Division counter-attacks

By 8 am most of the landings had taken place in the Anglo-Canadian sector and breakouts made beyond the coastal strip. Everywhere, the German coastal defence troops were being crushed and overwhelmed. Also, in the Sword Beach sector east of the Orne, the 6th Airborne Division already held a huge bridgehead. But where was the German armoured counter-attack that was such a source of worry to the Allies, what was the 21.Panzer-Division doing?

Having been in Paris in the arms of a woman and with his officers unable to contact him, Generalmajor Feuchtinger at last arrived at his HQ Saint-Pierre-sur-Dives at **5.20 am**, five hours since fighting with British paras had been taking place!

To the east of the Orne it was elements of Kampfgruppe Luck who took on some groups of paras. To the west of the river, Oberleutnant Braatz's

Colonel Hermann von Oppeln-Bronikowski, commander of the only available panzer regiment in the sector, Panzer-Regiment 22 of the 21.Panzer-Division. (Heimdal.)

TVollet
© Thierry Vallet / 2011

Opposite: Selbstfahrlafette für 7,5 cm Pak 40 auf Somua MCG S 307 (f). The troop commanded by Leutnant Höller (8./192) was equipped with three of these vehicles. They were sent in to counter-attack at Bénouville. (Illustration by Thierry Vallet.)

Below: Gefreite Atteneder who was with Leutnant Höller on 6 June 1944. The latter took this picture near the janitor's house at the Bénouville château. His face betrays the intense tension felt during this counterattack. (Coll. H. Höller.)

8./192 had vehicles armed with 75 mm anti-tank guns. They had been put on alert during the night and had set off to counter-attack, as early as 3 am, towards Bénouville where fighting had been signalled. This small unit confronted British paras in the vicinity of the Bénouville château. At **8 am** (7 am for the Allies), with the landings having taken place, the two tank battalions of Panzer-Regiment 22 at last received their movement orders, six hours after the first alert was given to the first of these battalions. They were still in the Falaise area, fifty kilometres from the coast! This panzer division was the only one in proximity to the landing sectors, despite the fact that Rommel had advised crushing the allied landings on the beaches! The Germans did not have the means to accomplish this at hand. All hopes now rested on this one division.

B-26 Marauder bombers. One can clearly see two bombs leaving the bomb bay of one of the planes. One seems to have been hit by flak as smoke is trailing from its starboard engine. (BA 493/3354/15a.)

The bombing of Caen on 6 June 1944 brought death and destruction to the great Norman city. There were very few German casualties in the second air raid early July, but more than 2,000 civilian deaths! This was a massacre which achieved very few real results... Seen here (below) is rue Saint Pierre where buildings still burn. (Archives Heimdal.)

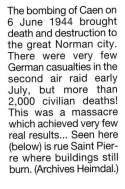

Already fighting, but alone as we have seen, the units of KG Luck and the two companies of Regiment 192 (including that of Leutnant Braatz) mentioned above, had received, at 9.12 am, the order to establish a defensive line between Périers sur-le-Dan and Saint-Aubin-d'Arquenay. Also, the tank destroyers of Panzerjäger-Abteilung 200, positioned astride the RN 13 road between Caen and Bayeux, were ordered at 8.05 am to assemble in the sectors of Matragny, Vendes and Basly; they would take on the Canadian tanks at around 11 am in the Seulles valley, but would be too late to help the II./726 coastal battalion which had been overwhelmed.

Attacks and counter-attacks in the afternoon

The tanks of the Staffordshire Yeomanry at last intervened at around 3 pm on the Périers crest with B Squadron and with C Squadron speeding towards Beuville. However, an armoured group of the 21.Panzer-Division had also at last arrived in the sector; it was spotted around Lebisey at approximately **4 pm**. General Marcks, commander of the German 84th corps, had first sent these elements towards the airborne bridgehead before redirecting them north of Caen, something which explains these delays. This panzer division was structured around three tactical groups; that of colonel von Oppeln Bronikowski (KG von Oppeln) with tanks, that of lieutenant-colonel Rauch (KG Rauch) with infantry and artillery and that of Major von Luck (KG Luck) with infantry and artillery, east of the Orne and against the airborne bridgehead. Despite the holdups and detours, von Oppeln's

panzers were north of Caen at 2 pm (3 pm for the Germans), between Lebisey and Biéville, and attacking the high ground at Biéville an hour later. Thus, due to a lack of initiative, the British had allowed the arrival of the panzers. The two attacks would run into each other and the panzers of the 21st division would hold on for a month, putting Caen out of reach when two hours earlier nothing could have stopped the British from taking it...

General Marcks, who had just celebrated his birthday, which is portrayed in The Longest Day, arrived, intervening red-faced and angry. The army corps commander held general Feuchtinger responsible for these delays and took over operational control, saying to von Oppeln: Oppeln, my friend, if you don't manage to push the English back into the sea, then I believe that we will have lost the war. Thus, the fate of the war depended on von Oppeln's 98 panzers! & The two tactical groups (KG von Oppeln and KG Rauch) attacked but the British had had time to set up their anti-tank guns, establishing a solid block in front of Beuville. However, further to the west, fourteen Panzer IV tanks of the II./22 got as far as Douvres-la-DÉlivrande, joined by grenadiers of the I./192. This tactical group slipped between the Canadian beachhead of Juno Beach and the British beachhead of Sword Beach, reaching the coast and arriving at **Luc-sur-Mer** at **8 pm**! There, they were supported to the east by the German position 108 at Lion-sur-mer which was still holding out in the east and by that of Langrune to the west, with the base at Douvres to the rear. However, an hour later (9 pm for the Germans and 8 pm for the British), a fleet of gliders passed over the sector (Operation Mallard) and landed on the plain between Saint-Aubin-d Arquenay and the canal. Fearing an

The area around the train station was badly damaged. German soldiers are seen here patrolling in the damaged streets. (Archives Heimdal)

At around 6.50 pm, 246 gliders, towed by as many aircraft, took off, bringing in the bulk of the 6th Airlanding Brigade and the heavy materiel that the 6th Airborne Division was still lacking. The weather had improved since the previous night and was now clear; the flight would be a lot better for the dozens of gliders crossing the Channel, one of which was overloaded. In the glider carrying Lieutenant Geoffrey Sneezum (A Company of the Devons), an overweight war correspondent had joined the passengers.

In the photo above we can see two large Hamilcar gliders coming in on Landing Zone N. The thirty Hamilcar gliders landed here at around 9 pm, bringing in precious materiel: 17-pounder anti-tank guns and light Tetrarch tanks. (IWM)

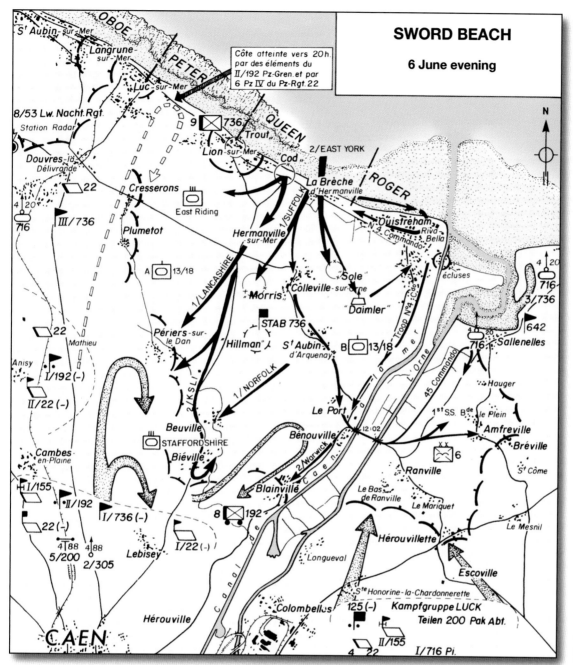

SWORD BEACH

6 June evening

Côte atteinte vers 20 h. par des éléments du II/192 Pz-Gren. et par 6 Pz IV du Pz-Rgt. 22

OBOE

PETER

QUEEN

ROGER

St Aubin-sur-Mer

Langrune-sur-Mer

Luc-sur-Mer

8/53 Lw. Nacht. Rgt.

Station Radar

9 736

Trout

Lion-sur-Mer

Cod

2/EAST YORK

Douvres-la-Délivrande

Cresserons

East Riding

La Brèche d'Hermanville

Ouistreham

N.4 Commando

Riva Bella

22

III/736

716

Plumetot

Hermanville-sur-Mer

13/18

écluses

"Sole"

Colleville-sur-Orne

"Daimler"

4 20

716

3/736

22

Mathieu

Anisy

I/192 (-)

II/22 (-)

Périers-sur-le Dan

"Hillman"

St Aubin d'Arquenay

STAB 736

B 13/18

642

Sallenelles

l'Orne

Hauger

A 13/18

Morris

45 Commando

Cambes-en-Plaine

I/155

22 (-)

4 88 4 88

5/200   2/305

Beuville

STAFFORDSHIRE

Biéville

I/736 (-)

8 192

I/22 (-)

Lebisey

Bénouville

Le Port

12:02

2/Warwick

Blainville

Le Bas de Ranville

Le Mariquet

Hérouvillette

Longueval

1st SS. B de

le Plein

Amfreville

Bréville

St Côme

6

Ranville

Le Mesnil

Escoville

Hérouville

Ste Honorine-la-Chardonnerette

Colombelles

125 (-)   Kampfgruppe LUCK

Teilen 200 Pak Abt.

II/155

4 22   I/716 Pi.

C.A.E.N.

N

operation to its rear, bringing in an entire brigade, the tactical group preferred to withdraw. In the Périers and Biéville sectors, thirteen panzers were lost. But although the 21.Panzer-Division had failed in counter-attacking, it now barred the road to Caen, with the Hitlerjugend arriving as reinforcements in the evening. Montgomery had failed and Caen would remain out of reach for more than a month.

This map shows how the fighting developed in the Sword sector and the British failure in front of Caen. Note the landings, the fighting of the commandos in Ouistreham, Lord Lovat's advance and the crossing of the bridges and the linking up with the paras, the failure of the 8./192, the panzer breakthrough to the sea and the final failure before Caen in the face of counter-attacks led by various elements, mostly those of the 21.Panzer-Division. (Heimdal.)

These photos, **bottom of the page opposite and below**, show some views of Landing Zone N and Landing Zone W. Note the way in which the Horsa gliders have been split in two to allow for the extraction of vehicles, and the roughly-painted 'invasion stripes' that were hastily applied to the gliders. The photo at the bottom of the page shows an aspect of Landing Zone W where the 'Rommel's asparagus' had not been removed, forcing the gliders to swerve amongst the obstacles. (IWM)

The evening of 6 June

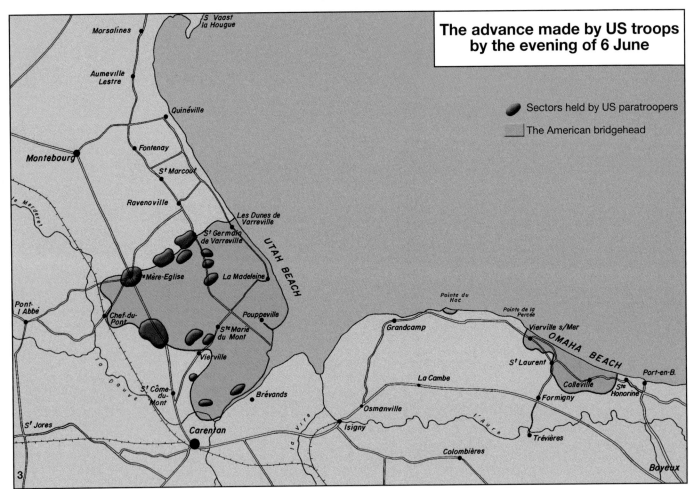

The advance made by US troops by the evening of 6 June

Sectors held by US paratroopers

The American bridgehead

By the evening the Allies had managed in establishing a more or less successful foothold in Normandy, but for the Germans it was already a failure because Rommel had stated that the battle had to be won on the beaches and that the panzers had to push the Allies back into the sea. This had failed because the sole panzer division available, the 21st, had intervened only by late afternoon. The general alert had, for various reasons, been delayed and above all, Rommel was not there. Sabotage had taken place in the chain of command. Also, several generals were not at their posts. General Falley and other senior officers were at a Kriegspiel, a tactical exercise taking place in Rennes and Falley was killed in an ambush as he arrived back at his HQ near Picauville. As for general von Lüttwitz, commander of the 21.Panzer-Division, he was in female company, as was Pluskat, and would only arrive late in the night, something which angered Major Hans von Luck, who had immediately put on the alert his 125th grenadier-regiment and which was rapidly in action against British paras. Finally, the 21.Panzer-Division succeeded in getting some of its panzers to the coast, as far as Luc-sur-mer, in a counter-attack that was withdrawn following the arrival of the 6th Airborne gliders in the evening. However, this armoured division did play an essential role in the British failure towards Caen.

Thus, in the east, facing the 6th Airborne Division paras, east of the Orne, and the British 3rd Infantry Division, a small bridgehead was established on both sides of the river. Everywhere else, following strong resistance on the beaches of the Anglo-Canadian sector of Gold Beach (British), Juno Beach (Canadian) and Sword Beach (British), the weak 716.Infanterie-Division had been destroyed and its remaining elements withdrew inland without putting up much of a fight. To the east, the British beachhead was faced by the only panzer division in the sector, the 21st. To the east of the Orne, the British paras were held back by Kampfgruppe Luck, mostly Panzergrenadier Regiment 125 of Major von Luck who held them there in a veritable 'cul-de-sac' for around two months...

In front of the martyred city of Caen, which was dying under the air raids, this D-Day objective pinned down the British 3rd Infantry Division for a little over a month. This was due to the 21st panzer division but also that of the 12.SS-Panzer-Division Hitlerjugend, the first elements of which began arriving in the Caen sector in the evening!

This bridgehead on each side of the river failed when faced by the panzers!

The Canadian sector of Sword Beach saw the biggest allied advance of the day. But this success was was only partial. The thin curtain of troops of the 716th division had been destroyed on the beaches and there was virtually nothing in front of the 3rd Canadian Infantry Division which had been considerably strengthened by tank regiments. Its advance was, however, held back by the huge jams at the beach exits. When night fell, it had reached the intermediate 'Elm Line', but halted when it was dark without reaching its 'Oak Line' of the RN 13 road. Instead of stopping for the night, the Canadian division should have pushed on and passed this objective without any opposition; there was virtually nothing left in front of it! Reinforcements began arriving at the front with, as we have seen, the Hitlerjugend division and, to its left, the Panzer-Lehr-Division...

1. This photo was taken on 6 June and shows a group of men of the 101st Airborne Division with civilians at the water pump in the square at Sainte-Marie-du-Mont where the Germans had pumped water only a few days before, as we have seen on page 9. (US Army)

2. This Coast Guards photo was taken from the top of the cliffs at Omaha Beach and evokes the losses suffered there on 6 June. (NA)

3. The two American beachheads were still fragile on 6 June 1944, especially that of Omaha Beach. (Heimdal map)

4. The two beachheads in the British sector of Juno Beach and Sword Beach had still not linked up, all the more so given the failure of the British 3rd Division facing Caen. (Heimdal map)

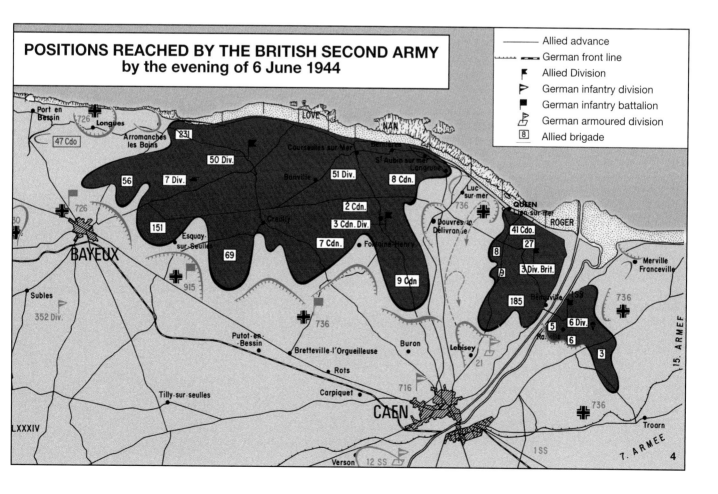

POSITIONS REACHED BY THE BRITISH SECOND ARMY
by the evening of 6 June 1944

Allied advance
German front line
Allied Division
German infantry division
German infantry battalion
German armoured division
Allied brigade

A rare colour photo of a Hitlerjugend grenadier. The German combatants fought back with determination, causing heavy losses to the Allies who were only able to break through the front towards the end of July. The Battle of Normandy would be particularly hard-fought. (Coll. Heimdal.)

Further west of this Anglo-Canadian sector, starting at Gold Beach, the British 50th Infantry Division, also strengthened by a tank brigade, was on the outskirts of Bayeux in the evening and entered the town the following morning with virtually no opposition.

Further west, facing a thin line of 716th division troops, reinforced by the 352.Infanterie-Division, the arrival of which was unknown to the Allies, the beachhead at Omaha Beach was very thin after the losses suffered there and there were still a few pockets of German resistance. Trévières, to the south, was a D-Day objective and should have already been reached; the same applied for Isigny for the coming day in order to link-up the two American beachheads. The small Rangers beachhead at the Pointe du Hoc, after heavy casualties, was threatened by German counter-attacks.

On the other hand, the Cotentin peninsula had seen the Americans establish a wide bridgehead. The flat coastline at Utah Beach had been flattened by bombs and put up little resistance; even the flooded area was not much of an obstacle. However, the penetration of the 4th Infantry Division from the coast, had been greatly assisted by the airborne operations of the night of 5-6 June. The 82nd and 101st Airborne Divisions did not, however, hold a continuous zone, but rather multiple strong-points over a wide area where there were still German and Georgian soldiers...

Opposite: This photo, taken by the Canadian army in June 1944, shows the centre of Creully, a Normandy town reached by the Royal Winnipeg Rifles as early as 6 June. Note the archway entrance of the Saint Martin hotel, bottom right, where Montgomery had his breakfast every morning at the beginning of the Normandy campaign. (PAC)

Field Marshal Montgomery, seen here wearing a paratrooper's camouflage Denison smock. At this time he commanded the allied ground forces that had landed. His HQ would be set up at Creullet, near Creully and he had his breakfast in the hotel that can be made out on the right... (PAC)

The 4th Canadian Armoured Division assembled south of Caen at Vaucelles, Colombelles and Fleury where these tank crew men are seen here. The German tanks were more efficient and better deployed than those of the Allies. However, the crushing air superiority of the Allies rendered this superiority to nought and the Battle of Normandy became a long drawn-out battle of attrition where the continuous arrival of allied reinforcements won the day. (PAC)

THE BATTLE OF NORMANDY
(7 June - 30 August 1944)

Darkness fell late on 6 June, two weeks before the summer solstice. The allied troops had succeeded in establishing beachheads and, contrary to what Rommel had recommended and who was absent on this fateful day, the troops that had landed had not been pushed back into the sea, even if catastrophe had been averted on Omaha Beach where evacuation had been envisaged. However, the British had failed in front of Caen and the arrival of nightfall paralysed the allied advance inland. Where were the German reinforcements? There would be everything to play for in the coming days.

Above: The first elements of the 12. SS-Panzer-Division 'Hitlerjugend' arrived north-west of Caen around midnight on 6 June and were only able to intervene the next day, too late to push the Allies back into the sea. However, the young soldiers of this division put up a determined defence of the front line. This young grenadier most were barely 18 years old from Panzermeyer's 25th regiment, is armed with a MG 42, a machine-gun with a formidable rate of fire. His face has been blackened for camouflage and he wears pea-dot pattern camouflage garments. This photo was taken in front of the Saint Norbert gate of the Abbaye d Ardenne. (Photo KB Woscidlo, coll. G.B.)

The photo **below** was taken on 8 June at the Pallières farm at Juaye-Mondaye, the furthest tip of the Panzer-Lehr-Division counter-attack. They reached the sector south of Bayeux two days late. Some of the men seen here belong to the divisional reconnaissance group. The man on the right could be Leutnant Gerstenmeier of this unit's 3rd company. The Panther tank in the background bears the name of Hesla. (ECPA.)

Where were the panzers?

As we have already seen, the 21.Panzer-Division, based in the Caen sector, only reacted the front late in the day on 6 June, stubbornly blocking the British in front of Caen. The 12.SS-Panzer-Division 'Hitlerjugend', made up of very young and motivated soldiers, also got under way late and its first elements, led by Kurt Meyer, known as 'Panzermeyer', only arrived north-west of Caen on the 6th at around midnight. The bulk of the Division only followed behind on 8 June. The elite Panzer-Lehr division was in the Le Mans and Perche region. It headed towards the front line with great difficulty and under the constant threat of fighter bombers. Its first elements only arrived at the front line at the end of 7 June and were not able to launch a first attack until 8 June but without its Panther tank battalion. As for the Tiger tanks of schwere SS-Panzer-Abteilung 101, in position east of Normandy at that time, they headed through Gournay-en-Bray at around 3 am on 7 June but the bridge over the Seine at Andelys was unusable and they had to turn round and make a detour via Paris; the powerful Tiger tanks would not reach the Argentan sector until the 10th. As for the 116. Panzer-Division, in the Rouen sector, it did not move and remained at the disposal of the men involved in the plot against Hitler...These men helped the allied victory, a fact which is not very well-known.

Seen here are some of the Panther tanks that the Division had at its disposal on 8 June. The others (of I./Pz.-Rgt. 6) had left for the Eastern Front and did not reach Normandy until 15 June. The tank seen here is a hybrid Panther equipped with the turret of an Ausf. A on an Ausf D hull. It bears the name of Christel, the girlfriend of one of the crew. (ECPA.)

On 7 June, after having been via Gournay-en-Bray, the formidable Tiger tanks went through Morgny. Seen here are two of them, belonging to the 1st company (see the markings on the hull). In the Schwimmwagen (amphibious vehicle) in the foreground, is SS-Unterscharführer Willi Röpstorff. However, these heavy panzers did not find a bridge to cross the Seine at Andelys and had to make a detour via Paris, only reaching Normandy, at Argentan, on 10 June. We will come across them later at Villers-Bocage! (BA)

Indian warfare...
7 - 10 June 1944

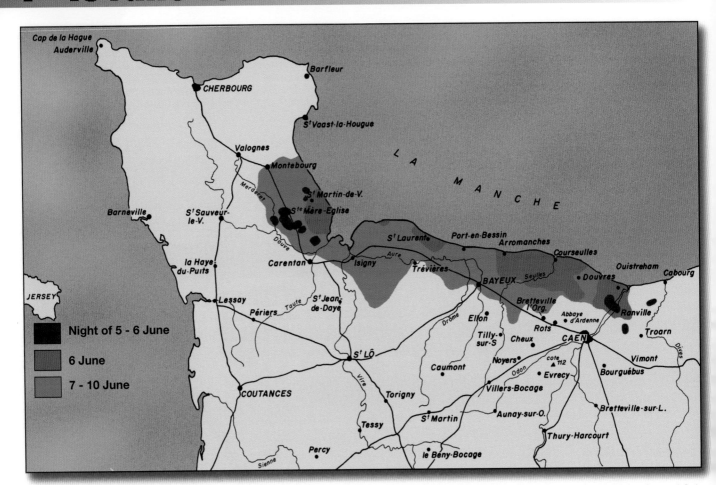

This map shows us the advance of the allied beachhead between 7 - 10 June. In the west and the Cotentin (Utah Beach sector), Major-General Collins' VII Corps strengthened its beachhead by now turning north to Montebourg, and west (capture of the Fière causeway over the Merderet on 9 June) and towards Carentan in the south. In the Omaha Beach sector, the 29th Division linked-up with the Rangers cut-off at the Pointe du Hoc and reached Isigny on 10 June in order to link-up with VII Corps at Carentan. In the east, the Americans linked-up with the British at Port-en-Bessin, north of Bayeux, as early as 8 June. In the British sector, starting from this town, the British 50th Infantry Division advanced south but was soon halted in front of Tilly-sur-Seulles by an elite armoured division which had arrived at the front on 8 June; the Panzer-Lehr-Division. In the centre of the Anglo-Canadian bridgehead, the 3rd (Canadian) Infantry Division had achieved the biggest advance south on D-Day and the German front there was wide open. However, from towards midnight on 6 June, and especially on 7 - 8 June, the 12. SS-Panzer-Division 'Hitlerjugend' reached the front line and halted all further Canadian advance. In the east, the British bridgehead of the 3rd Division to the west of the Orne and the 6th Airborne Division, to the east of the river, were in a cul-de-sac and also halted in front of Caen. The link-up between the Canadians and the British had been made but there still remained a German pocket at the Douvres radar station. (Heimdal map)

Since Omaha Beach. After fighting at the Pointe du Hoc and Omaha Beach, the Rangers remained in the bridgehead. Here a runner brings in a letter on horseback. This group's mascot wears the Rangers' insignia attached to its collar. (D.F./Heimdal)

In this 'Indian warfare' where the front lines had not been established everywhere and where deep raids could bring surprising success, or painful failure, a nighttime raid took place undertaken by a tactical group from the 'Hitlerjugend' division against Bretteville, where the solidly dug-in Canadians awaited... This photo bears witness to the fighting which took place during the night of 8 - 9 June. Seen here is the first Panther tank destroyed by the Allies during the Battle of Normandy as it was making its way up the main street in Bretteville-l Orgueilleuse from the west. It belonged to the 4th company of SS Panzer-Regiment 12 and was stopped by a PIAT projectile fired by Canadian Private Joe Lapointe. However, it was in fact finished off by a shot fired, in total darkness, from the Panther tank following behind, which explains the hole in the rear of the turret made by a German shell... As for the church tower, which had Canadian observers inside, it was destroyed by a shot from Panther '313' of the 3./12, commanded by SS-Uscha. März on the morning of 9 June. (IWM)

Sainte-Mère-Eglise, 7 June, paratroopers of 505 PIR (82nd Airborne) have gathered up horses and patrol the streets for this war correspondent's photo veritable 'Indian warfare' from 7 to 10 June.... (NARA/ Heimdal.)

At dawn on 7 June, the Allies had established four beachheads that they would stabilise by reinforcing the previous day's gains: those of the American paratroopers and seaborne troops of Utah Beach, that of the still narrow Omaha Beach, that of the Canadians and the British of the 50th Division, which was the biggest, and that situated astride the Orne estuary with British paras and the 3rd Division. By the evening of 6 June, the German coastal troops had been mostly wiped out or split up. In some sectors, the front was totally wide open and this allowed the allied troops to advance rapidly. In other sectors, defensive pockets or the arrival of reinforcement troops would halt, sometimes for several days, the seaborne troops. During this 'hazy' period which lasted from 7 to 18 June, the front was unstable. Also, up to 13 June, the Allies often did not know where the Germans were and vice-versa. It was real 'Indian warfare' which ended up with deep attacks and bloody failures... At the end of this period, the front line was more recognisable but with an advance that was generally slow in the face of progressively arriving German reinforcements.

Wednesday 7 June

It was only in the Anglo-Canadian beachhead (Gold and Juno) that any significant advances were made. To the east, the Canadian 9th Brigade wanted to continue its advance of the previous day, west of Caen. It advanced directly south with the objective of crossing the RN 13 road and taking the Carpiquet airfield. The Canadian armoured column advanced, however, under the gaze of elements of the Hitlerjugend which had arrived in the sector the previous evening and who were observing this column from the towers of the Abbaye

d'Ardenne. The Canadians had launched this attack at 6 am with the North Nova Scotia Highlanders and the Sherbrooke Fusiliers. But the Germans had set a trap whilst waiting for their first tanks, Panzer IV, which would not arrive near the Abbaye d Ardenne until 10 am, whereas the Canadians were already in front of Buron. At 12.30 pm, the Hitlerjugend counter-attacked with its tanks: the fighting would last until into the afternoon and was of unheard of intensity. Next to the panzers, the very young soldiers of the Hitlerjugend were caught by allied naval gunfire. The German counter-attack, initially victorious, was shattered by this storm of steel. The enthusiasm of these young soldiers gave way to despair ending in extremely violent combat. 43 Canadian prisoners were executed. The first clash was awful. However, despite the failure of the counter-attack in the end, the spearhead of the Canadian advance was broken; they had suffered 422 casualties (with 110 killed and 128 taken prisoner) and lost 7 tanks destroyed. Here, the Canadian front would from now on be static for a month opposite the Hitlerjugend who prevented any advance.

Thursday 8 June

Despite the failure of its counter-attack of the previous day, mostly shattered by naval gunfire, the 12.SS-Panzer-Division 'Hitlerjugend' wanted to attack again in order to finally throw the Allies back to the sea in this sector. The Panzer-Lehr-Division was to take part in this counter-offensive in the west, in the Bayeux sector. However, to the west of the previous day's sector, the Hitlerjugend wanted to attack in the Rots-Bretteville sector, by pushing up the Mue valley as far as the sea. But the Germans, as well as the Canadians, did not

With the Reginas dug-in at Bretteville (Foster Matheson) and Norrey (Major Tubb) facing east, D Company of this regiment (Captain Gordon Brown) was dug-in at the linen factory at Cardonville. One of these men has made his defensive position by opening up a hole in the thick stone wall around this linen factory and has dug a slit trench at the foot of it. He is looking south from where the II./26 HJ counter-attack will come. (PAC.)

Men of the Queen s Own Rifles are seen here waiting for a Hitlerjugend counter-attack. (PAC.)

1. In this rare colour photo, taken in the courtyard of the Ardenne abbey, one of the Hitlerjugend division's headquarters, we can see, from left to right: SS-Ostubaf. Karl-Heinz Milius, commander of the III battalion of SS-Panzergrenadier-Regiment 25 (in action on 7 June in the counter-attack to the north-west of the Abbaye d Ardenne), SS-Sturmbannführer Hubert Meyer, 1st staff officer of the Hitlerjugend division and behind him, SS-Oberscharführer Herbert Reinecker, the divisional war correspondent who, after the war, was the writer for the Inspector Derrick television series. (Photo KB Woscidlo/Coll. G.B.)

2. Following the heavy losses caused by the allied naval gunfire on 7 June, the III./25 was forced to postpone its counter-attack and hold the front line in front of Buron; something that it would do for almost a month. This rare colour photo taken by KB (war correspondent) Woscidlo, shows SS-Ustuf. (second-lieutenant) Franz-Josef Kneipp, signals officer of the III./25 (commanded by Milius). Kneipp wears here 'plane tree pattern' overalls first issued to Waffen-SS tank crews in the summer of 1943. (Photo KB Woscidlo/Coll. G.B.)

3. Among the 43 German dead from Kampfgruppe Meyer-Wünsche, killed in action during the night of 8 to 9 June in the Bretteville sector, was an NCO, SS-Oberscharführer Helmut Belke, an old companion of Kurt Meyer. In this colour photo taken by SS-Kriegsberichter Woscidlo, attached to the Hitlerjugend division, two soldiers from Regiment 25 have just finished his grave. (Coll. G.B.)

4. In the heat of the initial fighting, Hitlerjugend soldiers executed Canadian soldiers, but the extremely rough Canadians were not outdone, as we can see in this photo of a Hitlerjugend grenadier who has just been beaten up. (Coll. Heimdal.)

know yet know where their adversaries were. What then took place was real 'Indian warfare' where units virtually fumbled about without encountering any opposition, or falling into a trap set by the enemy...

Therefore, the Hitlerjugend command put together a tactical group led by Kurt Meyer, commander of SS-Pz.Gren.-Regiment 25, and Max Wünsche, who commanded SS-Panzer-Regiment 12. This would be known as Kampfgruppe Meyer-Wünsche which was to launch its counter-attack at the end of the day. They had, however, insufficient strength: two Panther tank companies (1st

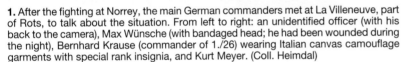

1. After the fighting at Norrey, the main German commanders met at La Villeneuve, part of Rots, to talk about the situation. From left to right: an unidentified officer (with his back to the camera), Max Wünsche (with bandaged head; he had been wounded during the night), Bernhard Krause (commander of 1./26) wearing Italian canvas camouflage garments with special rank insignia, and Kurt Meyer. (Coll. Heimdal)

2. Rudolf von Ribbentrop, with his arm in a sling due to his lung wound, seen here looking shattered after having seen his young soldiers wiped out, and Max Wünsche, wounded on the forehead a few hours previously, now leave La Villeneuve. (Photo W. Woscidlo/Coll. Heimdal)

3. War correspondents W. Woscidlo and Zschäkel took photos of grenadiers of 15./25 in a small alley between Villeneuve and Rots. It was approximately 2.30 pm and the 15./25 had returned from fighting at Norrey. The photographer came from the RN 13 road which passed through this locality and entered the alley looking towards the north. He first came across the face of Otto Funk. The latter is drunk with fatigue and his eyes and mind still filled with the horrors that he has just lived through: that of Canadian soldiers of B Company, Regina Rifle Regiment, crushed in their foxhole by the tracks of a tank and the 'crazed' screaming of burning tank crews. He was now a man scarred and crushed by the war whereas, three weeks earlier, he was still a 'kid' as seen in a photo taken in spring 1944. In German, Funk means 'spark'; and here the spark has gone from his face. The horrors of war have suddenly aged him. (Coll. G.B.)

4. The photographer then went into the alley to take pictures of the group previously seen in the background. (Coll. G.B.)

Berlin and 4th Pfeiffer) accompanied by a single grenadier company of Kurt Meyer's Rgt. 25, the 15./25, and a reconnaissance company.

In the meantime, the Hitlerjugend had received reinforcements from a grenadier regiment, SS-Pz.Gren.-Rgt.26, which was due to accompany, from the south, the attack led by KG Meyer-Wünsche which would be launched from east to west. Thus, it attacked towards the north against Rots and Norrey (where it failed against the Reginas' battalion led by Major Tubb), smashing into the strong-point of the linen factory at Cardonville, north of the railway line (Captain Gordon Brown, of the Reginas). On this day, in this 'Indian warfare', a British reconnaissance unit, C Squadron, Inns of Court, pushed deep into the lines of the Panzer-Lehr-Division, as far as Hill 102 where the HQ of the Lehr division's artillery regiment was situated. The Inns of Court captured the German officers, but their armoured vehicles were too small to take them away and the officers were shot on the spot. A surviving German officer, Major Zeissler, alerted the Hitlerjugend reconnaissance group at the Audrieu château; Canadian soldiers were shot in reprisal. These facts underline the extreme tension between the two adversaries in the first days.

5. The photographer is now at the end of the alley by the RN 13 road. In the foreground is Klaus Schuh with his MG, the butt of which is slightly burnt, he was part of Otto Funk's squad. On the right, with the grenade tucked into his belt, is the platoon leader, SS-Oscha. Wilhelm Boigk (who would be killed two weeks later south of Cheux along with Klaus Schuh). To the left, with the binoculars, is SS-Uscha. Wick, squad leader in IV platoon. In the background, by the barn, is Panther tank '326'. The commander of this tank was SS-Uscha. Eismann; he was cut in two (perhaps by a PIAT projectile) during the attack on Norrey. The gunner, Gerd Krieger, has got out of the turret in order to clean up the commander's blood. Later, Gerd Krieger asked his company adjutant, Post, for a new shirt to replace his bloodstained one. Post replied dryly, All you need to do is wash it! (Coll. Heimdal)

6. Grenadiers of 15./25 right, passing in front of the entrance to the Rots château, on their way to the western entrance to the village, beyond the road opposite Bretteville. Light tanks on Czech-made chassis are returning from the east. (Heimdal)

To the east and with night falling, the attack led by KG Meyer-Wünsche was launched to the west, passing through Rots to where the 1./26 had just advanced from the south, then drove across the plain to Bretteville in a 'cavalry' type raid as they had done in Russia. But the Canadians of the Reginas, led by Lieutenant-Colonel Matheson, had seen the German preparations and were waiting for them, on the plain and, above all, in the village where they were dug in. The Panther tanks would burn throughout the night. Lacking in infantry, the German attack failed and they withdrew. At the same time, south-west of Bretteville, Captain Brown's company confronted the 2./26 assault at the Linen factory at Cardonville. The close-quarter fighting was extremely violent and when it came to an end, German prisoners were finished off in the scutching room, their skulls shattered; this Canadian company had former convicts in its ranks.

Friday 9 June

After this night of hell, which ended in total failure for the Germans, the latter would attack again following the arrival of reinforcements from the 3rd company (Panther tanks) of SS-Panzer-Regiment 12. This unit was placed under the command of SS-Ostuf. Rudolf von Ribbentrop, the son of the Minister for Foreign Affairs. However, he had been wounded on 3 June (see page 7) and had been temporarily replaced by Hauptmann (Captain) Lüdemann. Following the failed attack on Bretteville, this new attack was launched against a village south of the railway line, Norrey. However, here too was a dug-in company of the Reginas, that of Major Tubb. At 12.30 pm, the 3./12 Panthers set off with their enthusiastic young crews, across the plain and heading directly west towards Norrey, accompanied once more by grenadiers of the 15./25. As one of war's fates would have it, Major Tweedale was arriving at the same time with nine new Sherman tanks of the Elgin Regiment. They would take on, from the north-west, the Panther tanks and seven panzers were knocked-out one after the other. The attack was another failure. Apart from the Panther tank losses, the smell of the burning tank crews wafted back to Rots.

In the airborne bridgehead east of the Orne

Opposite: Kampfgruppe Luck, a tactical group of the 21. Panzer-Division, placed under the command of Major Hans von Luck (see page 31) was facing the 6th Airborne Division paras and launched a counter-attack as early as 7 June against paras who were well dug in, but who were now stuck east of the Orne in a bridgehead which was, for now, a dead end. Seen here is a leutnant wearing the feldgrau wrap over assault artillery jacket, but with panzer death's head insignia. This must be an officer of Major Becker's assault gun group. The three soldiers around him wear camouflage smocks and helmet covers. (BA 495/3435/38a.)

Below: From the same set of photos: officers and two NCOs from the same unit examine the front line situation with military maps. Two officers wear the assault artillery wrap over tunics but, this time, with collar Litzen. (BA 493/3358/16a.)

21.Panzer-Division insignia painted on this division's vehicles. (Heimdal.)

A 10,5 cm le FH 18/40 auf Geschützwagen 38 H (f) advances across the plain between Colombelles and Escoville. This hybrid vehicle was made, 48 in all, by Baukommando Becker using the chassis of French Hotchkiss tanks. It was armed with a powerful 105 mm, 10,5 cm FH, German howitzer that usually equipped two-thirds of the artillery regiments. Twenty-one of these vehicles were sent to the assault gun group of the 21.Panzer-Division, StuG-Abt. 200. Despite their high profile, these roughly made and hard-wearing vehicles proved their worth, especially during Operation Goodwood; only five were lost during the battle. (BA 493/3359/34a.)

7 June 1944. Military police of the 6th Airborne Provost Company, Lance-Corporal A. Burton (foreground) and Lance-Corporal L. Balnett, guard a crossroads from their trench near Ranville. They are equipped with the Sten Mk V which was reserved for paratroopers. The number '46' indicates the 20th Anti-tank Regiment of the neighbouring 3rd Division. The Germans signposts still in place indicate the road around Caen via the north and south. They prove that these routes around the city rendered pointless and criminal, the bombardment of Caen that was deemed as being an essential road junction. (IWM)

The British airborne operation during the night of 5 to 6 June had been a success; the units had arrived at their objectives and had rallied much better than the American sector where the planes had been scattered by flak. This airborne bridgehead was reinforced during the day by the commandos of Lord Lovat's 1st Special Service Brigade with piper Bill Millin leading the way. Thus, on 7 June, this bridgehead was solidly installed east of the Orne, around Ranville and Amfreville. Facing them, to the north-east, were a few elements of the 716.ID who were soon joined by the 711.ID but, above all, in the south and south-east by Kampfgruppe Luck led by Major Hans von Luck, commander of Panzergrenadier-Regiment 25, one of the 21.Panzer-Division regiments (see pages 31 and 39). This tactical group comprised of Major von Luck's regiment, strengthened by Major Becker's powerful assault guns (Sturmgeschütz-Abteilung 200), a clever mix of captured French armour with German guns, but also the Panzer IV tanks of the 1st tank battalion of the 21.PD, the I./22, as well as artillery. Major von Luck launched a counter-attack as early as 3 pm on 7 June with the Panzer IV tanks of 4./Panzer-Regiment 22 and the divisional reconnaissance group. This reconnaissance unit was commanded by Major Waldow who had just returned, at dawn, from Berlin where had just got married; he was killed in this counter-attack which was repulsed by the airborne troops who had already dug in. This German failure would soon be followed by British ones. The fighting in this bridgehead was more often than not just a series of raids. Despite British reinforcements which arrived a little later, from 12 June onwards, with the 152nd Infantry Brigade of the Scottish 51st Highland Division. However, this brigade's actions were disastrous and its commander was sacked. What followed was a month of tough war of attrition in this sector which had become a dead end, but which would prove its worth as a jumping off point for Operation Goodwood (see further on).

Shoulder patch of the commandos and the cap badge of the Free French commando. (Coll. Nicolas Bucourt and Heimdal.)

Above: The French commandos at Amfreville immediately struck up a good relationship with the local population. Seen here is a group chatting with the Michèle family. From right to left: Nicolas Poli, Guillaume Guillou, Otto Zivolhava,?, Roland Gabriel and Louis Lanternier, concealed. (IWM.)

Opposite: Still at Amfreville, Laot and Priez, moved by a young Norman girl. (IWM.)

Major von der Heydte's command post (Fallschirmjäger-Regiment 6) was set up in the Marie house at the crossroads south of Saint-Côme-du-Mont which became known as 'Dead Man s Corner' (now a museum). This house overlooked the crossroads and the road leading to Carentan. Seen here is a diorama at the museum of the German paras' HQ. (Photo F. Coune/Heimdal.)

From Sainte-Mère-Eglise to Carentan

The Cotentin beachhead was now solidly instal-led with the arrival of reinforcements that had lan-ded at Utah Beach. From the latter, the offensive had been pursued in three directions. In the north, lieutenant-colonel Keil solidly blocked the Ameri-can advance towards Cherbourg. In the west, the beachhead had broken out thanks to the crossing of the Merderet river via the La Fière causeway on 9 June. But with the advance halted in front of

The German paratroopers, Fallschirmjäger, would be among the most formidable adversaries for the American soldiers. The men of von der Heydte's Fallschirmjäger-Regiment 6 fought against the American paras as early as 6 June paras vs paras and would be known as the 'Lions of Carentan'. Seen here is a combat squad armed with a MG 42, cove-red with ammunition belts to feed this machine-gun gun which had an incredible rate of fire. (DR)

This photo shows three American soldiers sear-ching the shop of Jules Lemencier in the church square at Sainte-Mère-Eglise. This photo was staged for propaganda purposes as the Ger-mans had already left this famous town during the night of 5 to 6 June... (Coll. Heimdal.)

The first 'Germans' encountered by the American paratroopers during the night of 5 - 6 June were in fact.... Georgians from the Caucasus, of Ost-Bataillon 795 (see page 30). These troops were positioned around Turqueville, between Saint-Mère-Eglise and Sainte-Marie-du-Mont, and fought back ferociously against the Americans until 7 June when they surrendered. Seen here is one of their officers, a lieutenant in German uniform with the nationality arm shield on his sleeve. This photo was used by American propaganda to show a 'German officer collaborating with the Allies'... (Coll. Heimdal.)

This young FJR6 para carries a formidable MG 42 on his shoulder. This light machine-gun was introduced in 1942 in order to gradually phase out the well-proven MG 34, also with an impressive rate of fire: 1,200 rounds per minute for the MG 34 and 1,500 for the MG 42. 350,000 MG 42 were produced up until the end of the war. It is probably the best light machine-gun ever made and continued to be used after the war by the Algerian National Liberation Front against the French army and, in a modified calibre NATO version by the Bundeswehr and other European armies. This young para looks worriedly at the sky as the threat from the air was constant in Normandy. (DR)

Prisoners, mostly Georgians, are gathered on the beach. The Americans would hand them over to Stalin...who would send them to concentration camps. (NA/Heimdal.)

Montebourg, the crossing of the Merderet allowed for a breakout towards the west with the objective of cutting the Cotentin peninsula in half, before turning north towards Cherbourg. In the **south**, the 101st Airborne paras fought against other paras, the very tough Fallschirmjäger adversaries of Major von der Heydte's FJR6. They now had to breakout of the peninsula and marshes via another causeway... the objective would be Carentan!

Widening the Omaha Beach bridgehead

After the landings at Omaha Beach which took place in terrible conditions and almost ended in tragedy and failure, the thin beachhead gained by the evening of 6 June was the jumping off point for a huge advance. On **7 June**, with the landing of three American infantry divisions, the 1st Infantry Division, 2nd Infantry Division and 29th Infantry Division, Major General Leonard T. Gerow's V Corps was a powerful force, soon strengthened by the tanks of the 2nd Armored Division, and which would push deep into the Bessin sector south of the coast against weak German elements and some elements of 716. ID and remnants of

Above: 9 June 1944, 1/175 of the 29th Infantry Division enters Isigny. However, this small town, destroyed by artillery and naval gun fire, still had to be mopped-up. Men of the 29th (the divisional shoulder patch can be seen on the man in the foreground) patrol in the main square still covered by the smoke from fires. (Coll. Heimdal.)

Opposite: An American soldier talks with locals. There were mixed relations between the local population and the American soldiers; in some sectors they were excellent and in others strained where the bombardments had caused painful losses, such as at Saint-Lô where stones were thrown and where there were cases of rape. (Coll.Heimdal.)

This photo was taken in the main square at Trevières after the fighting. A German body can be seen left lying there in the foreground. (Coll. Heimdal.)

the 352.ID. 7 June first began with the widening of the Omaha Beach bridgehead. The following day saw the linking up to the west with the Rangers surrounded at the Pointe du Hoc. The advance south was undertaken by the 115th Regiment (29th ID) which had just crossed the marshland of the Aure, advancing south on **9 June** and reaching the Elle river near Sainte-Marguerite d Elle on **10 June**. On this day, another 29th ID regiment, the 175th IR, reached and took Isigny; something which allowed for an advance south along the west bank of the river Vire as far as Airel (see map). To the east, the 38th Regimental Combat Team (tactical group of the 38th Infantry Regiment) also advanced directly south, taking Trévières and reaching the outskirts of Cerisy on the 10th. Thus, V Corps had succeeded in making a deep advance that allowed it to reach the sector situated northeast of Saint-Lô, an essential starting point for the capture of this town. However, German reinforcements were also arriving there, including paras of the 3.Fallschirmjäger-Division who would halt the advance in terrible hedgerow fighting that became known as 'Hedgerow Hell' to the GIs.

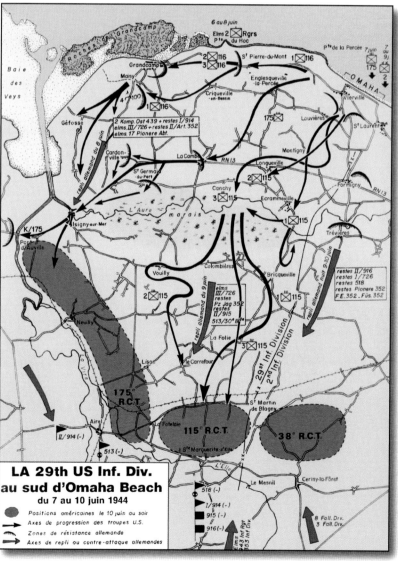

This map shows the rapid advance undertaken south of the Omaha Beach sector from 7 to 10 June, beyond the marshlands of the Aure valley, the capture of Isigny and that of Trévières, then the alignment of the front line along the Elle and Eure valleys as planned. (Heimdal)

LA 29th US Inf. Div.
au sud d'Omaha Beach
du 7 au 10 juin 1944

⬤ Positions américaines le 10 juin au soir
➤ Axes de progression des troupes U.S.
↷ Zones de résistance allemande
➡ Axes de repli ou contre-attaque allemandes

A view of the artificial port at Arromanches (Mulberry B), from the coast at La Vierge, shows us the concrete Phoenix caissons offshore that act as breakwaters protecting the artificial port. We can also see the unloading quays that are linked to the shore via floating roadways. (IWM)

Supplies

The question of supplies was an essential and decisive factor. By 7 June, the allied beachhead was firmly established on the Normandy coastline. But could it hold on if the Allies were not able to bring in enough troops, ammunition and fuel for the vehicles and tanks to hold out against German counter-attacks and then advance. As early as 6 June, 13,400 tonnes of fuel, in jerrycans, was landed on the beaches. This amount corresponded to a reserve of seven days. The British and Americans had forecast 2,000 tonnes per day during the first days. Landing supplies on the beaches was a way of ensuring the arrival of what was required and was mostly carried out with flat-bottomed LST craft that allowed the unloading of vehicles and machines via their bow doors. The capture of the deep-water port of Cherbourg was also an objective, but it would only start to be operational at D+40. Another complementary means had been put in place by the British and was one of the Landings' 'secret weapons'. These were the artificial ports, even if the term 'prefabricated ports' is more appropriate. Thus, the British engineers had designed prefabricated elements concrete 'Phoenix' caisson breakwaters (those that can still be seen off Arromanches). Then, in the harbour, there were artificial quays with unloading ramps that rose and fell with the tide on metal legs that rested on the sea bed. Their floating roadways led to the shore. All of these elements were built in England amidst the utmost secrecy.

Thus, the installation of two artificial ports by the Allies on the coast of Normandy was a remarkable technical exploit that was without precedent. In order to win the Battle of Normandy, the enormous quantity of allied materiel, mostly American, was vital for supplying and reinforcing the units engaged and those that were constantly arriving.

The entire campaign would depend on this struggle for speed in reinforcement and supply. It was the rapidity of bringing in allied materiel and reinforcements and the slow arrival of German reinforcements that decided the fate of the battle in favour of the Allies. The key role played by the allied air forces (destruction of rail hubs, bombing and strafing roads and German columns making their way to the front) which made the supply situation so difficult for the Germans and which allowed for the considerable increase in tonnage of materiel landed for the Allies.

Seen here (below) are light vehicles disembarking from the deck of a LST and driving down the unloading ramp to the quays, whereas other vehicles, tanks and heavier vehicles, could land directly from the open bow doors of the LST. (IWM)

(1) Read: *Quand l'or noir coulait à flot*, by Philippe Bauduin, Editions Heimdal, 2004.

Convoys use the long floating piers to leave the quays and make their way to the shore, here between Asnelles (left) and Saint-Côme (right), to the east of the huge Arromanches harbour. (IWM)

The artificial port elements (Mulberry A at **Saint-Laurent** in the American sector, and Mulberry B at **Arromanches**, in the British sector) were brought over as early as 6 June, but the assembly of the prefabricated parts (quays, floating piers, breakwaters and so on) required several weeks and the Admiralty had only forecast the completion of the artificial ports for 27 June. They were partially usable before this date and, in the American sector, the first LST unloaded its vehicles on **17 June** on the first quays of Mulberry A. By the very next day, this Mulberry recorded the disembarkation of 11,000 men, 2,000 vehicles and 9,000 tonnes of supplies for **18 June**. However, the great storm of 19 to 22 June broke up the elements to such an extent that Mulberry A at Saint-Laurent was rendered totally useless and only Mulberry B at Arromanches could be repaired. The assembly of the Arromanches artificial port was finally finished in early July by bringing in unused materiel from the Saint-Laurent artificial port that had been destroyed in the storm. However, even though these artificial ports played a considerable role, there were other ways of landing materiel and increasing the tonnage, thus rendering the permanent closure of one of the ports less dramatic and the delays in the use of the Arromanches artificial port less of a hindrance. The LCT, LCI, LST craft landed materiel directly onto the beaches, including **Utah Beach**. Some small fishing ports were used too: **Barfleur, Saint-Vaast, Carentan, Isigny, Grandcamp, Port-en-Bessin, Courseulles**. The port of Ouistreham remained under fire from German batteries until around 15 August. At the beginning of July there would only be a difference of 20 to 30% (according to materiel and supplies landed) compared to what had been forecast and what had been landed. On average, there were 185 ships a day since 7 June (1,442 LCT, 905 LST, 570 Liberty ships, 1,260 various types of ships, between 7 to 30 June). At this time, the port of Cherbourg (given the scale of the destruction caused by the Germans before general von Schlieben surrendered) was still unusable; the first four Liberty-ships would not be able to berth there until 26 July.

An American tanker berthed at the harbour wall in Port-en-Bessin. (IWM.)

9

The Americans advance 11 to 18 June

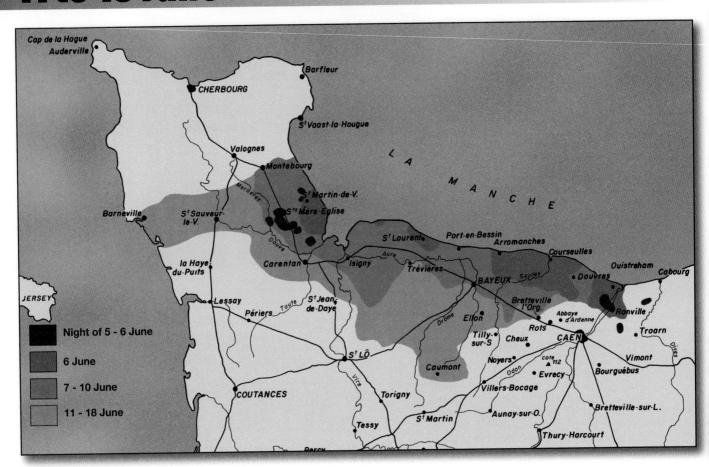

Starting from the narrow bridgehead, the Canadian sector formed a salient, in the Norrey area, on the evening of 10 June. But the Canadian advance was halted by the arrival in the front line of the 'Hitlerjugend' division which solidly held the front here, as was the case, to the east, opposite the British 3rd Division in front of Caen. The other salient was formed in the American sector by the 29th Infantry Division, to the south of Omaha Beach. From 11 to 18 June, facing a German front that was largely 'open' the advance was even more spectacular, going as far as Caumont, the high ground of which dominated the sector. This was by far the most southern advance and the most spectacular. However, with the arrival of reinforcements, those of the 2.Panzer-Division and the paras, it became once more a dead end for almost two months... Further west, the link-up was made at Carentan between the two American beachheads; shortly before the arrival of a new German division, the 17.SS-Panzergrenadier-Division 'Götz von Berlichingen' which would also block the front there. On the other hand, from the Utah Beach/Sainte-Mère-Eglise beachhead, the Merderet river had been crossed at the La Fière causeway and, with Montebourg solidly blocking the advance north to Cherbourg, it was via the west that Major-General Collins would undertake his breakout. After Saint-Sauveur-le-Vicomte, the west coast was reached on 18 June near Barneville, the Cotentin peninsula was now cut in half, thus cutting off the remains of four German divisions around the next objective, Cherbourg! (Heimdal map)

The lines had stabilised. In the Anglo-Canadian sector, three panzer divisions had now plugged the front line, even though they had failed in their attempt to throw the Allies back to the sea. The Panzer-Lehr-Division was facing the Tilly-sur-Seulles sector. The 12.SS-Panzer-Division 'Hitlerjugend' was then in the line as far as north of Caen. Then, it was the 21.Panzer-Division, from the north of the capital of lower Normandy to the bridgehead east of the Orne. To the west, apart from the Carentan sector, held by von der Heydte's paras and soon joined by the 17.SS-Panzergrenadier-Division 'Götz von Berlichingen', the Germans did not yet have any elite units to oppose the American advance to the west and east of this defensive breakwater. However, the 2.Panzer-Division was also on its way.

A dual British failure

Montgomery would fail twice against the three panzer divisions, two of which were elite. Firstly, given that the capture of Bayeux had been easy, the advance towards Tilly-sur-Seulles and beyond would be a first failure with the front stabilising there from 10 June onwards; the phase of 'Indian warfare' was well over. It was only the arrival of the Americans at Caumont, to the west, that allowed any advance in this sector to Lingèvres four days later. This was Montgomery's first failure. However, on 11 June the front had not entirely stabilised. Before the arrival of the 2.Panzer-Division, the front still remained 'open' on the right flank of the Panzer-Lehr-Division. A new British division, the 7th Armoured Division, slipped through with its tanks as far as Villers-Bocage. Montgomery aimed at carrying on as far as the river Orne, crossing it and taking Caen from the south. However, fate had just placed two companies of powerful Tiger tanks near the Norman town, schwere SS-Panzer-Abteilung 101, and the Tigers, led by tank ace, Michael Wittmann, were heading down the road into the town centre, destroying ten tanks and numerous vehicles. The victorious advance of the 7th Armoured Division was halted there and it withdrew north-east of Villers-Bocage to bolster the east of the American salient of Caumont-l'Eventé. The front here would remain static for almost two months. Montgomery's hopes of taking Caen from the south evaporated once more. He would, however, make other attempts, but these too would also fail. Despite a crushing materiel superiority, he found himself faced by a determined adversary.

A double victory in the American sector

The phase of 'Indian Warfare' in the airborne bridgehead ended thanks to the linking up with the troops who landed at Utah Beach. In the north, Montebourg was a solid defensive strong-point held by lieutenant-colonel Keil. To the south, the line of marshes was an obstacle held by the paras of Von der Heydte's 6th regiment. But the American paratroopers advanced along the road leading the Carentan where the German paras, out of ammunition, pulled back during the evening of 11 June. The paratroopers of the 101st Airborne Division thus entered Carentan the next day and were able to link up with the men who had landed at Omaha Beach; the two American beachheads were now joined making a first success. East of the river Vire the American troops had made a spectacular advance. Moving off from the first salient made by 10 June and advancing as far as Sainte-Marguerite-d Elle, for the 29th Division and more to the east for the 2nd Division, V Corps, with the 1st Division 'The Big Red One', reached Caumont on 13 June, just before the German paras of the 3.Fallschirmjäger-Division arrived in this sector. This elite German unit would block the German front in this sector for almost two months. The American effort would, from now on, be made in the 29th Division sector with the objective of taking Saint-Lô.

In the Cotentin peninsula, the front was blocked to the north and a link up made to the south. Therefore, Major-General Collins decided to break out after the Merderet was crossed. However, the lack of efficiency shown by these divisions (especially the 90th) opposite Pont-l'Abbé, forced Collins to keep the 82nd Airborne Division paras in the front line. The latter crossed the Douve and took Saint-Sauveur-le-Vicomte on **16 June**. From there the advance continued until the coast was reached at Barneville on **18 June**. The peninsula was now cut off, trapping the remains of four German divisions (77.ID, 91.ID, 709.ID). However, elements from three of these divisions (77.ID, 91.ID and 243.ID) had escaped being encircled, sometimes in dramatic circumstances (including the epic escape of colonel Bacherer). The German troops cut off in the north now began to fall back on Cherbourg for the final battle.

16 June, Cristot, north-east of Tilly-sur-Seulles, where hard fighting took place against the Panzer-Lehr-Division.

Monsieur Henri Bellière's farm is seen burning here after having been heavily bombarded by the British. The KOYLI soldiers can only take stock of the damage. The hand pump could not be used to put the fire out as most of the civilians had been evacuated by the Germans on 15 June. Animals, such as cows, paid a heavy price due to bombardments. The Bellière farm buildings, as they were in 1944, have disappeared but the farm was rebuilt. (IWM)

Carentan 12 June

After heavy fighting along the causeway in the middle of the marshes, between Saint-Côme-du-Mont and Carentan, by the American 101st Airborne paratroopers and the German paras of FJR6, the latter, out of ammunition, finally withdrew from Carentan during the evening of 11 June and the American paratroopers entered the small town without a fight. Seen here is Rue Holgate leading into the town centre. The railway crossing can be seen in the background. (US Army)

Bulldozers were at work as early as 7 June near the La Londe farm, two kilometres to the east of Sainte-Mère-Eglise, in order to set up an air field that would become operational seven days later, close the front line. (NA/ Coll. Heimdal.)

The Battle of Carentan

On Sunday **10 June**, with the first elements of the 29th Infantry Division arriving in Isigny, on the east bank of the Vire, the west saw the 101st Airborne Division paratroopers launch their attack towards Carentan with tough fighting along the causeway that rose above the marshes leading to the small town. There was desperate fighting against the German paras (Fallschirmjäger-Regiment 6) led by Major von der Heydte. When the latter were out of ammunition, they pulled out of Carentan on the evening of 11 June and took up positions south of the town where they linked up with the 17. SS-Panzergrenadier-Division Götz von Berlichingen which had began arriving at the front line from the Loire valley. This division, along with Von der Heydte's paras, blocked the land bridge in the middle of the marshes. Thus, the American 101st paras entered the evacuated town with a fight, there would be no final battle for Carentan. However, the American war correspondents would use their photos to magnify the capture of this small town six days after the landings.

As the American paratroopers entered Carentan, other 101st elements, men of the 327th Glider Infantry Regiment linked up with K Company of the 175th Regiment, 29th Division at Auville-sur-le Vey. The two American beachheads were now joined, six days after the landings!

At 5.30 am on 13 June, the Götz von Berlichingen division began artillery preparation for a counter-attack on Carentan. The advance started well but was halted by the American paratrooper positions at around 9 am south-west of Carentan. Also, the Americans brought up tanks, those of CCA2 of the 2nd Armored Division, which had started landing at Omaha Beach on 11 June. This unit's tanks were in action against the 'Götz' assault guns from 10.30 am onwards. The German counter-attack was definitively halted in front of Carentan where the American link up was now solidly established. However, what would now begin was a very tough and slow American advance south of this town.

Opposite: This well-known photo shows American paratroopers with a captured German VW-Kübelwagen turning right down Rue Holgate. These men arrived via the causeway which can be seen in the background at the end of the road coming from Saint-Côme. To the left is the Désiré Ingouf café and the railway crossing. Note the German signs still in place. (DAWA/Coll. Heimdal.)

Below: This photo, taken after the German counter-attack, on 18 June 1944, shows an American self-propelled 105 mm gun of the 14th Artillery Battalion of the 2nd Armored Division, returning from the front line and seen here at the railway crossing before passing in front of the Désiré Ingouf café. (US Army/Heimdal.)

7th Armoured Division

I.SS-Pz.-Korps

Michael Wittmann

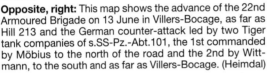

Above: This photo, taken on Hill 213, shows a destroyed Sherman and Cromwell tanks. (BA)

Opposite, right: This map shows the advance of the 22nd Armoured Brigade on 13 June in Villers-Bocage, as far as Hill 213 and the German counter-attack led by two Tiger tank companies of s.SS-Pz.-Abt.101, the 1st commanded by Möbius to the north of the road and the 2nd by Wittmann, to the south and as far as Villers-Bocage. (Heimdal)

Below: This map shows the flanking movement undertaken by the 7th Armoured Division on the western flank of the British front, from the rear of the 50th Infantry Division and using the American advance at Caumont-l Eventé (see front line on 12 June). This division at first advanced as far as Livry, then headed towards Villers-Bocage on the 13th with the aim of skirting around the German front. (Heimdal map)

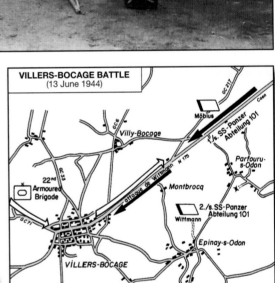

VILLERS-BOCAGE BATTLE
(13 June 1944)

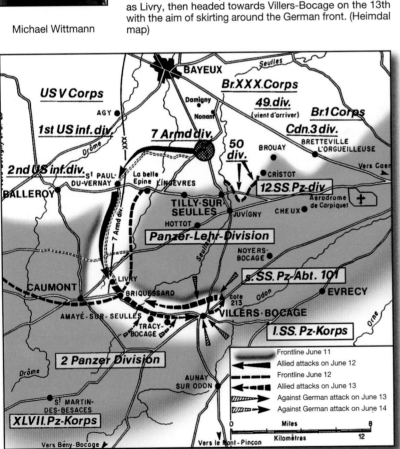

Villers-Bocage (12-13 June)

On **12 June** and in light of the situation of the American 2nd Infantry Division's advance as far as Caumont l'Eventé, Montgomery decided to put together Operation Perch which would allow for the German front and Caen to be encircled from the south. This operation would use the British 7th Armoured Division which had illustrated itself in North Africa. This division set off on this day at 3 pm and, instead of being sent in against Tilly as originally planned, it formed a long column which arrived at Livry in the evening (see map) having lost the lead tank of the 8th Hussars. The column then headed towards the south-east and the advance resumed at dawn (5.30 am) on 13 June towards Villers-Bocage, with A Company of the 4th CLY (4th County of London Yeomanry, the Sharpshooters) and B Battery of the 5th RHA then A Company of the Rifle Brigade at the front. The advance was rapid and the spearhead element reached Hill 213, overlooking the sector east of Villers at 8 am! The column halted there. However, fate was about to play a role. Two Tiger tank companies of schwere SS-Panzer-Abteilung 101 (see page 115) had just reached the sector and intended spending the night there: the

The entrance to the town.

Three tanks were knocked-out on the bend in Rue Clemenceau going down towards the town centre, The first was a Cromwell then a Panzer IV (634) belonging to II./Panzer-Lehr-Regiment 130 which had come to support the heavy battalion and which was destroyed there. Finally, heading towards the town centre was the wreck of Captain Dyas' Cromwell. We can also see a Schwimmwagen of the I. SS-Panzerkorps driving down Rue Clemenceau and passing in front of the wrecks of these three tanks. Note, on the wreck of the Panzer IV '634' the heraldic shield of the von Schönburg-Waldenburg family. Prince von Schönburg-Waldenburg commanded the II battalion (equipped with Panzer IV tanks, of II./Panzer-Lehr-Regiment 130) until his death on 9 June. His family crest was painted on the turrets of his battalion's tanks. (BA)

1st company was led by SS-Hauptsturmführer Rolf Möbius, to the north of the road and, the 2nd, by SS-Obersturmführer (lieutenant) Michael Wittmann, one of the panzer aces who had illustrated himself on the Eastern Front. They had been warned by the Panzer-Lehr-Div. that an attack was underway, due to the encounters of the previous day but they did not know from which direction it was coming. Suddenly, they found themselves near the armoured column. They launched an immediate counter-attack. Wittmann sped down the road heading towards Villers-Bocage, destroying the entire halted column as far as the town centre. Ten tanks and numerous vehicles were destroyed and the exploit would be exploited by German propaganda. The attack was halted on the outskirts of the town by British elements which had set up defensive positions. However, the attack by the 7th Armoured Division was shattered and it definitively pulled back from the town in the evening. The front would remain static to the west of Villers-Bocage until the beginning of August when the Germans began a general withdrawal following the American breakthrough!

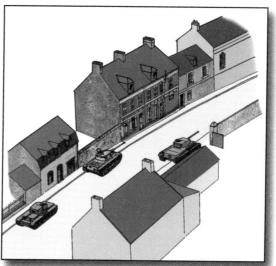

Illustration showing the positions of the destroyed tanks (B.Paich/Heimdal)

Photo taken at the foot of Hill 213 at the crossroads before the entrance to the town. We can see a long line of Rifle Brigade vehicles and weapons. This photo was published in the German Signal magazine. (Heimdal)

Villers-Bocage (12-13 June)

Above: Tiger 111 of Ostuf. Hannes Philipsen, seen here in the main road after its attack. This tank was hit in its running gear by a shot from one of Bill Cotton's tanks, hidden near the town hall. The Tiger, out of control, ended up in a shop front in Rue Pasteur. The left of the tank bears the 1st company markings and, on the right, that of the battalion, it has a green and brown camouflage scheme. In the background can be seen, also knocked-out, a Panzer IV (left) belonging to Kampfgruppe Ritgen (Panzer-Lehr-Division) and Tiger 113 (SS-Oscha. Heinrich Ernst) also hit by fire from tanks of B Squadron, 4th CLY. Philipsen managed to get out of his Tiger but Ernst was killed. It was here that the victorious advance of the panzers was halted by a British defensive position. (BA)

1. Photo of Captain P. Victory's burnt out Cromwell straddling Rue Curie. Blocked in this narrow street, it was hit by a shell from Michael Wittmann's Tiger 212 which was advancing down the main street and fired into this side street. The fire from the tank has spread to the building. On 13 June, the Germans lost six tanks (of which four were write offs) for s.SS-Pz.-Abt. 101, five Panzer IV (3 of which were write offs) for the Lehr division, making a total of seven definitive losses. Losses for the British were: 5 Sherman, 17 Cromwell, 3 Stuart, 3 Humber Scout Cars, between 9 and 11 half-tracks, 3 to 4 Loyd Carriers, making a total of 40 to 43 armoured vehicles. (BA)

2. Evening 13 June, a group of around fifty 7th Armoured Division prisoners left Hill 213 and made its way up the Caen road in a column of three with their personal items, escorted by a few men of the 4th company, s.SS-Pz.-Abt. 101. They avoided using the main road as it was too dangerous due to allied planes so took small roads via Esquay, Vieux and Amayé-sur-Orne, as seen in these photos. The long column is seen here making its way through the village of Vieux.

3. Another photo shows the prisoners passing in front of the village's church

4. Finally, the head of the column is seen here guarded by a few feldgendarmes of the I.SS-Panzer-Korps.

(Photos BA.)

Above: This aerial photo, taken looking towards the east, shows us the ruined town of Saint-Sauveur-le-Vicomte, overlooked by its medieval castle with its large keep (top, left). At the bottom of the photo we can make out the road coming from Pont-l'Abbé and the river Douve (which can be seen behind the castle), which was crossed by the paratroopers using assault dinghies. (Coll. Heimdal)

Below, left. Lieutenant Kelso C. Horne (1st Platoon, I Company, 508th PIR) poses for the war correspondent's camera with his Garand. This photo would become famous. Despite having fought for ten days, the American paratroopers displayed exceptional combat capability, helping pave the way for divisions that had stalled. (Coll. Heimdal)

Below, right. Saint-Sauveur, 16 June, 505th PIR paratroopers advance down Rue Bottin-Desylles, amidst the fires, towards the train station which is still in German hands. (Coll. Heimdal)

Towards the west: Saint-Sauveur-le-Vicomte

To the west of the Merderet, the 90th Infantry Division, which had taken Picauville on 10 June, lacked drive and experience and had stalled. The advance was weak on **12 and 13 June**. The 357th Infantry Regiment lost 150 men per day! Faced with the obstinate German defence, the Americans bombarded Pont l'Abbé at around 5 pm on 12 June. They at last entered the ruined and empty town during the night of 12 - 13 June. Following

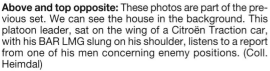

Above and top opposite: These photos are part of the previous set. We can see the house in the background. This platoon leader, sat on the wing of a Citroën Traction car, with his BAR LMG slung on his shoulder, listens to a report from one of his men concerning enemy positions. (Coll. Heimdal)

the failure of his offensive Maj. Gen. McKelvie was relieved of his command and replaced at the head of the 90th Infantry Division by Maj. Gen. Eugene M. Landrum. Also, the VII Corps commander, Maj. Gen. Collins, put the already tired 82nd Airborne Division back into the line in order to support the inexperienced men of the 90th.

At dawn on **14 June**, the men of the 82nd advanced to the west of Pont-l'Abbé, as far as the Bonneville sector. On 15 June, the 82nd Abn. advanced again, on both sides of the road leading to Saint-Sauveur-le-Vicomte. The attack on the town began at dawn on 16 June. The Americans were facing this town overlooked by its strong medieval castle; they held the east bank of the river Douve. The latter was crossed and they were in Saint-Sauveur by nightfall. Further north, on the right flank, the 9th Infantry Division had pushed through the German lines in the Orglandes sector and advanced on the same day to Sainte-Colombe and NÉhou with the objective of reaching the sea and cutting off the Cotentin.

This other photo shows us Lieutenant-Colonel Van Dervoort with his crutch in Rue du Vieux Château in Saint-Sauveur. One can see the road sign in the background indicating the way to La Haye-du-Puits which would take almost a month to reach. (NA/Heimdal)

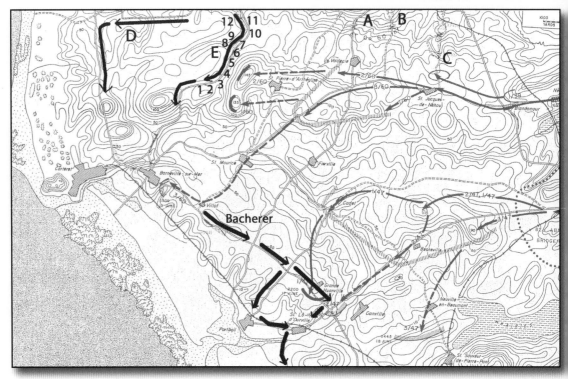

This map shows the German breakout attempts which took place on all available roads on 18 June between 3 and 4 am and which were halted by American road blocks: at the Saint-Paul bridge (A), the Gonneville bridge (B), the Jacquin hamlet (C). A retreating column reached Vretot (D), Barneville and another via the road leading from Bricquebec (E). The numbers indicate the areas where the German column suffered damage. We then see the Bacherer column passing through the American spearheads. (Heimdal map on top of a US Army map)

The peninsula is dramatically cut off

With the Americans advancing towards the west, some of the encircled German forces would regroup to the north around Cherbourg in a Kampfgruppe Cherbourg, whereas the bulk of the 77.Infanterie-Division (which had just arrived as reinforcements from Brittany), and the 91. Luft. L. Div. and 243.Inf. Div. were placed under the command of the leader of the latter unit, general Hellmich, with the task of breaking through to the south. This, however, meant going through the American spearheads in dramatic conditions. Generalleutnant Stegmann, commanding the 77.ID, was killed on 17 June near Bricquebec by an American patrol. As for general Hellmich, he was killed near Canville-la-Roque, also on 17 June, during an air attack. Thus, after general Falley (91.LL.Div. killed on 6 June), two other German generals were killed on 17 June. All three now lie at rest in the German military cemetery at Orglandes in the Cotentin. During their withdrawal, the German columns suffered a veritable carnage, at the Jacquin hamlet or on the road from Bricquebec. However, colonel Bacherer succeeded in an incredible breakthrough with elements of the 77.ID, the command of which he took over following the death of general Stegmann.

Above: 18 June, contact is made in front of the town hall in Barneville between the first American troops and the civilians. This was a decisive moment, the west coast had been reached... (NA)

Opposite: Barneville, small groups of Germans were taken prisoner by American soldiers. For these men the war is over. They are almost all, apart from one, wearing the issue cap for this period, the Einheitsfeld mütze, inspired by the mountain cap with its practical flaps that could be lowered over the ears. (NA)

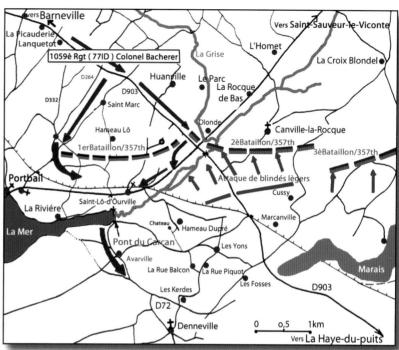

Generalleutnant Heinz Hellmich, at his HQ. He commanded the 243.Infanterie-Division, in the west of the Cotentin and was killed on 17 June at Canville-la-Roque (see map above) during an air attack. (Coll. Charita.)

This map shows the front line reached on the evening of 18 June 1944. The 9th Infantry Division cut off the Cotentin Peninsula by reaching Barneville. Elements of four German divisions (243rd, 77th, 91st and 709th) were now cut off and encircled in the north. Other elements of these divisions succeeded in withdrawing south and escaping encirclement. Three American divisions (9th, 79th and 4th), after the 90th was withdrawn, and the 82nd holding the line facing south, was sent off for rest, now advanced towards Cherbourg and the Germans who were falling back to the Festung. (Heimdal)

Colonel Bacherer's epic breakout

After the dramatic attempts by the 77.Infanterie-Division to break out, the situation was energetically taken in hand by colonel Bacherer. The losses had been suffered at the three crossing points at dawn on the 18th, with a few hundred men out of a division which numbered 10,505 men (with the Hiwis) at the beginning of June. Colonel Bacherer had to wait until the following night and darkness to get through. He had gathered together 1,500 men and at 1 am on 19 June, the column set off, probably by circling via the north. Doctor Schreihage, a staff officer, described this odyssey: Several Kübelwagen (Volkswagen), two of which were radio vehicles, led the way along the itineraries. The signals group kept the rear units informed as to how the advance was going. The column reached the hamlet of Villot (see map above). Bacherer has sent out the signal: *"Push on to Villot!"* Then, with dawn breaking ahead, we were at the Olonde stream (this was in fact the Grise near the Olonde manor house). It was here at 11 am, under a cloudy sky, that the column came across a camp of the American 2/357th IR. Colonel Becherer, behind two 243.ID assault guns, attacked in the old school way with the I./1050 with fixed bayonets, supported by the fire of a light machine-gun. Thus, 1,400 German soldiers battered their way through, bringing with them 240 American prisoners (American historians have since brought this number down to a hundred) with twelve jeeps! According to Jean Barros, Bacherer must have taken the following itinerary: the Duchemin hamlet, Saint-Lô-d'Ourville, the bridge over the Grise at Carcan again, Avarville (German lines), then Denneville.

Born on 9 February 1895 at Pforzheim, Baden-Württemberg and dying in the same region on 9 July 1964, colonel Rudolf Bacherer had seen action during the First World War with the Baden Dragoons regiment as a regular officer from 13 July 1914 to 1 January 1919. During the Second World War he took part in the Battle of France and the Russian campaign from 1941 to 1943. In the west, with the rank of Oberst (colonel), he commanded Grenadier-Regiment 1049 which he managed to push south through enemy lines .In the La Haye-du-Puits sector, he commanded the remnants of the division under the name of KG 77 ID or KG Bacherer. He tried to stop the Americans on 31 July at Pontaubault. He succeeded in withdrawing to Dinard (his unit had been previously stationed in the sector) where he resisted along with his men for a further ten days, only surrendering on 15 August 1944. He is seen here with his medals, including the German Cross in Gold, the Winter Campaign ribbon and the Knight's Cross of the Iron Cross awarded for his exploits in Normandy.

On the front line at Tilly-sur-Seulles, the 50th Division facing the Panzer-Lehr-Division

Following the rapid advance of the 50th Infantry Division, strengthened by two armoured brigades, the thrust was shattered by the arrival on the front line of the Panzer-Lehr-Division. The 2nd Glosters, one 50th Division's battalions, managed to set up positions at the Tilly crossroads on **11 June** but were pushed back by one of the Lehr regiments, the 901st. Also on this day, Prince von Schönburg-Waldenburg was killed in his Panzer IV during the fighting at Hill 103. The Panzer-Lehr-Division put up stiff resistance in this sector. But, on **13 June**, the rapid American advance in the

Men of the 6th Battalion Light Infantry (6 DLI), one of the 50th Division units, await a possible Panzer-Lehr-Division counter-attack. A radio-operator with a Sten sub machine-gun at hand, sends messages given to him by his officer who is observing with his binoculars. (IWM)

Private William Weatkley, of A Company, 6 DLI, in position with his Bren light machine-gun in the ruins of Douet de Chouain, a crossroads on the road to Tilly-sur-Seulles, near a place known as Jerusalem on the map opposite. (IWM)

Caumont sector, to the west, cleared the British right flank in the sector of Verrières and Lingèvres (see map) where the Panzer-Lehr-Division was forced to pull back. It was also threatened by the arrival of another British division, the 49th ID in the Cristot sector on 16 June.

Panzer IV type II of the II./130, one of the two Lehr tank battalions commanded by Prince von Schönburg-Waldenburg, killed on 11 June. This 5th company tank bears his heraldic shield. (Painting by Julio Lopez Caeiro)

Sergeant Trevor Ingram, 6th DLI, from Nantwich, Cheshire, is given first aid at the aid post after having been wounded at Verrières, northeast of Lingèvres, on 14 June whilst fighting against the 1st battalion of Panzergrenadier- Regiment 902 (see map below). Note the 'TT' badge of the 50th Division on his shoulder. (IWM)

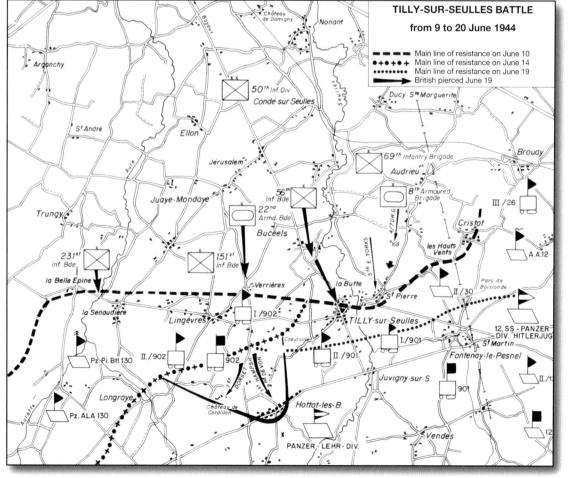

This map shows the tough fighting undertaken by the British (50th Infantry Division strengthened by two armoured brigades, the 8th and 22nd) against the Panzer-Lehr-Division during the Battle of Tilly-sur-Seulles between 9 and 20 June; a slow advance through the hedgerows during these eleven days of combat. (Heimdal map)

Success and failure for the panzers

The German success was multiple with the very progressive arrival on the front line of the panzer divisions. On 6 June, the **21.Panzer-Division** had halted the British 3rd Division opposite Caen and the 6th Airborne Division in the airborne bridgehead east of the Orne. The **12. SS-Panzer-Division** had broken the Canadian attack of 7 June to the west of Caen and had locked down all of the Canadian front and would continue to do so with as much success. It had, however, failed in all of its counter-attacks, on 7, 8 and 9 June as we have seen. The **Panzer-Lehr-Division** had blocked the 49th Division in the Tilly-sur-Seulles sector and had played a role in the German success at Villers-Bocage.

With the progressive arrival of the panzer units, which were often too late to play a decisive role, the Allies bombarded the Panzergruppe West HQ at **La Caine** on **10 June**, wounding its commander, General Geyr von Schweppenburg and killing several of his staff officers, thus depriving it of its leadership at a crucial moment!

On 17 June 1944, the allied beachhead in Normandy remained narrow and a race against time was engaged. The Allies had to bring in reinforcements in order to re-start the attack but the narrowness of the beachhead was a handicap. The Germans, who should have pushed the Allies back into the sea on D-Day, as Rommel had stipulated, had to bring up reinforcements in order to win back the initiative, but the Allies had air superiority and this slowed down the transportation of the panzer divisions which could only travel a few hours each night at a time when these were the shortest nights of the year.

Thus, on **17 June**, Adolf Hitler held a conference deep in the bowels of his underground HQ at Margival near Soissons in the Führer-Hauptquartier built in 1940 for the command of operation Seelöwe, the planned for invasion of England. Present at the conference was Generaloberst Alfred Jodl, the Wehrmacht chief-of-staff, OKW, but also field marshals von Rundstedt and Rommel, with their chiefs-of-staffs, generals Blumentritt and Speidel, as well as several OKW and Ob.West officers. According to the 'Ib' report of Heeresgruppe B, major I.G. Von Ekespare, Rommel presented the situation of the Allies and their impact on the German forces, talking of the heavy infantry losses and the delays in bringing up reinforcements due to allied air strength. He also underlined the lack of Luftwaffe support. Given the situation, he requested that the north Cotentin front be withdrawn to Cherbourg. This was accepted by Hitler as he had no other means to oppose the cutting off of the Cotentin peninsula. The large port of Cherbourg would fall ten days later on 27 June.

Hitler reminded them that a reversal of the situation would only be made possible by cutting off enemy supplies or by neutralising allied naval forces. He ordered the navy and the Luftwaffe to lay more mines between Le Havre and the eastern coast of the Cotentin.

As for AOK 15, the 15th army sector in the Pas-de-Calais, Hitler considered that the German forces there were stronger than in Normandy but that there were not enough available forces in the event of a second landing and the defensive front in Holland was too weak. He also noted that a landing was easily possible in Brittany. Thus, the allied Operation Fortitude deception plan had done its job perfectly; the German high command overestimated the number of allied divisions (estimated at sixty) still available in Britain. It believed that the presence of V1 launch ramps in the north would force the Allies to also land in the AOK 15 sector.

However, they would also have to prevent the extension of the allied beachhead in Normandy, it would have to be cut to the east of Saint-Lô and then sweep it up towards the east or the west, depending on the situation. They all ate together when the conference was over and the Führer left at around 3 pm (1).

On **20 June**, the OKW came to the following conclusions based on two studies of the war in the west and which were issued by Rommel the previous day: *"1) The Führer's intention is for a concentrated attack with the 1., 2., 9., 10. SS, 2. Pz and Pz.-Lehr-Div. to be undertaken in order to destroy American forces in the Balleroy sector (II Corps). This is why the relief of the 2. Pz and Pz.-Lehr-Div. by infantry divisions is necessary and to communicate how this will be done and the timetables.*

2) Before this, the enemy positioned east of the Orne by strong defensive means must be destroyed so that the ground forces which will have taken part in this operation can be available for the main attack." (2)

The next day, on **21 June**, field-marshal Rommel issued the attack order of battle. It would be carried out under the orders of Panzergruppe West. On the right (to the east, in the Caen sector): I.SS-Pz.-Korps with 12.SS-Pz.-Div., 1.SS-Pz.-Div. and Pz-Lehr-Div. In the centre (Villers-Bocage sector): XXXXVII. Pz-Korps with 2.Pz.-Div., 276. and 277. ID. On the left (to the west, towards Balleroy and the Cerisy forest): II. SSPz.-Korps with 9.SS-Pz.-Div., 10. SS-Pz.-Div. and 2. SSPz.-Div.. However, the attack would not be able to be launched before 10 or 14 days (between 1 and 5 July), due to the arrival of units and ammunition supplies. Rommel's report also added: *"The attack east of the Orne depends, as the Führer stated orally, on the prior elimination of the naval artillery. Without this measure, the conclusion that I came to myself yesterday, is that any attack is doomed to failure."* He considered that it was indispensable to engage the 16. Luftwaffen-Felddivision and the 21. Panzer-Division to the east of the Orne, as the 346. Infanterie-Division had lost the bulk of its combat capability. Thus, Hitler had underlined the most serious threat: the power of the naval artillery which could crush any German troop concentration; an analysis which would prove particularly exact. Therefore, as long as it was not eliminated, these counter-attack plans remained theoretical. Also, only three armoured divisions (as well as the 21st east of the Orne) were ready, the four others would not be on the front line before July, the II.SS-Panzer-Korps being brought in from the east in Galicia as quickly as possible.

The Germans had not eliminated the naval threat and were losing the race against the Allies in bringing up reinforcements. Only the weather would be able to help them and this would turn out to be the case. A heavy summer solstice **storm** began on 19 June and lasted until 22 June, halting much of the maritime traffic during four days and therefore slowing down the allied reinforcements, the front of which would be paralysed, thus giving the Germans an unexpected respite. On **24 June**, with the storm over, field-marshal von Rundstedt advised *"to Check if, after the success of the attack on Balleroy and the sector situated north-east of this area, it is possible to continue the attack towards Carentan. Until the beginning of this big offensive, the sector situated around and to the east of Caen remains the most important for Ob. West."* The field-marshal still hoped that the counter-attack undertaken in the Balleroy sector would go ahead but he drew attention to the importance of the Caen sector, underlining: This is why we must be strong in this sector. (3)

However, the planned counter-attack would run into Operation Epsom. The latter would fail in its objectives but would nevertheless have an unexpected success by diverting the II.SS-Panzerkorps from this counter-attack and it was effectively crushed on its jumping-off positions by the allied naval artillery. The panzers had definitively failed in pushing the Allies back to the sea. They would now be confined to a defensive role where they would be formidably efficient, but at the same time prey to the fighter-bombers...

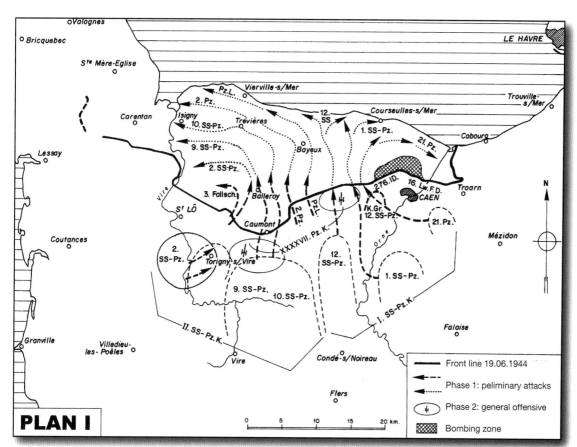

The two counter-attack versions proposed by Heeresgruppe B. In the first case, a strong artillery concentration would pin down the Allies north of Caen whilst the panzer divisions pushed towards the sea. In the second case, all of the forces would advance towards the sea then turn towards the American sector. (Heimdal maps made from archive documents)

PLAN I

⎯⎯	Front line 19.06.1944
⎯ ⎯►	Phase 1: peliminary attacks
⋯⋯►	Phase 2: general offensive
⬭	Bombing zone

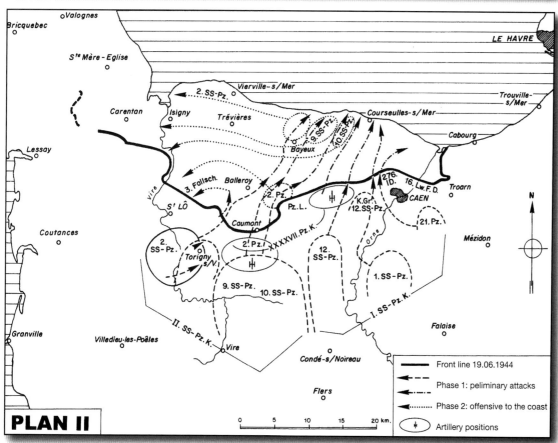

PLAN II

⎯⎯	Front line 19.06.1944
⎯ ⎯►	Phase 1: peliminary attacks
⎯·⎯►	Phase 2: offensive to the coast
⬭	Artillery positions

(1) For further details read H. Meyer, *12. SS-Panzer-Division Hitlerjugend*, Heimdal, pp. 257-258.

(2) *KTB Pz.-AOK 5, 63181/4. Fernschreiben Ob. West* to Panzergruppe West from 21.6-44.

(3) KTB Ob. West, B/, Bestand RH 19 TV/28, from page 140 onwards.

10

Cherbourg to the Odon...
19 to 30 June

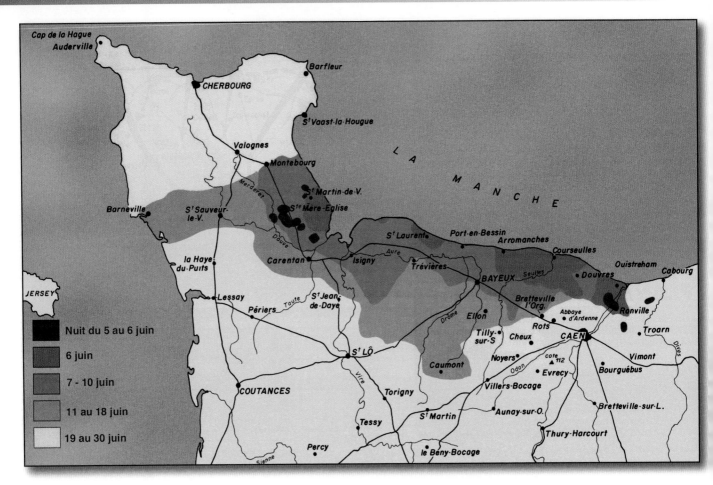

The advance was spectacular between 19 to 30 June with the capture of Cherbourg, "The first American victory in Normany". The advance remained weak in the British sector where the Battle of the Odon ended in failure on Hill 112, an area where the Germans had brought up an entire armoured corps, the II.SS-Panzer-Korps. The Battle of Normandy was turning into static warfare and hard fighting in the middle of the bocage, something which led the American high command to say: "This damned war could last for a century." (Heimdal map)

'The first American victory'

Once again, the three American First Army army corps advanced the furthest, first with VII Corps which went as far as Cherbourg, establishing a large bridgehead on the Cotentin peninsula. This 'first American victory in Normandy' also led to the capture of the first deep-water port essential for allied supplies. Despite the destruction carried out by the Germans before they surrendered, the port was operational again on 16 July. It was also the arrival point for the PLUTO undersea pipeline and the train station in Cherbourg would later be used as a starting point for allied rail supplies.

South of the peninsula, the battle for the capture of La-Haye-du-Puits allowed for, after tough fighting, a jumping-off position towards the south, even if, further east, the advance was particularly slow opposite Sainteny and Saint-Lô in the midst of 'hedgerow hell'.

Failure at Hill 112

In the Second British Army sector, the British offensive on the Odon had been delayed by the summer solstice storm and the consequent slowing down in the arrival of supplies. This battle of the Odon (Operation Martlet on 25 June then Epson starting the next day) was finally launched with the balance of power considerably in favour of the British. However, the bitter resistance of the young soldiers of the Hitlerjugend division, who continued to fight to the rear of the attackers once they had been passed, upset an offensive that should have been straightforward. The British chain of command was partially paralyzed, delaying operations and allowing some elements of the Hitlerjugend to set up positions on Hill 112 and forming a final obstacle, allowing German reinforcements of the II. SS-Panzerkorps to arrive in time. The two attacks ran in to each other and the 'Scottish corridor' found itself halted on Hill 112, a place which would become a veritable 'Norman Verdun'.

The storm of 19 - 22 June. A storm broke for the summer solstice and lasted between 19 to 22 June with a north-east blowing for 72 hours. Boats of all types and tonnages off the Normandy beaches were blown onto the shore. The prefabricated ports, particularly Mulberry A in the American sector, began to break up. The bombardon breakwaters broke in two and sank and the huge Phoenix caissons were pushed by the waves into the Mulberry harbours. It was only the blockships that prevented the worst. There were landing craft beached all along the shoreline and more than 600 were lost; the shore was covered with all sorts of wreckage. Almost all of the landing operations had to be halted. On 18 June, 24,412 tonnes of ammunition and supplies arrived in Normandy, a high point in the supply statistics. On 20 June, only 4,500 tonnes were landed, mostly at Mulberry B at Arromanches which was better built, thus suffering less damage. All operations slowed down during this period. In this photo, taken after the storm, we can see Mulberry B (Arromanches with the floating roadways thrown onto the coast and sunken ships presenting a picture of desolation. The Arromanches Mulberry was able to be repaired, in part thanks to elements recovered from Mulberry A at Omaha which was not repairable. (IWM)

Great hopes were placed in Operation Epsom. Seen here, at dawn, is 12 Platoon, B Company, 6th Royal Scots Fusiliers (15th Division) heading towards Saint-Manvieu. These hopes were dashed against Hill 112. (IWM)

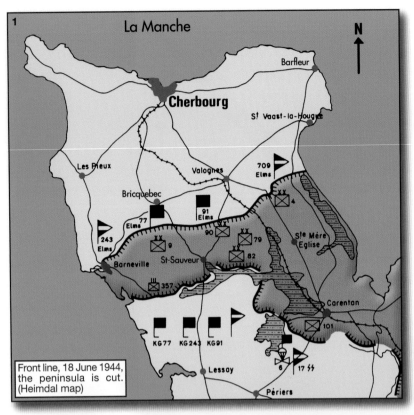

Front line, 18 June 1944, the peninsula is cut. (Heimdal map)

1. This map shows the new front line on 18 June. The 9th Infantry Division has cut the Cotentin peninsula in two by reaching Barneville. Elements of the four German divisions (243rd, 77th, 91st and 709th) are now cut off and encircled in the north. Other elements of these divisions were able to withdraw south and escape the encirclement. Four US divisions, then three (9th, 79th and 4th, from east to west) will now advance towards Cherbourg against the Germans withdrawing to the Festung. (Heimdal)

2. Near Bricquebec, medics of the 39th IR, 9th ID, give a glass of wine to a German soldier who has received a neck wound. This must be one of the 77. ID soldiers hit by American fire on the road from Barneville to Bricquebec. Note the stencilled markings on one of the medics' helmets used by the men of the 39th IR, AAAO, meaning *Anytime Anything Anywhere Nothing*. (NA)

3. A helmet bearing this inscription. (Private collection)

9th Infantry Division shoulder patch. (Heimdal)

Objective Cherbourg

After having succeeded in its campaign in the Cotentin peninsula, Major-General Collins' VII Corps now aligned its four divisions to towards the north, from east to west: 9th ID (Maj. Gen. Eddy), 90th ID (Maj. Gen. Landrum), 79th ID (Maj. Gen. Wyche), 4th ID (Maj. Gen. Barton). And finally the 90th ID which had failed miserably opposite Pont-l'Abbé and consequently removed from the front line. As for the Germans, their command

decided to make a general withdrawal to Festung Cherbourg. The large military port of the Cotentin had, however, the bulk of its defences facing the sea, but also had a semi-circle of defensive positions around the town with anchor points in the west (Westeck) and another in the east (Osteck). The order to pull back was given at midday on **19 June**. The withdrawal was carried out under the noses of the Americans who would advance into the empty space fearing that a trap had been laid. Valognes, abandoned by the Germans, was vic-

Cloth 79th Infantry Division shoulder patch.

On 24 June 1944, the 79th Infantry Division captured, in its assault, the final strong-points on the way to Cherbourg. In order to reach the Fort du Roule, the last defensive position overlooking the port and town, the infantrymen of this divisions had (in particular those of the 315th and 314th Infantry Regiments) had to attack, with the help of aircraft, the concrete strong-points of 'Chèvres' and 'Mare aux Canards'. After having blown the bunker door that we can see here, they mopped up the position (opposite). A little further on, a GI looks at the corpse of German corporal on a concrete pillbox. (NA/Coll. Heimdal)

tim of a heavy allied bombardment, the 'petit Versailles normand' was nothing more than a pile of ruins where the rubble held up the traffic... Advancing carefully, the 9th ID arrived to the west of the Festung on **20 June**, cutting off German positions in La Hague. On this day, the German general, Wilhelm von Schlieben, in command of all German forces in the Festung, with admiral Hennecke, put into place his defensive elements. On **21 June**, the Germans awaited the Americans but held little hope. It would be a delaying battle with the aim of stopping the large port, essential to the Allies, from falling into their hands for as long as possible.

During the night of 21-22, Major-General Collins sent an ultimatum to general von Schlieben and laying out the hopelessness of his situation. This ultimatum expired on **22 June** at 7 pm. On 23 and 24 June, the American assault stalled opposite the German positions. On **25 June**, the Fort du Roule, dominating the town, at last fell at 10 pm after an audacious raid led by Lieutenant Carlos C. Ogden and Corporal John D. Kelly; the Americans could now enter the town. On the **26th**, the situation was dramatic in general von Schlieben's underground HQ and he was forced to surrender the same day at 2 pm. The town fell but Fregatten-Kapitän Witt carried on fighting in the fortified arsenal and in the harbour forts. The town was taken on the **27th** but fighting still continued in the last fortified strong-points. The Osteck position ceased fighting on the **28th**. Witt surrendered at 9 am on the **29th** in one of the forts situated on

The last fighting for Cherbourg was particularly tough. Colonel Van Fleet's 8th Infantry Regiment (a regiment of the 4th Infantry Division) suffered such heavy losses that it was detached from the division and sent off to rest.

Opposite: An American infantryman digs a foxhole facing Cherbourg in the 'Mare aux Canards' sector. The German mortars were particularly efficient and such a precaution was worthwhile. This GI's face betrays fatigue and discouragement. His comrades are dispersed around the area. (USIS/Heimdal). However, if the German mortars and guns were formidable, those of the American artillery were even more so as they could line up a much larger number of barrels. This photo (below) was taken south of Cherbourg on 25 June 1944 near La Pierre Butée (9th Infantry Division sector). Officers from the three divisions and artillery observers are there to direct the fire of their respective artillery regiments, but also that of the allied ships firing on German positions in Cherbourg on this day. (NARA/Heimdal)

the large breakwater. In the La Hague peninsula however, lieutenant-colonel Keil, who had solidly defended Montebourg, was now at the Westeck position with 6,000 men. However, he also had to surrender on **30 June**. All fighting now ceased. The following day, 1 July, it was all over. The Americans had taken 39,000 prisoners during the battle for the Cotentin and this was **their first victory**. They had obtained a large bridgehead, the biggest in the allied sector with a deep-water port, but the latter had been systematically destroyed by the Germans before they surrendered. The capture of the port, planned for D+15 (21 June) had taken place on D+21 or D+25. Another exploit would be the re-use of the port three weeks later with

the first ship bringing in supplies, the USS Owl, berthing there on 16 July after the mine clearing of the port had been completed four days earlier. The final battle was also a race against time between the American services wishing to implement the AMGOT occupation structure, and the teams led by Général de Gaulle to re-establish legitimate national authority... a race that the latter would win.

Opposite: At 2 pm on 26 June, the 39th IR, 9th Infantry Division, opened fire on general von Schlieben's underground HQ, forcing his surrender. His tall and impressive outline is seen here shortly afterwards, followed by admiral Hennecke wearing a cap and greatcoat. They were taken to Major-General Collins' HQ at the château de Servigny in Yvetot-Bocage near Valognes where the act of surrender was signed. However, total surrender would not be effective: Fregattenkapitän Witt still held out in the Arsenal and port forts, Osteck to the east and Westeck in La Hague where lieutenant-colonel Keil continued fighting. (DAVA /Heimdal.)

Below: Tuesday 27 June, the fighting has ceased in Cherbourg and Captain W.H. Cooper, commanding I Company, 314th IR, 79th ID (who would be killed at the beginning of July in the fighting for La Haye-du-Puits) along with some of his men, escorts a column of German prisoners with the officers at the front. They are seen here marching up Avenue de Paris in Cherbourg passing in front of the town sign at the foot of the 'Montagne du Roule'. The column is heading south where it will join POW camps set up along the plateau of the 'Montagne de Roule' heights, near the La Fieffe farm. (DAVA-6048/Heimdal)

Allied air superiority

More than 11,000 aircraft and 3,500 gliders were engaged by the Allies in the landings and the Battle of Normandy between 5 June and the first half of August 1944. This was the biggest air concentration of all time and was the culmination of almost total allied air superiority in the skies of Europe. Nowhere was the German fighter and anti-aircraft component capable of stemming the flow of RAF and US Air Force bombers and fighters which hit, day after day, the towns, industry and infrastructure of the 3rd Reich. Without the support of allied air forces, the landings and the Battle of Normandy would probably have been a lot more costly and longer as the German ground forces could have moved around more freely and have arrived at the battlefield in a much better state. The fighters, fighter-bombers, heavy and medium bombers of the RAF and 8th and 9th US Air Force literally 'boxed in' Normandy.

The role played by allied aircraft in the Normandy fighting was crucial to the successful outcome. Up to that point in time, the German forces had never been confronted by such an absolute aerial threat and surveillance. More than on any other front, the Wehrmacht suffered in the West, due to aircraft, losses in men and materiel that represented almost 1/3 of its total losses between 5 June and the end of August 1944. However, the air war in the West, particularly over Normandy, was no 'picnic' for allied air forces. Losses were heavy. During the night of 5 - 6 June and during D-Day itself, 127 allied planes were lost due to various causes. In July, the 2nd Tactical Air Force and the 9th Air Force alone lost 312 planes shot down.

Above: Allied airfields in Normandy, designated with a letter A for the American sector and B for the Anglo-Canadian sector. (Map by F. Robinard/ J. Clémentine.)

Opposite: P-51 B Mustang, 353rd Fighter Squadron, 354th Fighter Group Shellelagh. (Profile by Jacques Clémentine.)

B-26 bomber bearing 'invasion stripes' on its wings that were used to identify allied aircraft during the Battle of Normandy. (US Air Force.)

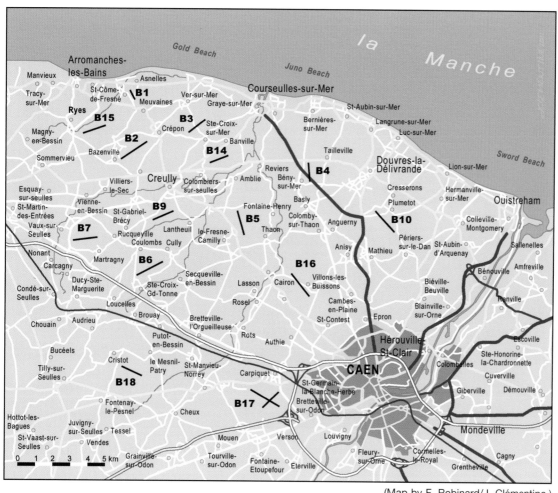

Anglo-Canadian airfields coded B

(Map by F. Robinard/J. Clémentine.)

Spitfire fighter

This Spitfire was flown by the French ace Pierre Clostermann who no longer flew with a FAFL wing (Free French) but with RAF 602 Squadron.

(Profile by Jacques Clémentine.)

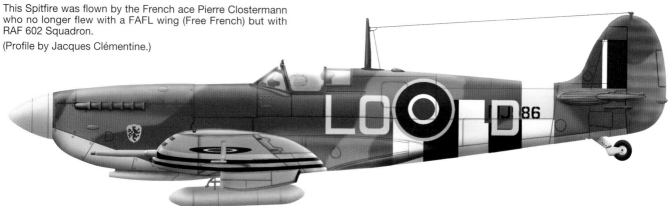

Typhoon fighter-bomber

This Typhoon was flown by of Squadron-Leader FAFL 198 Squadron, Yves Ezanno, an emblematic personality of the French air force who would go on to be a general.
(Profile by Jacques Clémentine.)

25 June, Fontenay-le-Pesnel. This dramatic photo was taken by Lieutenant Handford at Fontenay-le-Pesnel during the first phase of the battle on 25 June. On this road, coming from Tilly-sur-Seulles (behind us) and leading to Caen, is an abandoned German anti-tank gun (Pak 40) and the body of a Hitlerjugend soldier lying nearby. This gun was pointing towards the where the Hauts Vents road came out on that of Cristot, on the left, from where the British attack came. The Panther tank, destroyed a little further on the right also faced this attack. (IWM)

Below: The next day, **26 June**, saw the start of the main attack against Saint-Manvieu and the Odon valley. Seen here are two photos by Major Stewart who followed this attack. Here it is 7.30 am in the middle of the fields and the morning mist. Seen here is a Scottish soldier of 12 Platoon, B Company, 6th Royal Scots Fusiliers (15th Division) as he prepares to attack. (IWM)

The Battle of the Odon (25-30 June)

General Montgomery launched Operation Martlet on **25 June** to the east of Tilly-sur-Seulles, following his directive of 18 June: *"We must now capture Caen and Cherbourg, as the first step in the full development of our plans."* The storm had delayed this plan. He brought in a new corps, VIII Corps (15th Scottish Division, 43rd Wessex Division, and the tanks of the 11th Armoured Division). However, beforehand, he launched Operation **Martlet** to the west with the 49th West Riding Division, in order to clear **Fontenay-le-Pesnel**, but the outcome was not satisfactory as Rauray was still not reached. The main attack, Operation **Epsom**, was launched on **26 June**, it was supposed to cross the Odon valley and take the strategic high ground of Hill 112, then cross the Orne and take Caen from the south! The British had overwhelming superiority (60,000 men against less than 2,000) but this did not take into account the determination of the young Hitlerjugend soldiers... and the inertia of the British command. Isolated young grenadiers and a few panzers would considerably hold up the offensive. Behind a few Hitlerjugend 'plugs' there was nothing as far as Hill 112! And yet, the excessive prudence of the British allowed the Germans to bring up a few reinforcements to this strategic high ground.

Then, on **30 June**, German reinforcements from the II.SS-Panzer-Korps (9th and 10th Div.) began arriving and the two attacks ran into each other. With the Odon river crossed, the 'Scottish Corridor' became a dead end in front of Hill 112. Montgomery had lost this battle against all logic due to being overly prudent when his tanks could have broken through a wide-open front...

Above: This other photo taken by Major Stewart shows 12 Platoon (commanded by Canadian officer Lieutenant Robertson) now advancing through Saint-Manvieu. Despite the cool morning air, there is tension on the sweaty faces and the advance is proving very difficult against elements of the Hitlerjugend I./26, who would hold on to this village until nightfall. B Company suffered a 50% casualty rate, including its commanding officer, Major Agnew. (IWM)

Below: 11th Armoured Division tanks head towards the front line, behind the Scottish soldiers of the 15th Division, along the Fontenay-le-Pesnel/Carpiquet road. This photo, taken north of the road by Sergeant Laing, shows a vehicle carrying ammunition blowing up after being hit by a German mortar. (IWM)

Insigne d'épaule en tissu de la *15th (Scottish) Infantry Division*. (Heimdal.)

Above: During the start of Operation Epsom, a group of soldiers from the 2nd Battalion, The Argyll and Sutherland Highlanders (227th Brigade), led by their piper, head towards the front. Photo taken by Sergeant Laing. (IWM)

Below: Another photo taken by Sergeant Laing shows infantrymen of the 7th Seaforth Highlanders (46th Highland Brigade - 15th Scottish Division) advancing through a wheat field opposite a hedgerow that might conceal the formidable German machine-guns that the British called 'Spandaus'. This Highland battalion went into action on 26 June against the 15./25. It resumed the attack on 27 June. This photo is a good illustration of the type of fighting during Operation Epsom, mostly carried out by infantry with tank support. (IWM)

Rauray, 28 June. This hamlet, where the tank regiment HQ of Hitlerjugend (SS-Pz.-Rgt. 12) had been set up, was fiercely fought for. A German counter-attack was made there with a few Tiger tanks of s.SS-Panzer-Abteilung 101. Seen here are two British infantrymen of 70th Brigade (49th West Riding Division)looking at the still menacing wreck of one of the Tiger tanks with its long 8,8 cm gun. This is a type E of the 3rd company, N°334, attributed to SS-Oscha. Rolf von Westernhagen.

It seems to be in a strange position stuck against the hedge of the Rauray ch,teau, probably pushed there by a vehicle. (IWM)

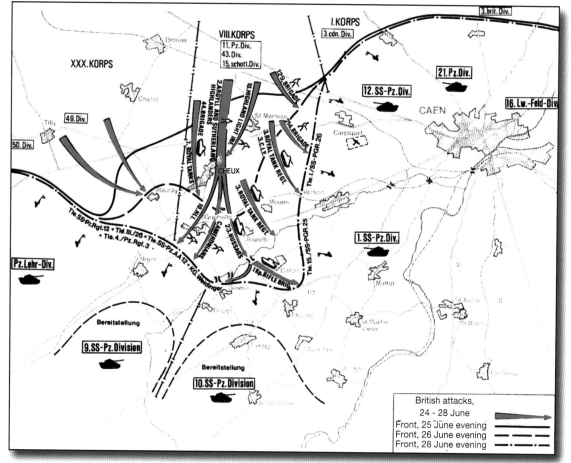

Opposite: This map shows the British advance along the 'Scottish Corridor', led by four divisions (15th Div., 43rd Div, 49th Div., and the 11th Armoured Division). However, three German divisions arrived to reinforce the sector and the 'corridor' would become a dead end. (Heimdal)

British attacks,
24 - 28 June
Front, 25 June evening
Front, 26 June evening
Front, 28 June evening

11

Before the final assault 1 - 24 July

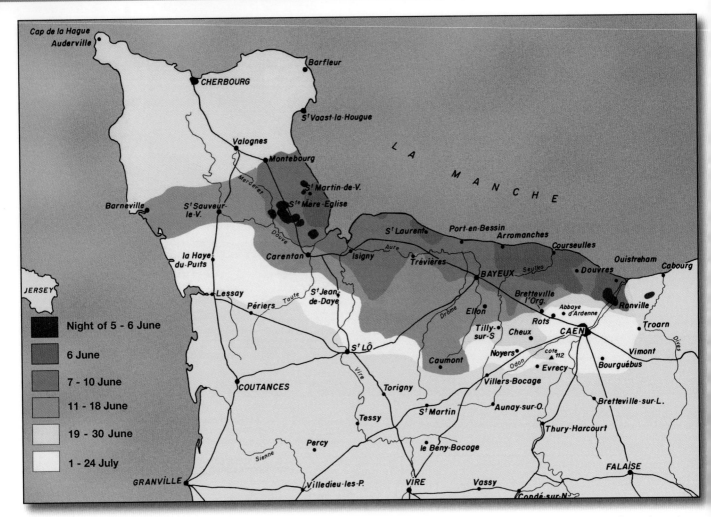

This map shows the very difficult advance of allied troops between 1 - 24 July. In the west, the Americans turned south from the Cotentin peninsula, capturing La Haye-du-Puits on the 8th, but also Saint-Lô in the east on the 18th. In the Anglo-Canadian sector, Caen finally fell, some 33 days late, but it was a dead end and Hill 112 remained an untakeable obstacle. For the allied soldier This goddam war could last a century, but he now had an overwhelming superiority in numbers... (Heimdal map)

After the fighting ended in the Cotentin peninsula on 30 June, the First Army would now turn south at the same time as the Germans had brought in reinforcements to the La Haye-du-Puits sector. The 1st US Army would encounter hard fighting there, especially in the Mont Castre sector where the American VIII Corps troops were pitched against FJR 15, a German paratrooper regiment. The Americans finally captured **La Haye-du-Puits on 8 July**. The advance in this sector would be halted along the 'water line' facing Lessay. A little further to the east, the advance was even harder and men would have to 'die for Sainteny'. Finally, east of the river Vire, Saint-Lô was a cornerstone, the capture of which was essential in order to break out south of the Cotentin. In the thick bocage where every hedgerow could be turned into a fortress, it would be 'hedgerow hell'. Lieutenant Edward G. Jones, commanding officer of 2nd Platoon, 29th Cavalry Reconnaissance Troop remembered: *"Throughout the weeks and months we would witness all the horrors of war and amongst all these dead there were more Americans than Germans. He also remembered what sort of warfare it was: Positioned at the angles (of the hedgerows), the automatic weapons (German) had very clear fields of fire. (...) The anti-tank guns remained around the lanes as did the mines that the sappers laid at night along each side. As it was practically impossible, even with artillery, to overcome these fortifications, only a tank, accompanied by infantry, was able, due to its firepower, to force out a deeply entrenched enemy."* Also added to this was the storm which had considerably delayed the arrival of reinforcements. Lieutenant-General Bradley, commanding American troops in Normandy, feared that the 29th Division, in the vanguard in the bocage, was approaching its brea-

king point. For many GIs, it seemed that *"This god-dam war could last a century...!"* Finally, after a lull in the fighting, the advance continued to Saint-Lô, a town fiercely defended by German 3rd division paras. **Saint-Lô**, known as the 'capital of ruins', fell to the 29th Division on **18 July**.

To the east, and some 33 days late, the town of **Caen**, also turned into a field of ruins like Saint-Lô, was finally taken in a last battle between **4 - 9 July** with the concentrated assault of the British 3rd Infantry Division to the north and that of the 3rd Canadian Infantry Division to the west. The attack, however, ended in a dead end on the banks of the Orne. Thus, in order to finally clear Caen from the south, new attacks were made against **Hill 112**, an area turned into a 'Norman Verdun' with Tiger tanks still preventing the capture of this strategic high ground. The latter was finally evacuated, without fighting, a few weeks later during the German withdrawal.

The casualty rate during this time was particularly bad for the allied command that was only advancing step by step at the price of heavy losses against particularly efficient and determined German combatants. However, the latter were reaching breaking point against a crushing superiority in manpower and materiel and, above all, due to a sky dominated by the Allies, preventing all German attempts to attack.

A somewhat surreal photo, taken on today's Boulevard des AlliÉs, showing an AFPU reporter wearing a battle jerkin and filming the gate post to the destroyed HÙtel Moderne bearing the hotel's plaque and a sign marked Feldkom-mandantur. (IWM.)

These three Canadian RCE soldiers, Bernard Hoo, John Mac Conville and R.J. Kostick, pose for the camera at last by the sign for Caen, reached thirty-three days after this D-Day objecti-ve. (PAC)

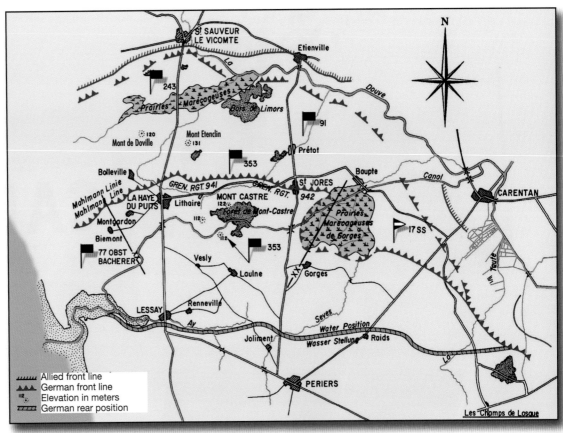

We see here the three defence lines set up by the Germans in front of La Haye-du-Puits: a belt of forward positions, the Mahlmann Line (the main resistance line anchored on the high ground of Montgardon and Mont Castre), the water line, Wasser Stellung (the withdrawal line). (Heimdal map using US documents concerning the 353. ID)

The final battle for La Haye-du-Puits (3 - 9 July)

La Haye-du-Puits, 9 July 1944. The Norman town has just fallen to the GIs of the 79th Infantry Division. A squad is seen here carrying, in several parts, a 80 mm mortar. These soldiers are coming from the front line and are heading back towards Barneville.

Following the American breakthrough to the sea at Barneville on 18 June, Major-General Collins launched his VII Corps directly north towards Cherbourg, but forgot about his southern front and beyond the belt of marshlands across the peninsula, thus losing an opportunity. Although the bulk of the divisions had driven south on 20 June, leaving behind a few elements to block Festung Cherbourg, La Haye-du-Puits and even Coutances could have been taken within a few days as the

8 July, the attack on La Haye-du-Puits was launched by the 314th Infantry Regiment, 79th Division. These GIs are now close to the town on the Barneville-Bolleville road to the north. However, despite the apparent tension, this photo was staged on 9 July.

Germans did not have many forces to stop them in the sector south of the peninsula. The terrible fighting that took place before Operation Cobra could have been avoided.

When VIII Corps, led by Major General Troy Middleton, with the 79th and 90th Infantry Divisions and the 82nd Airborne Division finally started to turn south on Monday **3 July**, with the objective of taking Lessay, general von Choltitz (LXXXIV. AK) had had the time to reorganise his troops, essentially three tactical groups which had escaped encirclement in the Cotentin, Bacherer's (KG 77 ID, KG 243 ID and KG 91 ID, but he had also placed in the centre an infantry division that had just arrived from Brittany as reinforcements, the 353.ID, and had established three defence lines (see map). He was also waiting for other reinforcements: elements of the 'Das Reich' division with the 4,000-man strong Kampfgruppe Weidinger (which arrived at La Haye-du-Puits on 5 July) the paras of Fallschirmjäger-Regiment 15 (Gröschke) who would hold Mont Castre.

Thus, it would take five days of hard fighting for Major-General Middleton's troops to arrive at La Haye-du-Puits and the global casualty rate for VIII Corps was around 15% (40% for the infantry). The final objective, the Lessay sector, was far from being reached as the offensive had only covered half the distance to the objective aimed for, but the conquered terrain comprised of the hardest obstacles and it would be flatter north of Lessay. The German troops had shown great skill and determination. On 7 July, the 79th ID had lost another 1,000 men and the 90th ID had already suffered 2,000 losses by the same evening over five days of fighting and six kilometres, one man for every three metres... The totally exhausted 82nd Airborne Division was removed from the front and replaced by the 8th Infantry Division, a unit that was lacking in experience. However, in this terrible hedgerow fighting, the Germans were even more exhausted. On 8 July, the 79th Infantry Division launched an infantry battalion into the attack on La Haye-du-Puits, supported by artillery, mortars and tanks. Despite heavy losses, the US infantry infiltrated the town. The night was lit up by fires and La Haye-du-Puits was mopped up on 9 July. The next objective was now Lessay.

Above: At the entrance to La Haye-du-Puits, near the railway crossing, two German prisoners look at one of their wounded comrades. This is to the east of the town.

American infantry now patrol in the town and pass in front of the post office.

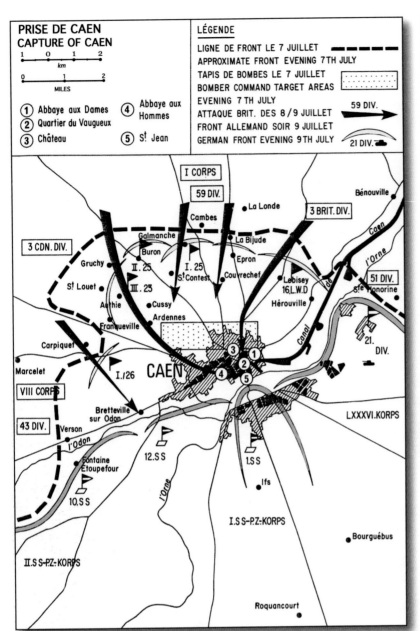

PRISE DE CAEN
CAPTURE OF CAEN

1 0 1 2
km

0 1 2
MILES

① Abbaye aux Dames
② Quartier du Vaugueux
③ Château
④ Abbaye aux Hommes
⑤ St Jean

LÉGENDE

LIGNE DE FRONT LE 7 JUILLET
APPROXIMATE FRONT EVENING 7TH JULY

TAPIS DE BOMBES LE 7 JUILLET
BOMBER COMMAND TARGET AREAS
EVENING 7TH JULY

ATTAQUE BRIT. DES 8/9 JUILLET

FRONT ALLEMAND SOIR 9 JUILLET
GERMAN FRONT EVENING 9TH JULY

59 DIV.

21 DIV.

I CORPS

59 DIV.

3 BRIT. DIV.

Bénouville

La Londe

Cambes

Galmanche

Buron

La Bijude

3 CDN. DIV.

Gruchy

II. 25

I. 25

St Contest

Epron

Couvrechef

51 DIV.

Lebisey

16.L.W.D

Ste Honorine

St Louet

III. 25

Authie

Cussy

Hérouville

Ardennes

Franqueville

21. DIV.

Carpiquet

I. 126

Marcelet

CAEN

Canal de l'Orne

VIII CORPS

Brette ville sur Odon

LXXXVI. KORPS

43 DIV.

Verson

l'Odon

12. SS

1. SS

Fontaine Etoupefour

10. SS

Ifs

l'Orne

I. SS-P.Z.-KORPS

Bourguébus

II. SS-P.Z.-KORPS

Roquancourt

The final battle for Caen.

Insignia of the 12. SS-Panzer-Division.

4 July, this grenadier of the Hitlerjugend I./26 has been wounded in the face and captured at the Carpiquet airfield. He is one of the rare prisoners taken on this day. (PAC)

Panther 438 turning in front of Venelle St-Nicolas in Caen. First aiders and French civil defence personnel look for survivors in the rubble of the buildings which have just been bombed. Many civilians were killed. (Coll. J-P. Benamou)

162

An excellent photo of a Sd.Kfz 232 armoured reconnaissance vehicle belonging to the 12.SS-Panzer-Division (the insignia of which can be seen painted on the hull) in Rue Saint-Pierre, heading west towards the Canadians in the final fighting. An NCO in camouflage clothing is sat on the side of the vehicle. In the background we can see the tower of Saint-Pierre church, the spire of which was destroyed by allied artillery. (Coll. H. Meyer/Heimdal.)

Caen, the final battle (4 - 9 July)

At dawn on **4 July**, with the front facing Caen blocked for almost a month, the 3rd Canadian Division attacked Carpiquet to the west of the large Norman city as part of Operation **Windsor**. The Winnipegs (RWR) attacked from Marcelet with the Régiment de la Chaudière on their left flank, then the North Shore Regiment near the railway line. The tough Canadian soldiers advanced across open fields towards the positions held by I./26 (Hitlerjugend); the losses were heavy. The attack continued on **5 - 6 July** on the village of Carpiquet and the outskirts of the airfield where the HJ grenadiers held out in positions and bunkers that were cleared with flame-throwers.; there would be very few prisoners.

On **7 July**, north of the Carpiquet and the RN 13 road, the North Nova Scotia Highlanders sent its spearhead to Authie. The Canadians lost twenty tanks to a German counter-attack (III./25, 5./12 and 6./12). This was the prelude to a new offensive launched north-west of Caen as part of Operation **Charnwood**. The latter had considerable means at its disposal with three infantry divisions: 3rd Canadian, British 3rd and 59th Divisions, with many support units and a considerable artillery force, representing a total of 115,000 men against approximately 10,000 Germans in this sector, making a superiority of at least eleven to one for the Allies. The 3rd Canadian Division continued its attack on Buron and the Ardenne abbey on **8 July** with a tank battle taking place on the flat terrain. The Germans and the last elements of the Hitlerjugend in the abbey were forced to withdraw to Caen. The Canadians had just taken the last strong-point west of the city and they entered the latter late morning on **9 July** after the Germans made the decision to pull back to the other side of the Orne, making the occupation of the city a formality. However, Caen had become a dead end, the Germans had shortened their front and overlooked the city centre from the high ground on the other side of the river. The great Norman city had at last fallen, a month after D-Day, but Montgomery would have to strike elsewhere in order to break out of this dead end.

Opposite: A British infantryman helps an old lady out of the rubble. She has only taken with her the bare essentials. As for the British soldier, he is covered in white dust from the chalk stone in the city. (IWM)

Forward position held by the 1st KOSB in the St. Pierre square. Scottish soldiers return from a patrol in Rue St. Pierre, the church of St. Sauveur (Notre-Dame de Froide Rue) which has remained intact, can be seen. Destruction is everywhere. (IWM)

Above: A photo taken from the ramparts south of the castle. A soldier of the Royal Ulster Rifles patiently waits for a German sniper to emerge from his hiding place. The destroyed spire of St. Pierre church emerges from the smoke. (IWM)

Opposite: The Quatrans borough, at the foot of the castle, was totally destroyed; the roofs have been caved in and walls collapsed. Some of these houses were between three and five-hundred years old. (IWM)

Civilians in Caen took refuge in the numerous underground quarries; 2,000 civilians were killed by the bombardments. (IWM)

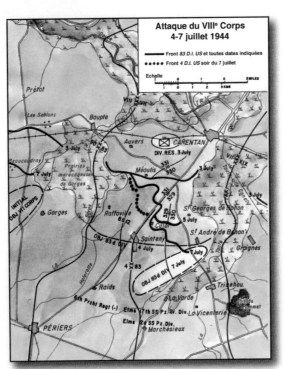

Fallschirmjäger-Regiment 6 paras in the Méautis sector (south-west of Carentan), sheltering under a hedgerow. (Coll. J.Y. Nasse.)

German paratrooper badge.
(Private collection)

Attaque du VIIIᵉ Corps 4-7 juillet 1944

Above: This map shows how narrow the front was south of Carentan, stuck between the Gorges and Taute marshes, favouring the German defenders.

Opposite: Map showing the operations to the west of the Vire, crossed on 7 July at Airel by the 30th ID and 3rd AD. This attack was countered by the Panzer-Lehr-Division brought in from the Tilly-sur-Seulles sector. Tribehou is where the two maps join together. (Maps US Army/Heimdal.)

Dying for Sainteny (4 - 11 July)

After Carentan finally fell on 12 June (see pages 20 and 21), the front remained blocked by von der Heydte's paras and the grenadiers of the 'Götz' across a land bridge stuck between two marshy areas (see map below). However, in this region, Collins now had three infantry divisions (4th ID, 9th ID, 83rd ID). The first two had seen action in the battle for the Cotentin and the 83rd began landing at Omaha Beach from 18 June onwards. Collins relaunched the attack at dawn on **4 July** south of Carentan and the 'Götz' with FJR6 to its left, came under a deluge of steel, but the poorly-led 83rd Div. suffered heavy losses with the commander of the 331st IR, Colonel Barndollar, shot in the heart and killed. Casualties were very heavy, even though the 330th IR had advanced over a kilometre to the east. On the 5th, the sector remained very narrow and Collins could not deploy the other two divisions; 83rd Div. would suffer a further 750 losses added to the 1,400 of the previous day opposite Sainteny. On the 6th, the 83rd Div. sector was halved in order to engage the 4th ID on its flank to the west. However, the 83rd lost another 700 men, making almost 3,000 casualties for Sainteny!

But, on **7 July**, starting at 3.30 in the morning, the 2/117th IR of the 30th Infantry Division silently crossed the Vire at Airel opposite Saint-Fromond. It was followed by the 113th Cavalry Group and they only faced elements of KG Heintz. The tanks of the 3rd Armored Division prepared to cross on the **8th** but KG Wisliceny (elements of the 2.SS-Panzer-Division) with fifteen Panzer IV tanks (6./SS-Pz.Rgt. 2) would move to meet them for a small counterattack which was relaunched on the **9th** but the Germans came under a terrible artillery barrage and the CCB of the 3rd Armored Division reached Hauts Vents (see photo). However, faced with this crisis, the German command had brought back into the sector the Panzer-Lehr-Division which had previously been in action in the Tilly-sur-Seulles sector; this division arrived in the line on 9 July, along with the 13th para regiment led by Count von der Schulenburg (who would be killed on 14

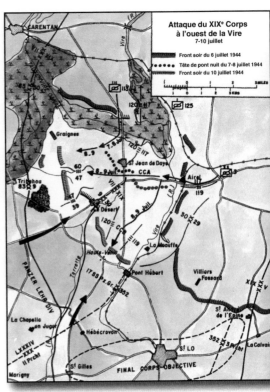

Attaque du XIXᵉ Corps à l'ouest de la Vire 7-10 juillet

July). The Panzer-Lehr-Division launched a counter-attack on **11 July** against this American bridgehead towards Le Désert and Saint-Jean-de-Daye (see map); with six against one, it advanced rapidly but, at around midday, the allied fighter-bombers shattered this attack led towards the Vire-Taute canal. The 'Lehr' would lose 500 grenadiers and 23 of its tanks. On the same day, the exhausted 'Götz' pulled back south of Sainteny...

Young paratroopers (aged 17 to 20) of Fallschirmjäger-Regiment 13 (Count von der Schulenburg) move up to the front line in the Champs de Losques sector, 9 July. (Coll. A. Pipet/Heimdal.)

Above: A SS-Unterscharführer of the 'Götz', probably from the reconnaissance group, seen here in the marshes. (Heimdal.)

3rd AD

11 July near Saint-Fromond, tanks and vehicles of the 33rd Armored Regiment (CCB), 3rd Armored Division, are seen here crammed together on a muddy road. A few hundred metres ahead, their comrades are holding off a counter-attack led by the Panzer-Lehr-Division from Hauts-Vents. The Stuart light tank in the foreground belongs to C Company, 33rd Armored Regiment and is named 'Carol'. (Photo US Army, collection Heimdal.)

This remarkable photo, taken by Sergeant Jones on 10 July 1944, shows a group of infantrymen advancing near Verson, probably at Fontaine-Etoupefour. Despite the obvious staging of the photo, where the photographer has made the three men in the background take up somewhat insistent poses, the faces of the men in the foreground are anxious as they will soon be thrown into the battle. The Sergeant's comment states that they were under mortar fire. This is a reserve platoon of the 4th Dorsets attacking from Verson and Fontaine-Etoupefour towards Eterville. The shield of a 6-Pounder anti-tank gun can be seen in the foreground. (IWM)

During the course of a patrol between the lines, two Waffen-SS carefully approach an abandoned Panzer IV. Kneeling in a wheat field with one of his grenadiers, the squad leader takes a long look around with his binoculars before moving towards the tank. (Musée Mémorial de Bayeux)

Hell on Hill 112

On Saturday **1 July**, following the failure of Operation Epsom, the 9.SS-Panzer-Division 'Hohenstaufen' arrived as reinforcements but also failed due to the naval artillery fire, the guns of which could reach this area! It was relieved on the **9th** by the 277. ID infantry division. The front would now become static here in veritable trench warfare. But, after the fall of Caen the previous day, Montgomery relaunched the attack in this sector, with the same objectives as Epsom, as Caen had become a total dead end on the left bank of the Orne. This was Operation **Jupiter**, launched at dawn on Monday **10 July** from Verson with a single division, the 43rd Wessex Division. The château of Fontaine-Etoupefour was first taken against a battalion (II./22) of the 10.SS/Panzer-Division 'Frundsberg'. However, on the right flank, to the west, 129 Brigade failed at Hill 112. The Germans received reinforcements of Tiger tanks of s.SS-Panzer-Abteilung 102 which pushed back the attack, despite the success of the 4th Dorsets at Eterville, the Hampshires opposite Maltot and the engagement of the 15th Scottish Division further to the west. With his Tiger tank, SS-Oscha. Will Fey also notched up some successes. Also, the 'Frundsberg' relaunched at counter-attack against

This photo was also taken by Sergeant Jones on 10 July. Seen here are 5th DCLI infantrymen, one 214th Brigade's battalions which attacked in the centre, as the second wave, to the right of the 4th Dorsets. These Cornwall infantrymen are digging foxholes with their entrenching tools in order to take cover from German artillery fire. Digging in such terrain was a tiring job as the layer of earth was not very thick before encountering chalk. The combatants on both sides had to undertake this tiring task in order to survive... (IWM B 6851)

Maltot, Eterville and the château at Fontaine-Etoupefour at dawn on **11 July**. The Hohenstaufen counter-attacked at Hill 112, where it suffered heavy losses. Operation Jupiter was a failure. Hill 112 changed hands several times but was never definitively taken by the British who generally held the northern side of the hill, whereas the Germans held the southern part. Thus, Herbert Fürbringer, a messenger with the Hohenstaufen division, recalled the vision of horror when he reached the top of Hill 112 with torn off legs and arms of bodies dismembered by the incessant artillery fire.... like at Verdun. He was wounded shortly after and had to crawl back from the terrible hilltop. Hill 112, the top of which was barely noticeable alongside the neighbouring Hill 113, nevertheless overlooked

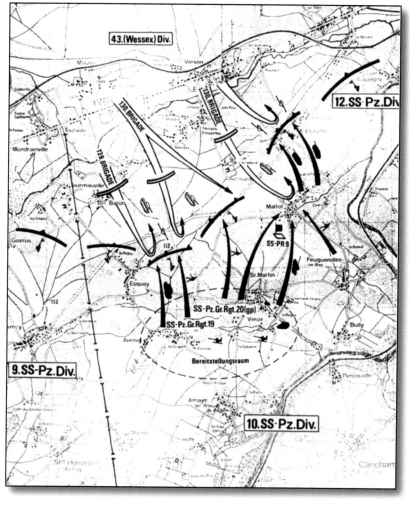

This map shows the attacks carried out by the 43rd Wessex Division on 10 July and the successful counter-attacks launched by the 9.SS-Panzer-Division 'Hohenstaufen' on 11 July at Hill 112 (SS-Pz.Gren.-Rgt. 19, supported by tanks of I./SS-Pz.Rgt. 9) with SS-Pz.Gren.-Rgt. 20 counter-attacking from Vieux to Maltot, then Eterville, supported by II battalion panzers. (Map HF/Heimdal)

SS-Oberführer Heinz Harmel, commander of the Frundsberg, on a Befehls-Funkpanzer at Feuguerolles, 10 July; he led the fighting as close as possible to the front. (Musée Mémorial de Bayeux)

After the battle

Above: Shortly after the fighting ended, two Caen civilians, Serge Varin and friend (his future brother-in-law) walked over the battlefield and took some remarkable photos that have gone down in history, including three of these four photos. These destroyed Sherman tanks in the Great Orchard are probably from the Royal Scots Greys who supported the resistance of the 5th DCLI near Hill 112. The trees have been stripped by artillery fire. (S. Varin/Heimdal)

Opposite: British prisoners captured in the Hill 112 sector have to empty their pockets. The period text states that they contained a large quantity of 'invasion money' and 'counterfeit francs'.

1 T.Vallet
© Thierry Vallet / 2011

EIN MITTELPUNKT DER SCHLACHT SÜDLICH CAEN

HÖHE 112

Wie bei Verdun: Wochenlang geht der Kampf um einen einzigen Hügel

So sieht die vorderste Front aus

Mühsam wurde ein Loch in den steinigen Boden gewühlt, dann mit Bohlen und Steinen abgedeckt. In diesem Loch lebt, schläft und kämpft der deutsche Grenadier

Das ist die vielumkämpfte Höhe 112 bei Caen

„Tascheninhalt vorzeigen!"

1. Tiger 211, a 2nd company tank of (commanded by SS-Hstuf. Endemann). This s./SS-Panzer-Abteilung 102 company was particularly involved in the fighting on Hill 112 on 10 July with the 1st company on its right, between Maltot and the top of the hill. (Illustration by Thierry Vallet)

2. *Hamburger Illustrierte*, an illustrated magazine published in Hamburg in the summer of 1944, shows the fighting on Hill 112. We can see a 5th company Panzer IV of the Frundsberg tank regiment.

3. The period text states that: Front line life is thus. A hole has been dug with difficulty in the stony ground, then covered over with logs and stones. The German grenadier lives, sleeps and fights in this hole.

(Documents B. Jasniak/Heimdal period photos taken by SS-Kriegsberichter Schulz, Kriegsberichter Lutz Koch and the photographer Raudies of the Agence Atlantik.)

the entire plain leading down towards Caen which could be seen from this awful hilltop. This veritable 'Norman Verdun' would never fall in bitter fighting to the British who still found the way south to Caen blocked off. Despite a fresh attack by XII Corps on **15 July** (Operation Greenline), it was shattered the following day by a counter-attack led by II.SS-Panzer-Korps, 'Frundsberg', supported by the 'Hohenstaufen' and Tiger tanks. Thus, the battle for Hill 112 remained a German victory. The top of the hill was finally abandoned to the 53rd Division without a fight when the Germans withdrew on 4 August.

3

Saint-Lô sector
An observation position on the front line in the Saint-Lô sector, sheltered by a hedgerow. This battle would be above all that of hedgerow hell. (Coll. Heimdal.)

11 July, a Technician 5th Grade carries in his jeep Private Vincent Lucas, hailing from Braddock in Pennsylvania, wounded by a mine explosion and taken to the aid post. We can see the stencilled 29th Division emblem painted on the driver's helmet. (DAVA/Coll. Heimdal.)

'Hedgerow hell' north of Saint-Lô

South of Omaha Beach, the three divisions which landed there (of V Corps) had initially made a good advance against weak German opposition (mostly the remnants of the 352.ID see pages 126 and 127). As early as 13 June, elements of the 1st Infantry Division (Big Red One) had reached the Caumont-l'Eventé sector (strategic high ground), allowing the British 7th Armoured Division to undertake an audacious encircling manoeuvre as far asVillers-Bocage which ended in failure (see Villers-Bocage p. 134 to 137). To the west, 29th Division crossed the Elle on 12 - 13 June but at the cost of 547 casualties. Despite the death of General der Artillerie Erich Marcks (commanding LXXXIV.AK), killed on 12 June by a fighter-bomber, the German front stiffened with the arrival of reinforcements: the 2.Panzer-Division in the Caumont sector, and a para division, the 3. Fallschirmjäger-Division north of Saint-Lô. Thus, on 20 June, after seven days of hard fighting, the 29th Infantry Division (Blue and Gray) remained blocked to the south-west of Couvains, around six kilometres from Saint-Lô, opposite the salient of **Villiers-Fossard**, where the capture of each hedgerow became a costly battle in the midst of the bocage and hedgerow hell.

A month of hard fighting now began, made worse by the equinox storm that destroyed the artificial port at Omaha Beach between 19 and 21 June, considerably slowing down the arrival of reinforcements and materiel throughout several days and postponing all attacks.

Therefore, a month after the landings, Saint-Lô appeared to be out of reach. The Germans held on in the dominating high ground to the north and

Generalmajor Richard Schimpf (with his back to the camera), commanding officer of the 2. Fallschirmjäger-Division paras, listens to a report from a captain (left) under his command. The general carries a Fallschirmgewehr 42, a specific German paratrooper weapon which was issued in small quantities. The photo opposite shows one of the German paras who fought with determination. With a few fern leaves around his helmet, a mud-covered face and his rain-soaked smock, he looks intensely at the ground he has been tasked with holding. This is probably a NCO as he is equipped with MP40 magazine pouches and a pistol holster. (Photos BA.)

the hollow where the town was built, mainly on Hills 122 (to the north) and 192 (to the north-east). On its rocky outcrop, the town of Saint-Lô, the administrative capital of the Manche, had its old fortified part on a spur overlooking the Vire which was surrounded by a ring of hills dominated in the north by high ground that controlled its access and which had to be captured. To the north, Hill 122 was the objective of the 29th Infantry Division. Further east, Hill 192 was covered by the 2nd Infantry Division, then the 1st, as far as Caumont. On **12 July**, the 29th ID, now supported by the newly arrived 35th ID (started arriving on 9 July), faced Hill 122, a German strong-point strengthened by the Carillon position. The 29th ID only advanced a little to the east on the Martinville crest, at a cost of 1,000 men lost in two days. On this day, the 2nd ID lost 69 killed, 328 wounded and 8 missing. The bocage really was hell.

The battle for Saint-Lô (13 to 18 July)

The awful hedgerow fighting on the way to Saint-Lô continued on **13 July** when the inexperienced 35th ID continued its effort at Hill 122, assisted by the 30th ID which gave it covering fire from the west bank of the Vire. The sector was defended by a German paratrooper corps, II.Fallschirmjä-

19 July, La Bascule crossroads in Saint-Lô

Task Force Charlie arrives in Saint-Lô at the La Bascule crossroads where the roads converged from Bayeux, Isigny, Torigni-sur-Vire and those from the town centre. The troops arrive accompanied by tanks and will head off to the right towards the town centre. (US Army/Coll. Heimdal)

Below: A German sergeant with a leg wound has been captured in the middle of the ruins of Saint-Lô. As we can see in the second photo, he is loaded into a 13th Cavalry Group half-track, a unit temporarily attached to 29th Division from 18 to 20 July. In the third photo in the series we see the sergeant wincing with pain. (Coll. Heimdal)

ger-Korps led by Gen.Lt. Meindl with the remnants of three infantry divisions (KG 266, KG 352 and KG 353) and the paratrooper 3.Fallschirmjäger-Division. On **14 July**, the joint attacks of all the American divisions coupled with formidable artillery fire, finally broke the German front; in two days, KG 352 had suffered 840 wounded from US artillery fire, not counting the dead! On **15 July**, the 35th ID continued its attack and overran the Germans to the east of Mesnil-Rouxelin, then threatened Saint-Georges-Montcocq, only two kilometres to the north of Saint-Lô. After a hail of steel and fire, Hill 122 was at last taken, pushing the German soldiers in the sector back to the Vire and forcing their withdrawal. In the centre, the 29th ID made little progress except at the Madeleine crossroads (where today's Credit Agricole offices are) to the east of Saint-Lô, still under fire from the Martinville crest; Major Bingham's battalion was surrounded.

On **16 July**, the German front had reached breaking point. On the **17th**, the left flank of II.Fj-Korps collapsed under the fire of the 35th ID, but the honour of being the first to enter Saint-Lô fell to the 29th ID. As early as 18 July, Maj. Gen. Corlett (commanding XIX Corps) ordered the commanding officer of the 29th ID (Maj. Gen. Gerhardt) to send a Task Force into the town to take control of it. The Task Force was placed under the command of Brig. Gen. Cota who had distinguished himself at Omaha Beach. The force left Luzerne at 15.10 pm and arrived at Saint-Lô via the northeast (today's D6 road). By 7 pm, the ruined town was in American hands. Major Howie had been killed attacking the Martinville crest with his 3/116; his men carried his body to the Sainte-Croix church in Saint-Lô, he would become the 'Major of Saint-Lô'. On **19 July**, the 35th Division also entered the 'capital of ruins', taking over from the exhausted GIs of the 'Blue and Gray' division. This hard-fought victory freed-up First Army's left flank and would allow Lt. Gen. Bradley to launch Operation Cobra.

This colour photo, taken from the tower of the Notre-Dame church in the upper part of the town, shows Saint-Lô turned into a field of ruins with Rue Torteron on the left, the Hôpital crossroads (or Alluvions), La Vaucelle. (NA/Heimdal.)

Opposite: This other colour photo, taken in the summer of 1944, gives us a better understanding of the scale of destruction in the Saint-Lô 'capital of ruins'. A lake has been formed due to the Dollée stream being blocked by rubble. The road passing along the foot of the upper town has been cleared for American vehicles. (US Army/Heimdal.)

Operation Goodwood

In a conference held on 10 July, Bradley, the First Army leader, spoke of a plan for a new attack that aimed to break out of 'hedgerow hell'; Operation Cobra. However, as usual, Montgomery wanted to win the laurels of success for himself and when he learned of this new plan, he wanted to beat the American general to it and, on **12 July**, he informed Eisenhower that Dempsey, commanding British Second Army, would attack to the east of the Orne from the airborne bridgehead in what would be called Operation Goodwood. This operation had Falaise at its objective.

However, this was exactly where Rommel was expecting Montgomery, across a plain that favoured a tank attack south-east of Caen and he had set up three defence lines there. The infantry would be the first line (272.ID, 16. LFDD, 346.ID), then the second line with Kampfgruppe Luck and the Major Becker's assault guns and the Tiger tanks of s-Pz.-Abt.503. The third line would consist of artillery and the formidable 8,8 cm flak guns (used in an anti-tank role) of Flak-Rgt.Moser (III.Flak-Korps). For his offensive, Montgomery was lacking in infantry after the heavy losses previously suffered and despite the arrival of reinforcements. He would launch his VIII Corps with a thousand

The Manneville château grounds

At dawn on 18 July, the 12 operational Tiger tanks of 3./s.Panzer-Abteilung 503 were hidden in the grounds of Manneville stud farm grounds and would find themselves beneath a carpet of bombs. A tank received a direct hit (that of Unteroffizier Westerhausen) and blew up immediately, killing all the crew. Another Tiger ('313' of Feldwebel Sachs), weighing 58 tonnes, was turned over with its tracks in the air. Leutnant von Rosen, the temporary company commander, also had his tank damaged.

Opposite: 2nd company, s.Panzer-Abteilung 503, Tiger '213' tipped over after the bombing in a ditch at the Manneville ch,teau; its crew attempted to pull it out.(© Heimdal)

Below; This spectacular photo shows Feldwebel Sachs's Tiger '313' turned over from the blast of an explosion, despite weighing 58 tonnes. Two of the crew were killed and the three others rendered unconscious for several hours. They were eventually freed after many efforts to open the rear right-hand turret hatch, that used by the loader. (IWM)

tanks and the three armoured divisions (Guards Armoured Division, 7th and 11th Armoured Divisions). This armoured spearhead was supported in the east by I Corps and in the west (to the east of Caen) by the II Canadian Corps. All of these units were at their start positions on **17 July**. On **18 July**, 942 British bombers arrived over their objectives of the first German line at 5.35 am. The impact was awful for the Germans. The explosions threw vehicles into the air, even the heavy Tiger tanks in the grounds of the Manneville château. The 16. Luftwaffen-Feld-Division was wiped-out under the effects of the carpet bombing. At 7.45 am, the tanks pushed through the first line, the

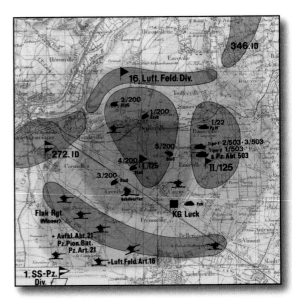

This map shows the German positions which would be bombed, mainly those on the first line: 272. ID, 16. LFD, 346. ID. KG Luck was on the second line and the artillery was spread out to the rear along the Bourguébus ridge. The orange-shaded zone shows the sectors situated under the bombing areas. (Heimdal)

A rare colour photo showing a Cruiser Cromwell III of the reconnaissance regiment of the 6th Airborne Division temporarily attached to the 1st Canadian Army for Operation Atlantic, on the left flank of Goodwood. (PAC)

A Ford Canada vehicle turned over in a bomb crater. In the background is the steel works at Colombelles. Fires would rage throughout the factory. To the left are the blast furnaces. However, the British photo reports give a false view of the situation. The images of German vehicles turned over in bomb craters are spectacular but they do not show any destroyed British tanks and Montgomery had lost 314! (IWM.)

3rd Royal Tank Regiment (11th Armoured Division) in the vanguard encountering a few assault guns (StuG) and at 10;15 am, hit in the flank by a 8,8 cm flak battery of Major von Luck firing over a flat trajectory from north of Cagny. The tanks had already suffered heavy losses from the 8,8 cm guns and Major Becker's assault guns when they reached the second line.

However, at **midday**, the British Second Army received enthusiastic reports, announcing that the 11th Armoured Division tanks were already approaching the Bourguébus ridge. But the reality on the ground was very different. The infantry was far behind and still fighting in Démouville against unexpected areas of resistance. And now, the 3rd RTR was halted in front of Hubert-Folie, the furthest point of the British advance when the 11th Armoured Division had Bretteville-sur-Laize for its objective! The Guards were supposed to take Vimont and the 7th Armoured Division then speed on towards Falaise. The latter finally attacked at **5 pm** but, the Leibstandarte also arrived in a counter-attack with Peiper's Panther tank battalion (I./1) pushing back the tanks of the 23rd Hussars. On the western flank, Operation Atlantic, launched by the II Canadian Corps, was halted by just the 346.ID. The operation had already failed. It would continue until **19 July**, but with further losses for the British who would finally lose a total of **314 tanks** out of the thousand engaged if Montgomery launched another two offensives like this he would have no tanks left! On **20 July**, rain finally brought this offensive to a definitive end which resulted in a brilliant defensive victory for the Germans, to such an extent that it was used post-war in the field as an example for Swedish cadets. After this failure, Montgomery would now need Canadian and Polish armour to relaunch his attacks...

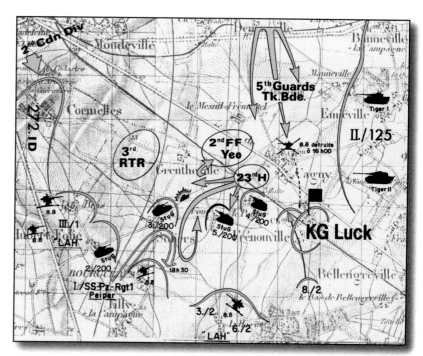

German counter-attack and stabilisation of the front: Panther tanks of Peiper's I./SS-Pz.Rgt.1 counter-attacked at the foot of the Bourguébus ridge. In this attack, they were supported by 21.PD Stug assault guns. On the western flank of the front, the men of LAH III./1 strengthened the German positions at Bras and Hubert-Folie. In the direction of Bourguébus, the defenders were grenadiers of 3./1. The British thrust was shattered by, amongst other things, the 8,8 cm flak guns, destroyed at 4 pm, and which had hit the tank columns in the flank, causing them heavy losses. It would have been suicidal to continue an attack that had already cost nearly 200 tanks. (Heimdal)

Cagny, 19 July. This photo shows a company of the 1st Welsh Guards at the eastern entrance to Cagny, a village that they had just mopped up at 10.30 am. Suddenly, at FrÉnouville, to the south (to the left in this photo), Germans of the Waldm¸ller battalion (I./25),KG 'HJ', have just appeared. The lieutenant is pointing out enemy positions to the company commander. (IWM)

179

Historical falsehoods

What we know about the Landings and the Battle of Normandy has evolved considerably over half a century and we are proud to have played a large part in this. Thus, when we began our work as historians and publishers on the subject back in 1976, available documentation was mainly limited to *The Longest Day*, both the book and the film, and few first-hand accounts. The blockbuster film at least created great interest in D-Day all over the world and helped veterans reconcile themselves with their history, even reinstating them as they had often been forgotten post-war in a Europe that needed rebuilding in the midst of Cold War tension. However, *The Longest Day* was more of an idealised adventure film, filled with many errors that historians, specialists such as Jean Quellien and myself, revealed throughout the years. Also, do not forget that in wartime, propaganda is also a weapon of war and that the nascent history of this battle was still influenced by wartime propaganda.

Also, the German army was still, in 1976, 'the army of the shadows'. The public could only read *'Invasion! They're coming!'* by the former German war correspondent Paul Carell, which at least had the merit of existing in the wilderness. Also, with the publication of a great many monographs, often very detailed and produced by allied units, American and British historical services and associations, the vanquished were not heard.

However, starting in the nineteen sixties, monographs began appearing in Germany, often published by veterans' associations. This work was nevertheless patchy as many German archives had disappeared in the chaos of the end of the war.

But there were still many veterans around for researchers and we were lucky enough to be around during this fantastic period where there were so many eye witnesses, allowing us to rebuild the past with great detail and bringing it back to life. We then undertook a veritable monastic work and this publication is the result of more than forty years of research. On the German side, details of their operations were still fragmented and their photos in a total muddle. The rolls of film taken by German war correspondents were seized by the Americans and the French without their reference files that are now lost. Thus, the archives had two million photos that said nothing. We then began work on identification, something that is still continuing today. On rolls of film, road signs, identifiable buildings and unit markings allowed us to make identifications. We have, therefore, been able to caption numerous photos (look at the caption for photos 3 and 4 on page 120, in 1984, which we still believe were taken at Virson on 25 June   a meeting with the veteran Otto Funk allowing us to bring history back to life).

Among the grey areas, apart from those of the German soldiers who were no more than ghosts, was that of the totally forgotten, at the time, fate of the Normandy civilians. Only German sources spoke of 2,000 civilian dead in Caen. But was this figure reliable? We did not mention it during those years when mentioning civilian dead was, for some 'well-meaning' people, damaging to the image of the allied liberators. This was censorship. However, valuable research was undertaken, village by village, with the elderly population. This research was published (1). The reality was terrible; there were more Normandy civilians killed than British soldiers in Normandy!

However, although the history of this battle has become more exact over the decades, there is also a certain amount of falsehoods, most of which come from some veterans. Everyone remembers the famous scene in *The Longest Day* where we see Major Pluskat looking at the allied fleet at dawn on 6 June; the scene being filmed at one of the best conserved batteries at Longues. It would take until the nineteen eighties for the truth to come out: Major Pluskat was not at his post on 6 June at dawn but was in the arms of a woman in Caen. He had overstated his role to Cornelius Ryan, much to the indignation of his veteran comrades. There were also false-real veterans, including the case of Howard Manoian who passed himself of as a 82nd Airborne paratrooper dropped over Sainte-Mère-Eglise. A former Detroit policeman, he had moved near the Normandy town to spend his retirement there and became a local 'hero' who was interviewed by international media each 6 June. Howe-

(1) Mémorial des victimes civiles en Normandie, unicaen.fr

(2) Article by Philippe Wirton published in issue n°216 of 39/45 Magazine, Editions Heimdal.

(3) Publlished in French by Editions Heimdal in 2013 the German edition was published in 1989.

(4) French version by Editions Heimdal summer 2017.

(5) A magazine, *Normandie 1944 Magazine*, deals with the history of the Battle of Normandy and this can be read in issue N°14 in the part dealing with John Gorman. Among the 'new' subjects is the question, amongst others, of war crimes. Those of the Germans were documented. Those of the Allies, which are numerous, especially on 6 June are increasingly better known, especially in light of accounts by American paratroopers.

ver, an American researcher, intrigued by this story, found his records in the US Army archives and discovered that he was in fact in a rear-echelon unit tasked with cleaning.

Let us now talk about a case that we uncovered, that of Lieutenant **Gorman** who was in action during Operation Goodwood on 18 July 1944 as a troop commander, 2nd Squadron (Sherman tanks) of the Irish Guards (Guards Armoured Division). After having crossed the stream coming from the Manneville stud farm and then heading towards Cagny, his troop was halted and alone. It was then that: *"Looking over to my left, to my great dread, I saw the easily recognizable outline of a Königstiger that had just emerged from a hedgerow barely 200 yards away and was heading towards my Sherman. I ordered my gunner to: 'Turn left halt fire.' He fired and I saw, with consternation, that the 75 mm shell had hit the front of the Tiger and ricocheted off the glacis plate. I ordered the gunner to fire again, but from down below, a voice echoed out: 'Gun problem Sir.' (...) I watched the Tiger in great apprehension and saw, with fright, its long gun slowly turning towards me.»* He is then supposed to have ordered to drive towards the Tiger and ram it in 'naval fashion'. The two tanks remained stuck in the field. Gorman returned on foot, told his story and was welcomed as a hero. He was subsequently awarded the Military Cross for this supposed feat of arms and took part in ceremonies held in his honour and a monument was placed on the scene of the action bearing the following inscription, translated from French: *"The first King Tiger to be destroyed in Europe took place here in an action by Lt. John Gorman, 2nd Squadron, Irish Guards."*

However, a civilian took numerous photos of the wrecks, showing that the Tiger II was not heading towards Gorman. These photos (which now belong to Editions Heimdal) were passed around in the meantime and faced with this proof, John Gorman rendered a second account which differed, but which nevertheless validated the supposed attack. We validated Gorman's story up to October 2004 (2). However, in a book written collectively by German veterans of s.-Panzer-Abteilung 503 (3), the truth emerged in an account by Hans Joachim Thaysen: *"122, the panzer in which I was gunner, was fighting with an English tank when we came under fire from another. This led my Kommandant (a novice without any combat experience), almost in a state of panic, to reverse the panzer. We reversed and went through one of the many hedgerows common around those parts. In any case, the Kommandant was in a bit of a muddle as he should have seen that behind the hedgerow there was another tank. Anyway, there was an impact and we were stuck on an English tank. In no way had we intended to ram the enemy, especially as I was busy looking towards 12 o'clock and the Tommy who was firing at us."* Wolfgang Schneider, a tank instructor officer in the Bundeswehr, panzer historian and writer of several books wrote the following on page 119 of *Tiger in Kampf*: *"Gorman probably hoped that we would swallow his version without any problems. Luckily, we do not need to rely only on suppositions. A photo in the Canadian archives, unpublished up to now, shows without any shadow of doubt what took place. In front of the Tiger are clear track marks of the latter, showing that it reversed with a sharp turn to the left (therefore in front of the Sherman). This proves that they hit the Sherman. It is also visible via the lowering of the track behind the sprocket wheel that the Tiger was reversing. When a panzer is moving forward, the track is tight."* It was, therefore, a simple 'traffic accident' and the Tiger II was even knocked-out by a German anti-tank shell that was meant for the Sherman (confirmed by the gunner's account). These laurels of victory were therefore claimed for dishonestly... There are other similar cases, as told by Helmut Konrad von Keusgen in his recent book on Pegasus Bridge and the Merville battery (4). Lieutenant-colonel Ottway also 'made up' his story concerning the guns at the Merville battery which remained intact and managed to cross the Seine during the retreat.

Thus, research is ongoing and is progressively allowing us move on from 'epic legends' to history...there are still many surprises in store. (5)

Of the many photos showing the rammed tanks, this one clearly shows the track tension of Tiger II '122' which hit Lieutenant Gorman's Sherman as it reversed. Gorman's version of events state that he saw the panzer heading towards him (head on therefore), something which is not true. Note also the hole in the Sherman's running gear, a shell probably fired by a German anti-tank gun which knocked-out the Tiger by mistake. (© Heimdal.)

Preparing for 'Cobra'
(14 - 24 July)

The First Army now how certain advantages for launching this offensive. The infantry had gained experience in the struggle against tanks. The bazooka had proved to the GI that he was not defenceless against panzers. Also, on 5 July the 79th ID had designed a type of hedgecutter, which was then improved by Sergeant Curtis G. Curlin Jr. of the 102nd Cavalry Reconnaissance Squadron. This cutter comprised of teeth set at the front of tanks that could cut through hedgerows and they were made from German beach obstacles. Tanks equipped with these cutters were named 'Rhinoceros', then more simply 'Rhinos'. The 23rd Armored Engineer Battalion of the 3rd Armored Division, also claimed to have invented this device. When 'Cobra' was launched, three out of five tanks were equipped with hedgecutters but, in order to retain tactical surprise, Lt. Gen. Bradley forbade their use before the operation.

Four armored divisions and four infantry divisions had now arrived as reinforcements. The First Army had four army corps making a total of fourteen divisions. Maj. Gen. Collins' VII Corps made up the spearhead of the attack and had it been seriously strengthened. He disposed of two infantry divisions in the front line (9th and 30th ID) through which would leapfrog two armored divisions (3rd and 2nd AD), then two reinforcement infantry divisions (1st and 4th ID). He was supported in the east towards the Saint-LÙ sector, by XIX and V Corps. In the west, the attack would be joined by VIII Corps (Maj. Gen.Middleton) with two other armored divisions (4th AD and 6th AD) and four infantry divisions.

These considerable forces would push through a gap opened by a huge carpet of bombs 6,000 yards wide and 2,500 yards deep. This bombardment aimed at **crushing the German lines** along the front line sector where the remnants of the

The hedgerows posed a formidable problem to the American tank units. In order to allow them to move off the narrow roads, the engineers had to blow up a section of the hedgerow. Some tanks, the Tank-dozers, were equipped at the front with a bulldozer blade. Although these tanks were effective, they were not widely available and were less manoeuverable than the other tanks. One of these tanks of the 3rd Armored Division is seen here. (DAVA/Coll. Heimdal.)

After the fighting experienced at Villiers-Fossard and Hauts-Vents, the engineer battalion of the 3rd Armored Division, the 23rd Armored Engineer Battalion, invented a device with teeth attached to the front of tanks; the hedgecutter tank was thus born. This device was made by cutting up and welding together the readily available German beach obstacles. It was both straightforward and ingenious. Seen here is a Sherman of the 3rd Armored Division that had just driven through a hedgerow. (DAVA/Heimdal)

A close-up of a hedgecutter on a Stuart light tank. (Coll. Heimdal.)

part! 1,800 heavy bombers would crush the saturation zone for over an hour with a carpet of bombs. 350 fighter-bombers would strafe and bomb a narrower strip at the moment of the attack. Ten minutes later, 396 medium bombers would bomb the southern half of the zone for 45 minutes. During the entire operation, this aerial armada would be protected by 500 fighters. Then, in order to exploit any breakthrough, Lt. Gen. Patton would launch his 3rd Army into the breach; his spearhead units were already in the Valognes region by **22 July**. However, General Montgomery also wanted 'his' offensive and he launched 'Goodwood' on **18 July**!...

23 July, a 4th Infantry Division unit marches towards the lines, watched by a Norman farm woman as they pass by the farm at the La Maison Basset hamlet in Hommet d Arthenay. Here too, the men follow the 'One Way' roadsigns. (DAVA/Heimdal)

Panzer-Lehr-Division was positioned with 5,000 men, of which 2,500 were combatants with forty tanks, as well as the remnants of FjR 13 of the 5th parachutist division and those of Kampgruppe Heintz, then **shatter the German lines of communication**, neutralise their reserves and **reduce their will to fight** with terror. Bradley was in England on **19 July** to finalise this air support; in all he would have **more than 3,000 planes** taking

This diagram shows the positions of American units shortly before the offensive. We can see the vital role given to VII Corps with two infantry divisions both respectively supported by two armored divisions, the 3rd and 2nd, and two infantry divisions in reserve, the 1st and 4th. To the west, the other future point of the pincer comprised of four infantry divisions, the 79th, 8th, 90th and 83rd with an armored division for penetration, the 4th, and another in reserve. (Heimdal map)

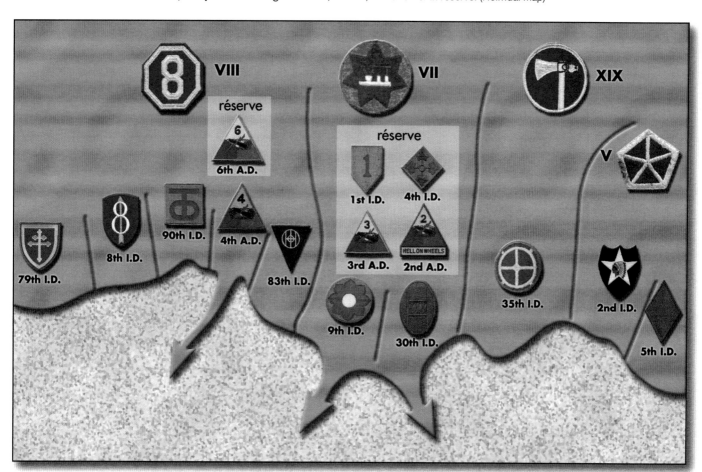

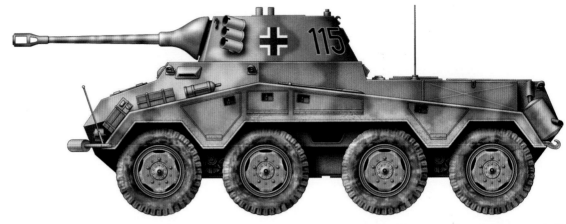

Panzer-Lehr-Division Puma reconnaissance vehicle. This rare eight-wheel armoured vehicle was with this division's reconnaissance group, Panzer-Aufklärungs-Abteilung 130. It was armed with a 50 mm gun, the 5 cm KwK 39/1 L/60. The turret was made by Daimler-Benz AG, originally planned for use with the Leopard reconnaissance vehicle. It carried fifty-five 50 mm shells, weighed 11.74 tonnes and had a crew of four. It was powered by a V-12 Tatra 103 engine. Its maximum speed was 90 km/h and it had a remarkable range of 1,000 kilometres on road and 600 kilometres off-road. It consumed 40 litres of fuel per 100/km and 60 off-road. The fuel tank had a capacity of 360 litres. Its braking system was made by Knorr. It was 6.88 m long, 2..33 m wide and 2.38 m high. Frontal armour was 30 mm thick, 8 mm on the sides, 10 mm at the rear and 30 mm on the front of the turret. The entire 1st company of Pz.AA.130 was equipped with 26 Radspähwagen 'Puma' or SdKfz 234/2. According to its turret markings, this is the 5th vehicle, 1st troop, 1st company. Three-hundred pre-production examples of these remarkably modern reconnaissance vehicles and one-hundred production examples (of which 26 were just for the Lehr!) (Illustration by Julio Lopez Caeiro.)

Panzer-Lehr-Division SdKfz 251/9 Ausf. D. This half-track was armed with a short-barrel 75 mm gun (Stk 37L/24) and was mostly used in panzergrenadier battalions. Thus, each I./901 combat company was equipped with two, as was II./901. The same applied for Panzergre-nadier-Lehr Regiment 902, making a total of twelve vehicles for each of these regiments. The 3rd pioneer company, Panzer-Pionier-Bataillon 130 also had two of these vehicles. The four-number marking with the two first being '11' corresponds to this pioneer battalion. (Illustration by Julio Lopez Caeiro.)

6th Armored Division Sherman. Note the markings: Number 6 and a triangle symbolising the 6th. Armored Division. The divisional emblem is painted on the side. This Sherman is a cast hull M4 A1 or Sherman II. Its total combat weight was 31,500 kilos. It was 5.90 m in length, 2.62 m wide and 2.67 high. It had a maximum road speed of 42 km/h and an autonomy of 160 kilometres. The frontal armour was 51 mm thick and 38 mm on the sides. It was armed with a 75 mm gun and carried 98 shells. It had a crew of five, three of which were in the turret. (Illustration by Julio Lopez Caeiro.)

M8 75 mm HMC attached to the 82nd Armored Reconnaisance Battalion of the 2nd Armored Division. This 75 mm howitzer is equipped here with a frontal hedge cutter. (Illustration by Julio Lopez Caeiro.)

US Army anti-tank missions in France mostly fell to the Tank Destroyer M10, until the arrival of the M18 and M36 after the Battle of Normandy. Seen here is a mid-production M 10 TD of the 612th US Tank Destroyer Battalion. (Illustration by Julio Lopez Caeiro.)

The M16 corresponds to a M3 half-track equipped with a Maxson quadmount with four M2HB 12.7 mm machine-guns, a gunner's seat, two circular aiming sights, a forward armoured shield and a small generator for traversing or raising the gun without using the vehicle's engine. 2,876 of these vehicles were made, not counting the 777 made by transforming other half-tracks. (Illustration by Julio Lopez Caeiro.)

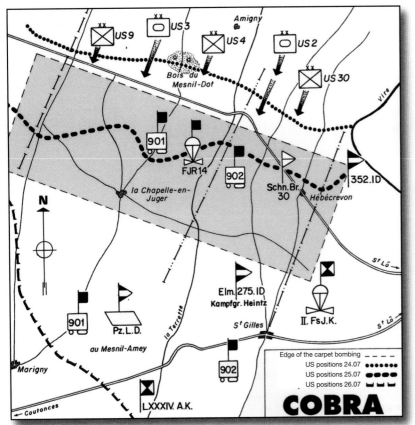

The Cobra carpet bombing sector. The 9th ID and tanks of the 3rd AD would pour over the sector held by Regiment 901, Panzer-Lehr and FJR 14. Then the 9th ID would be leapfrogged by 4th ID. The 30th ID and 2d AD (Hell on wheels) would drive through the sector held by Regiment 902 of the Lehr, the Schnelle Brigade and KG Heintz. The objective for the first was Marigny and Saint-Gille for the second. (Heimdal)

Cobra - the carpet bombing (24 to 26 July)

The bombardment was set for 1 pm on **24 July**. Approximately 1,600 bombers took off from England (six fighter-bomber IX TAC groups and three 8th US Air Force wings). Major-General Collins had withdrawn the men of the 9th and 30th Infantry Divisions in the forward lines 1,200 yards (1,100 metres) to avoid them being too close to the bombing zones. But visibility was bad in England

The 25 July bombardment also hit American positions. Medical officers are seen here trying to free GIs buried by earth thrown up by the bombs. (DAVA/Coll. Heimdal)

The 25 July bombardment

At 9 am on 25 July, 1,500 B-17 and B-24 bombers were over their objectives and dropped 3,300 tonnes of bombs over the saturation area between Montreuil-sur-Lozon and Hébécrevon. Hell fell from the sky and there were also heavy losses in the American ranks: 111 killed and 490 wounded, almost the strength of a battalion! Medics are seen here extracting GIs who have been buried by earth thrown up by the bombs.

The death throes of the 'Panzer-Lehr'

The war correspondent, George Greb, followed the American breakthrough towards Marigny on 26 July 1944. He took many exceptional photos bearing witness to the cataclysm that fell on the Panzer-Lehr-Division. He photographed at least three Panthers, a Panzer IV and two half-track vehicles. Seen here is a 45-tonne Panther which has been thrown like a piece of straw into a bomb crater. (Coll. Heimdal)

and Air Chief Marshal Leigh-Mallory decided to postpone the bombardment. However, all the groups could not be contacted and some bomb runs were carried out in poor conditions, killing 25 men and wounding 131 in the 30th ID. Mistakes concerning procedure led to controversy. Surprise had been lost but it was essential to not allow the Germans time to take preventive measures. Paradoxically, they took this failed bombardment for a real attempt and did not pull back their lines. Bradley made the decision to launch Cobra at 11 am.

25 July - At 9 am, 1,500 B-17 and B-24 bombers were over their targets and dropping 3,300 tonnes of bombs on the saturation area. There were further losses in the American sector (111 killed and 490 wounded; Lieutenant-General McNair being among the killed and combat fatigue bringing US losses to 814 in two days). Naturally, losses were heavier on the German side. The Panzer-Lehr-Division now only had 7 operational tanks out of 40, those it held in reserve. The American battle corps attacked but came up against areas of resistance held by a handful of survivors. Two panzers and a line of grenadiers held up a battalion of the 8th IR, 4th ID. The latter only arrived at Chapelle-en-Juger at nightfall. Major-General Eddy would be surprised by unexpected resistance and hesitated in engaging all of his 9th ID. After the failure of Goodwood, was this large-scale offensive also on the point of failing?

26 July - The German command, however, had few reserves and there was virtually nothing left behind these last areas of resistance, even if the Lehr got some tanks working again; it now only had 14 with another 14 joining later. In the first hours of the day, the situation was not great for the Americans and they had only made small gains on the ground. However, the final areas of resistance gave way. On the left (to the east), the 30th ID headed east and cut off the Coutances/Saint-Lô road in the afternoon and by nightfall was closing in on the Canisy - Saint-Lô road. Its commanding officer, Major-General Hobbs, was ecstatic. Given this good news, Maj. Gen. Collins had to decide how to use his tanks. Thus, he engaged to the right (west) the 3rd Armored Division CCB and to the left (east) the 2nd Armored Division CCA, the latter reaching Canisy. Further west, VIII Corps also attacked. General von Choltitz, commanding the German troops, ordered the troops on his left flank to pull back to Coutances.

Saint-Gilles was an important objective on the Saint-Lô/Coutances road south of the area that was carpet bombed (see map). Arriving from the north, just before the crossroads on this road, is a 2nd Armored Division (Hell on Wheels) Sherman, passing next to a Panzer IV of 5. Kompanie (II./130), Panzer-Lehr-Division. The German tank has been cut in two and its upper section thrown next to the hull. (Coll. Heimdal)

This map shows the breach opened in the German front with the breakthrough of the 3rd AD in the west, and that of the 2nd AD in the east, respectively accompanied by the 9th and 4th AD. Three villages were destroyed and, under the carpet of bombs, the front line held by the Panzer-Lehr-Division in front of Marigny and Saint-Gilles. (Heimdal)

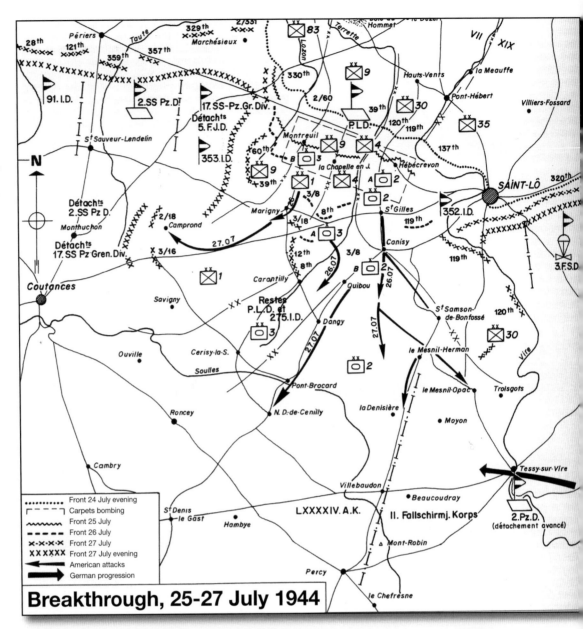

`················`	Front 24 July evening
	Carpets bombing
`∿∿∿∿∿`	Front 25 July
`- - - - -`	Front 26 July
`×-×-×-×`	Front 27 July
`××××××`	Front 27 July evening
→	American attacks
→	German progression

Breakthrough, 25-27 July 1944

Mechanised infantry of the 2nd Armored Division wearing camouflage clothing, were at Canisy on 27 July and Pont-Brocard on the 28th. (Coll. Heimdal)

Following on the heels of the 3rd Armored Division's tanks, infantry enter Marigny at the end of 26 July. Note the German tactical signs on the pole on the right: the upper sign is that of the 2. SS-Panzer-Division 'Das Reich' and below, the direction towards Kampfgruppe Heintz. The church square can be seen in the background, as well as the grain store and bakery. (Heimdal)

M8 Light Armored Car of the 2nd Armored Division reconnaissance squadron (C Squadron) seen here entering Canisy where a house, hit by artillery fire, still burns. The American artillery fired on the village before the troops entered. (US Army/Heimdal)

Cobra, exploitation

The exploitation of the breakthrough was rapidly continued on **27 July**. In the east, the 2nd Armored Division advanced even faster, as there was no opposition, and fanned out in a deep penetration past Mesnil-Herman, reaching Mesnil-Opac with its CCA and Pont-Brocard with its CCB. In the west, the exploitation also took place rapidly with the 3rd Armored Division's CCB as the northern pincer, attempting to block the withdrawal of the 'Das Reich' and 'Götz' which were establishing lines of resistance to the north and east of what would become the 'Roncey Pocket'. On this day, near Neufbourg on the road east of Coutances, SS-Uscha Barkmann of the 'Das Reich', knocked out nine Shermans and several vehicles with his Panther in a few minutes.

Cobra, from 28 to 31 July

The American offensive achieved unhoped for success on **28 July**. To the south-east of Coutances, the 2nd Armored Division reached Saint-Denis-le-Gast, encircling from the south the Germans in the Roncey Pocket. To the north-west, the 90th

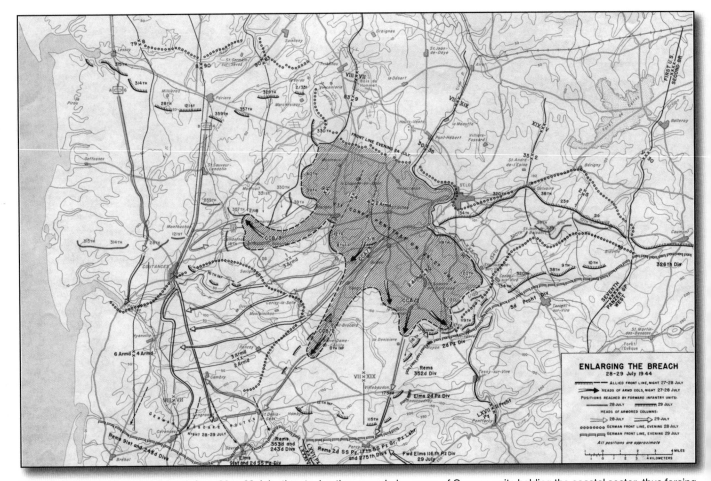

ENLARGING THE BREACH
28-29 July 1944

ALLIED FRONT LINE, NIGHT 27-28 JULY
HEADS OF ARMD COLS, NIGHT 27-28 JULY
POSITIONS REACHED BY FORWARD INFANTRY UNITS:
28 JULY
29 JULY
HEADS OF ARMORED COLUMNS:
28 JULY
29 JULY
GERMAN FRONT LINE, EVENING 28 JULY
GERMAN FRONT LINE, EVENING 29 JULY
All positions are approximate

Widening the American breakthrough from 28 to 29 July, threatening the rear echelon areas of German units holding the coastal sector, thus forcing them to withdraw. Two armored divisions, to the west, the 6th and 4th, were hot on their heels, with the 4th entering Coutances as early as 28 July. However, the 2nd Armored Division carried out a scything movement and caught many German units in the trap of the Roncey Pocket, south-east of Coutances. The Germans withdrew on the evening of the 29th to the BrÉhal-Gavray-Percy line. (US Army Center of Military History)

Marchésieux, Montcuit, Saint-Sauveur-Lendelin, 28-29 July 1944

1. When Cobra was launched, the Marchésieux sector, opposite the 83rd ID, was held by the remnants of the 17. SS-Panzer-Grenadier-Division 'Götz von Berlichingen'. 29 July, a 105 mm HM2 howitzer, mounted on an armoured 'Priest' chassis from an American unit, passes in front of the grave of SS-Unterscharführer (sergeant) Josef Richtsfeld, born on 9 August 1914 and killed near Saint-Gilles on 17 June 1944 whilst serving with the 9th battery of the 'Götz' artillery regiment (SS-A.R. 17). This battery was commanded by lieutenant Günther Prinz and was armed with heavy 15 cm guns. Sergeant Richtsfeld was killed by fighter-bombers. (Coll. Heimdal)

2. A GI looks at a destroyed amphibious 'Schwimmwagen' vehicle. Given the presence of the stencilled 'Fist' on the rear left-hand side, we know that this vehicle belonged to the 'Götz von Berlichingen'. The painted tactical sign on the right indicates that it belonged to the headquarters company of the divisional engineers battalion. This is, therefore, one of the four 'Schwimmwagen' of the company's reconnaissance squad. This company was commanded by captain Müller. (Coll. Heimdal)

1

2

The Roncey Pocket, 29 to 31 July

This map shows the scything movement towards the south-west undertaken by the 2nd Armored Division's CCB, thus trapping numerous German units in the 'Roncey Pocket'. In the pocket were the 6th parachute regiment (6.F.J.R.), 2. SS-Panzer-Division with the 'Deutschland' regiment ('D'), elements of KG 91 and KG 353, 17th artillery regiment of the 'Götz'. Most of these units were elite. To the north, another American armored division (the 3rd Armored Division), closed the pocket to the west, along with the 4th Armored Division who sped on to Coutances. The pocket was closed on the evening of 29 July and the 2nd Armored Division would cause 1,500 German casualties and capture another 4,000. However, during the night of 29 to 30 July, numerous German elements pushed their way out via Saint-Denis-le-Gast and withdrew to a line going from Bréhal, Gavray, Percy, Beaucoudray, Moyon, Troisgots, Torigni-sur-Vire. (Heimdal map from Stöber.)

Inf. Div. had taken **Lessay** and Périers the previous day, opening the way for two new divisions, the 6th Arm. Div. arriving four kilometres from Coutances with its tanks in the evening whilst, coming from **Saint-Sauveur-Lendelin**, the 4th Arm. Div. reached it at the end of the day.

On **29 July**, the Americans at last won the race against time that they had been engaged in with the Germans who were trying to establish a solid front line south of Coutances (see map). The 4th AD passed through **Coutances** as the **Roncey Pocket** was closed around the remains of at least five divisions. The Germans tried to break out during the night with many succeeding and a lot remaining trapped: 2,500 killed, 5,000 prisoners, 539 vehicles, including more than 100 tanks and 150 half-tracks. As Martin Blumenson said: *"There were sufficient troops (Germans) gathered on a line from Percy to the sea but the difficulty lay in*

that these men were exhausted. This line was broken through on 30 July at Hambye by the 3rd Arm. Div. CCB. Gavray, to the west, was taken and a bridge was layed over the Sienne river. Lt. Gen. Patton's Third Army then took over, charging without a break and passing Avranches on 31 July. The 4th Inf. Div. reached the gateway to Brittany at Pontaubault. The breakout had succeeded!"

Prisoners from the Roncey Pocket, 30 July. When mopping up the Roncey Pocket on 30 July, the Americans took 5,000 German prisoners, most of whom belonged to elite units. In this famous photo there are only Waffen-SS officers and paratroopers (a parachutist lieutenant-colonel on the right). The bearing of these captured men shows the determination that they had shown in attempting to break out of the pocket.

The 4th Canadian Armoured Division assembled south of Caen at Vaucelles, Colombelles and Fleury where these tank crew men are seen here. See also the photo of the same report in the page 113. (PAC)

Operation Bluecoat, then Operation Spring and the 9.SS-Panzer-Division counter-attack in the 272. ID sector from 25 to 31 July 1944. (H. Fürbringer/Heimdal)

Operation Spring (25 to 26 July): All for nought!

At the same time as Operation Cobra was launched so was another on **25 July** at 3.30 am east of the Orne: Operation Spring. The objective of this attack was, one, to reach the May-sur-Orne/Verrières/Tilly-la-Campagne line and, two, the Fontenay-le-Marmion/Hill 122 line (7th Armoured Division). The third objective was to push towards the south and Cintheaux (Guards Armoured Division). Advancing behind a powerful artillery barrage and under artificial moonlight created by searchlights, the Canadian Corps made an initial advance of one kilometre. To the east of the Falaise road (RN 158), 9th Brigade, 3rd Division suffered heavy losses against elements of the Leibstandarte: the artificial moonlight had shown the outlines of the Canadians to the defenders. The North Nova Scotia Highlanders had 140 casualties. To the west of the RN 158 road, 2nd Division launched its 4th Brigade against Rocquancourt and its 5th Brigade against May-sur-Orne. This sector had many mine shafts and tunnels which allowed the Germans to counter-attack to the rear of the Canadians! Furthermore, the Canadian advance was spotted by the Germans from Hill 112 west of the Orne, laying down artillery and Nebelwerfer fire. Hohenstaufen elements counter-attacked from 1.05 pm onwards with a Kampfgruppe (commanded by Otto Meyer the tank regiment commander) with the bulk of the panzers, III./20, a pioneer company and a flak battery towards Rocquancourt and Tilly. Another KG (Zollhöfer), with the remnants of the division's grenadiers, attacked towards the west against May, Saint-Martin and Saint-André. **May** (to the west) and **Tilly** (to the east), remained impregnable.

The Hohenstaufen continued its counter-attack on the **26th** and KG Zollhöfer took the villages of Saint-Martin and Saint-André after four hours of furious fighting. On the right, the panzers of KG Meyer were attacked by Typhoons and Hill 88 was not recaptured until nightfall. In this second day of counter-attack, the Germans had retaken almost all of the

Canadian soldiers silhouetted by the artificial moonlight during the night of 25 July near Fleury-sur-Orne. (PAC)

May-sur-Orne, this man, probably from Fusiliers Mont-Royal, takes aim with his Sten from behind a pile of brushwood. (PAC)

terrain that the Canadians had captured and even approached Fleury and Caen. Canadian losses numbered 1,500, 307 of whom were from the Black Watch. The 2nd Canadian Infantry Division units were progressively taken back to Fleury and Ifs to be reformed with young and inexperienced soldiers before returning to the front line. The Canadians suffered new failures opposite May-sur-Orne, with heavy losses against the Hohenstaufen, from 1 to 5 August. It would not be until 8 August, and Operation Totalize and the dropping of 3,500 tonnes of bombs on the German positions, that May and Tilly were retaken from the 85.ID; the Hohenstaufen having moved to another sector.

1. 26 July in the British 1st Corps zone. The protective wings over a convoy seen here as a RAF Typhoon takes off from an airfield as a convoy makes its way to the front. Allied air superiority was total throughout the entire Battle of Normandy. (IWM)

2. Shortly after, an ammunition truck has just been hit by a shell. Men immediately take cover behind one of the trucks belonging to the 1st Corps armoured car regiment (Inns of Court, C Company seen here) as the truck that has been hit blows up. (IWM)

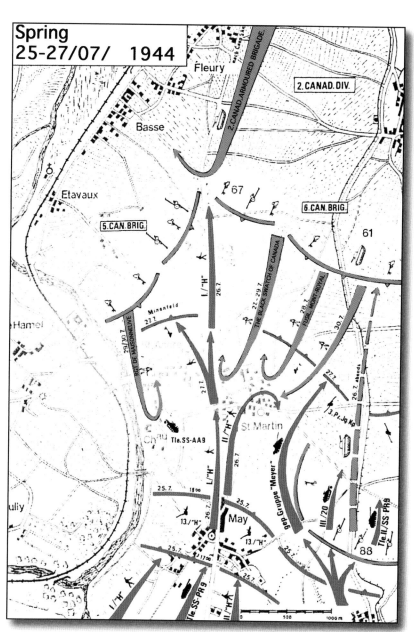

Operation Spring, carried out from 25 to 26 July and repulsed by the Hohenstaufen, was an allied failure. (Map H. Fürbringer/Heimdal.)

12

The final battle
1 to 30 August

With the Third US Army breakout in Normandy following Operation Cobra and on the verge of breaking through at Avranches, before pushing into Brittany and the Loire valley, Montgomery was still attempting to do the same in the Caen sector where he sent in the First Canadian Army south of the large city of lower Normandy. The Canadians were sent in to attack following the British losses suffered during Operation Goodwood. But, with the Americans breaking through at Avranches, Hitler sent his panzer divisions, mostly from the Anglo-Canadian sector, to take part in a counterattack at Mortain with the aim of cutting off the American armies at Avranches. However, Lüttich, the counter-attack at Mortain, was launched with insufficient strength and was crushed by fighterbombers.

In the meantime, the Third Army advanced south of Normandy virtually unopposed. The threat to the Germans was now one of being pushed into a huge pocket. The Lüttich attack was definitively halted on **10 August**. The German army would now progressively withdraw towards the east.

However, in the north, pressure was placed again on the German lines in the Caumont sector with Operation Bluecoat, launched by two British corps across difficult terrain and one which saw initial success thanks to overwhelming numerical superiority, before being slowed down by the arrival of German reinforcements (Hohenstaufen, Frundsberg, 21.Panzer-Division, s.Panzer-Abteilung 503, Panzerjäger-Abteilung 654). These units had been sent by the Germans in order to protect Lüttich and they would now pull back in the general withdrawal, initially carried out to the east of Flers and which was undertaken on **16 August**.

The battle had taken an unexpected turning point in August. Whereas allied progression had been slow, very difficult and often despairing between 6 June and 25 July, against a very motivated and efficient adversary, the sudden breakout that began on 26 July upset what the Allies had forecast for Overlord; a fast advance but one that was also progressive. The Third Army's stampede beyond Avranches across a huge swathe of countryside, would open up unexpected prospects. The rapid conquest of Brittany (except for the pockets) and the Loire valley, would allow the American armies to push on the Seine. However, paradoxically, this spectacular success would save the Germans from disaster. Indeed, Allied aircraft dominated the battlefield, making German movement difficult and costly in terms of heavy losses. Air power had played a crucial role in the allied victory with its overwhelming firepower. Without this, victory would have been uncertain. Now, the allied air power was spread out over a huge theatre of operations and much of it was no longer in the skies over Normandy. Also, on 16 August, Eisenhower believed that the Germans had withdrawn, something that was partially true as 40% of their units were already near the Seine. He would neglect the advance north in order to link up with the Anglo-Canadians. German resistance against the latter was desperate, given the stakes at play, and was mostly undertaken by the rearguard elements of the Hitlerjugend on the flat terrain north of Falaise. During this time, the German withdrawal continued for another three days. The 'Falaise Pocket' was on the verge of being close on **19 August**. Despite the sacrifice of the Poles, this pocket would not be closed totally, partly due to the premature departure of the French 2nd armoured division in order to push on to Paris. Approximately half of the encircled troops escaped, mostly those of the best units, joining those which had already withdrawn. Retreating from the pocket was apocalyptic; pounded mainly by allied artillery, the Germans left behind around 5,000 dead in a vision of horror within such a confined area.

The German counterattack at Mortain. (H. Fürbringer/Heimdal.)

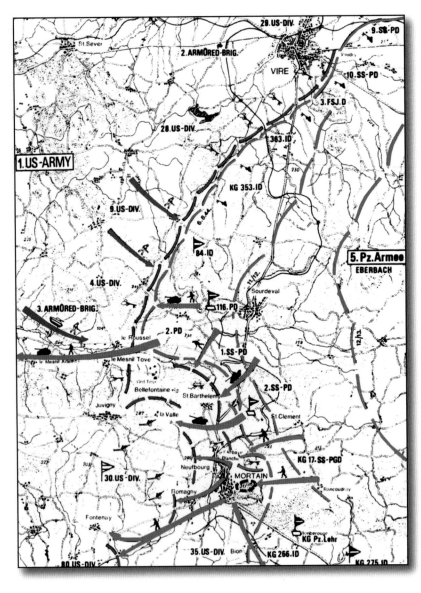

However, the Allies had grasped the situation too late and the bulk of the German army had withdrawn to the Seine. This was not, as Eddy Florentin stated, 'Stalingrad in Normandy', but more a 'Dunkirk in Normandy'. The latter was even more similar as the Germans left behind a lot of materiel.

Also, the Battle of Normandy did not end on 21 August when the last units escaped from the pocket, but rather came to an end later. Indeed, the fighting continued along rearguard lines as far as the Seine which was definitively crossed on 30 August. The troops that had withdrawn would be back together a few months later during the Battle of the Bulge. The Battle of Normandy, therefore, ended in an uncompleted victory.

The map **below** shows the successive withdrawals of German units from what would become known as the 'Falaise Pocket', and the bottleneck through which the last units managed to escape. (Heimdal)

Above: The German army withdraws to the Seine. A Panther tank is seen here near Bourgtheroulde in open country. The tank's driver (of the 2. Panzer-Division or the 9. Panzer-Division) observes the sky whilst the commander has climbed out to get his bearings. (BA)

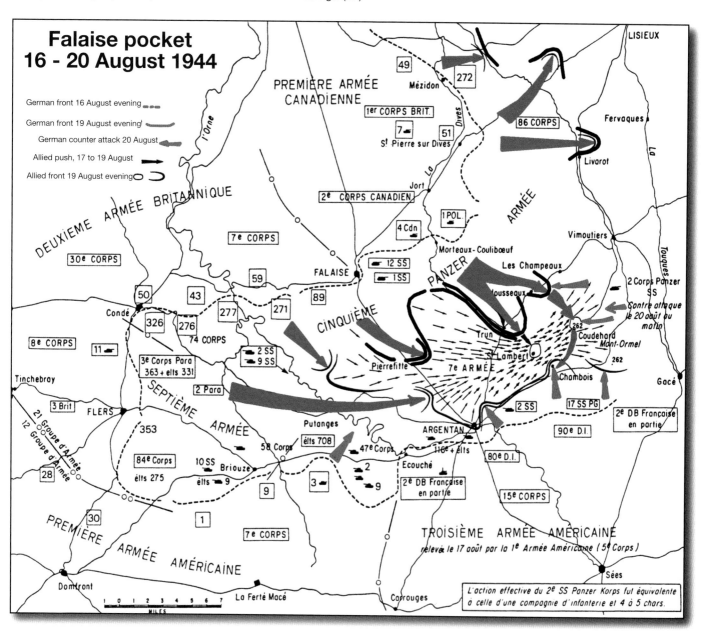

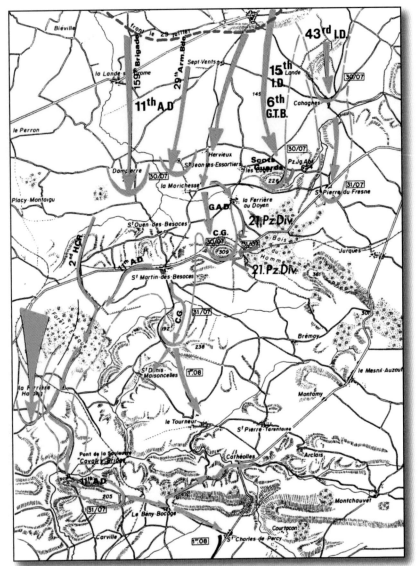

Operation Bluecoat (30 July - 15 August) Tanks stuck in the bocage

With the German front broken through in the west thanks to Operation Cobra and the thrust of the First US Army, Montgomery decided to accompany the movement. Following the failure of Operation Goodwood, then Operation Spring, the best opportunity was offered on the left flank of the American breakthrough. This would start from the Tilly-sur-Seulles sector with XXX Corps along with the 50th ID, attacking towards Villers-Bocage and Aunay-sur-Odon. It would be supported on its right by the 43rd ID and the 59th ID on its left with the 7th AD tanks in reserve. The main objective was Hill 361 (Mont Pinçon which overlooked the entire sector). To the west, from the Caumont-l'Eventé salient, VIII Corps would attack with the 15th Scottish Division supported by two armoured divisions, the Guards Armoured Division and the 11th Armoured Division which would have to slowly advance through dense and hilly bocage country. The objective being Saint-Martin-des-Besaces and Hill 309. All they had facing them were two German infantry divisions; 326.ID in the west and 276.ID in the east.

The offensive began at 6 am on **30 July** with a frontage of three brigades in each corps. In the

VIII Corps   XXX Corps

The start of Operation Bluecoat south of Caumont, 30 July. Following a powerful artillery barrage and strong air support, the tanks of the 4th Grenadier Guards/6th Guards Brigade support the 15th Scottish Division's attack. (IWM)

50th Infantry Division

43rd Infantry Division

15th Infantry Division

11th Armoured Division

The advance continues, 31 July. Seen here is the main road in Saint-Martin-des-Besaces; the village has just been liberated at midday by the 11th Armoured Division. (IWM)

east, the 50th ID advanced as far as Orbois whilst the 43rd ID was in Briquessard at midday. Cahagnes was reached at midnight. However, in the west, tanks, machine-gun carriers and half tracks were caught up in inextricable minefields, creating huge traffic jams that blocked 30,000 vehicles in the bocage of the Vire region! However, with the support of 174 tanks of the 6th Guards Tank Brigade, the 15th Scottish Division reached Hervieux and Hill 309 (north-east of Saint-Martin-des-Besaces). But there, it was counter-attacked by the formidable Jagdpanther tanks of Panzer-jäger-Abteilung 654 in the Hill 309 sector to the west of Bois du Homme. As soon as day broke on 31 July, the remnants of 21.Panzer-Division, accompanied by 65-tonne Tiger II tanks of s.Panzer-Abteilung 503, also counter-attacked in the Bois du Homme sector, but then came under attack themselves from 60 Typhoon fighter-bombers that knocked-out 30 panzers and 54 armoured vehicles. Further west, the 11th Armoured Division broke through as far as Saint-Martin-des-Besaces which it reached at midday. Better still, at 10.30 am, armoured vehicles of the 2nd Household Cavalry had found an intact bridge across the Souleuvre six kilometres south-east of this village! This captured bridge, at the boundary of two German divisions (3.FJD to the west and 326.ID to the east) allowed the tanks of the Guards Armoured Division to push through this breach. On 1 August, the 21.Panzer-Division continued with its counter-attacks but, coming under fire from artillery and fighter-bombers, it was forced to withdraw, pursued by the VIII Corps' Tommies. However, the 21.PD did not give up Le Tourneur to the 5th Guards Armoured Brigade until midday.

On **2 August** the 11th Armoured Division held Le Bény Bocage, covering its approaches to a depth of two kilometres and with its reconnaissance units having entered Vire the previous day. But the Hohenstaufen, having left the sector situated south of Caen (see Operation Spring), came to the

rescue. Otto Meyer's Kampfgruppe arrived at dawn and counter-attacked at Montchauvet in the afternoon. Its panzers fought the Guards' tanks. Other German reinforcements came in: the Tiger I tanks of s.SS-Panzer-Abteilung 102 and the Frundsberg. This blocked the front and the British advance came to a halt. The 7th Armoured Division failed at Aunay-sur-Odon against the Frundsberg. The front became static once more and British losses were very high in this sector. The line only moved again when Panzergruppe Eberbach decided to shorten the front line at 1 am on **3 August** so that it could pull back its panzers and make them available for operation Lüttich (the Mortain counter-attack). This would be the case further east where the British were able to enter, without a fight, Villers-Bocage (4 August), Aunay-sur-Odon and Evrecy, then Hill 112 (5 August), cross the Orne at Grimbosq (6 August) and thus get closer to Falaise. However, in this sector, the 11th Armoured Division, the Guards and 15th Division remained unable to advance, losing forty armoured vehicles a day, with 39 Sherman tanks destroyed on 4 August near Chênedollé by Will Fey's Tigers. The Germans would only pull back there on 15 August during the general withdrawal.

An 11th Armoured Division column waits for the order to depart at Saint-Charles-de-Percy during the breakout at Vire (2 August 1944). (IWM)

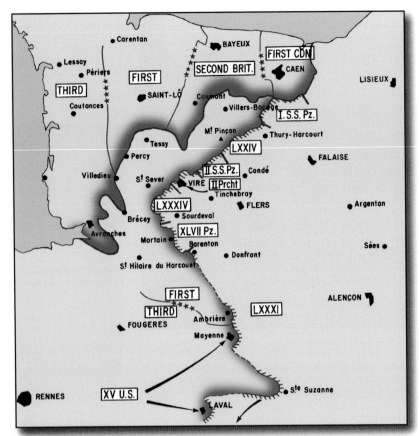

This map shows how the front evolved between 1 to 6 August 1944 with the deployment of Patton's Third Army next to the First Army which came under the command of Lt. Gen. Courtney Hodges at the beginning of August. The two armies were under the orders of 12th Army Group led by Lt. Gen. Bradley. During the six days of the breakout, the Avranches corridor was widened and the Third Army deployed in Brittany and the Loire valley, whereas the First Army widened the Avranches corridor as far as Mortain where the Germans launched a counter-attack on 7 August. (Heimdal)

The pursuit (1 - 6 August)

After the breakout at Avranches, a second American army, Patton's **Third Army**, was already in Brittany on **1 August** and advancing rapidly towards the Loire valley. It was in Mayenne and Laval as early as 6 August! In the meantime, the First Army had widened the breakout corridor at Avranches and advanced towards Percy and Villedieu-les-Poîles up to 6 August. The 2nd Armored Division's CCA found itself opposite Vire and the 4th Infantry Division was in the Saint-Pois sector. The 3rd Armored Division's CCB was in the Reffuveille sector and the 30th Infantry Division reached Mortain on **6 August**.

But Hitler had ordered a counter-attack at Mortain, the place where the 'American corridor' was the most narrow, starting from Mortain and heading towards Avranches. The objective consisted of totally isolating Patton's Third Army and cutting it off from its bases before wiping it out with the help of German divisions based in Brittany. However, what had been successful in Russia failed in the west due to the overwhelming allied air superiority. A German armoured force was quickly assembled for the counter-attack. The XLVII. (r.47) Panzer-Korps with the 116.Panzer-Division, 2. Panzer-Division, 2.SS-Panzer-Division 'Das Reich', 1.SS-Panzer-Division 'Leibstandarte' and a Kampfgruppe of the 17.SS-Panzergrenadier-Division. This armoured corps only had four divisions (some of which were very much weakened from previous losses), whereas Hitler had wanted to use seven. Allied superiority would have two consequences: the Germans were slowed down in bringing up by road their armoured forces and the latter would be confronted by the firepower of the fighter-bombers when they were in the line and attempting to deploy. So,

This photo was taken on 5 August to the west of Périers-en-Beauficel and Sourdeval, where the 4th Armored Division fought between 3 and 5 August. We can see here the results of this fighting. A type A Panther has been knocked-out and the body of one of its crew lies in front of the wreck. (NARA)

Below: Almost opposite the Landser of the 84. ID, this GI, loaded with grenades and armed with the heavy, but effective, Garand, takes a break on 4 August to the east of Villedieu. He belongs to the 12th Infantry Regiment, 4th Infantry Division. (Coll. Heimdal)

was this plan suicidal? In fact, Hitler had planned for heavy air support for his tanks, bringing in a thousand fighters from the air forces defending the Reich, but they were all chased off before they reached their objective.

These two photos show the reality of daily life for the basic soldier during this period where the front was moving.

Above: With the Third Army having broken through at Avranches and driving deep into Brittany and the Loire valley, Hitler launched operation Lüttich, the counter-attack at Mortain. German war correspondents followed the units as they headed towards the front line. Amongst these correspondents was Kriegsberichter Theobald who followed the advance of the 84. Infanterie-Division, between Beauchêne and Ger, north-east of Mortain, in all likelihood here on 30 July. Among the many photos that we have been able to identify following a long period of team work in our publishing company, the advance carries on here at the crossroads in Ger, in the direction of Essard; the place has not changed. These men are well-armed. They are 'tank breakers' and carry the German Panzerschreck bazooka and a Panzerfaust (the type here is the one that had to be fired less than thirty metres from the target) carried by the last grenadier. The latter also carries two rockets for the Panzerschreck carried by his comrade. In front of him is another grenadier armed with the very modern Sturmgewehr assault rifle that was still being issued to troops in very small numbers. (BA)

A little further on, an old Norman hands out cider to the grenadiers from a traditional jug. The photo report had previously shown country folk supplying soldiers with milk. These men are also heavily loaded. On 6 August, the 84. I.D. held the line between Saint-Pois/Chérencé-le-Roussel/

Saint-Clément, to the north-west of Mortain, finding itself in the vanguard. It would end up in the Falaise Pocket where it would be wiped out. Many of these men would die. (BA)

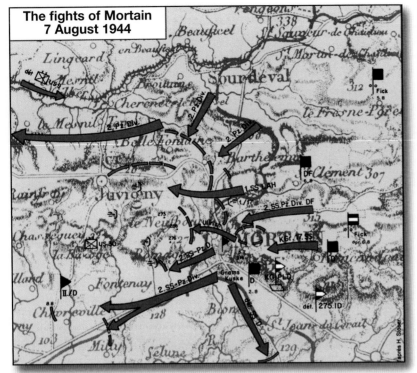

The fights of Mortain
7 August 1944

The Mortain sector.

1. We identified this photo back in 1988. It was taken as the 2. SS-Panzer-Division 'Das Reich' moved up to the front lines and shows several tank men of this unit with, in the centre, SS-Oberscharführer Johann Thaler, born on 6 February 1920 in the Tyrol. (three other photos where he is smiling in the same way led to this identification). He was awarded the Ritterkreuz on 14 August 1943 when driving a tank within the 'Das Reich' tank regiment. His actions led to the destruction of seven Soviet tanks. In this photo he is still with SS-Panzer-Regiment 2 ('Das Reich') which was engaged to the left of the 116. Panzer-Division during the Mortain counter-attack on 7 August. Johann Thaler got out of Normandy alive but was killed on 7 April 1945 by the Soviets during the battle for Vienna. (BA)

2. This other photo from the same set allows us to identify the location. This Sturmgeschütz 40 type G was photographed in the streets of Lonlay-l Abbaye. The abbey's church tower can be seen in the background. It might be a tank belonging to the 116. Panzer-Division. (BA)

3. Seen here is a group of soldiers of the 116. Panzer-Division. The divisional emblem is on the cap worn by the lieutenant on the right. To the right, in the background, we can see an American prisoner being questioned. (BA)

4. Men of the 116. Panzer-Division, probably belonging to the divisional reconnaissance group or the assault gun group. Two of them wear feldgrau jackets bearing death's head collar tabs. To the left of the photo, we can see the warrant officer seen in photo 3. (BA)

5. The previously seen 116. PD warrant officer. He is posing for the war correspondent by looking up at the sky. Indeed, the aerial danger was very high and the vehicles are covered with branches. This NCO wears numerous decorations: from top to bottom, Close Quarter Combat ribbon, ribbons of the Iron Cross Second Class, War Merit Cross, 1941 Eastern Front Medal, then the Iron Cross First Class and Close Quarter Combat clasp. (BA)

6. Two parachute unit sergeants (Vire sector) have picked up a stray puppy. The man on the rights bears the specialist's badge of a vehicle driver. (BA)

The Mortain counter-attack

The German armoured forces slowly headed towards the front line but, on 6 August, field-marshal von Kluge decided to push forward the start of operation Lüttich, the attack at Mortain. Only 145 panzers (which was not even the theoretical strength of a panzer division!) attacked **at dawn on 7 August**, even before the arrival of all the units. To the north of the attack, the 2. Pz-Div. advanced eight kilometres to the west, as far as Mes-

nil-Adelée. In the southern sector of the attack, the 2. SS-Panzer-Division advanced ten kilometres, as far as Fontenay and Milly. Around Hill 317, above Mortain, elements of the 120th Infantry Regiment (30th Division), found themselves surrounded. The 'Das Reich' division had already covered a third of the distance between Mortain and Pontaubault. However, the morning fog soon lifted and from midday onwards, fighter-bombers arrived in force and pinned down the German armoured force before it could even take on the

Mortain, 7 - 13 August. The small Norman town would be the pivotal area for several days of the counter-attack launched on 7 - 8 August towards Avranches. Seen here, on 7 August, is an American anti-tank gun awaiting the panzer attack. (Coll. Heimdal)

American tanks of the 3rd Armored Division which was in the sector. A large number of panzers (sixty) burned. The attack was shattered. By the evening, Maj. Gen. Collins had at his disposal two armored divisions and five infantry divisions for his VII Corps, his reinforcements having been swiftly brought up.

The next day, on **8 August**, and despite the losses of the previous day, this last-chance counter-attack was relaunched. The American forces were now superior in numbers. The German attack stalled and was continued, without success, until 10

August. On the evening of 8 August, Le Mans was reached jointly by the Third Army and the First Army on its left flank. It was from this town that the attack towards Alençon began. The Americans were turning the flanks of the German army in Normandy. On **10 August**, the Canadians were ten kilometres north of Falaise. In the south, the Americans (XV Corps, Third Army), were between Le Mans and Alençon, moving north and attacked by elements of the newly-arrived 9.Panzer-Division.

Mortain, 12 August 1944. American soldiers are seen here looking at German vehicles destroyed by allied fighter-bombers near the Mortain-Le Neufbourg train station following the failure of the offensive launched on 7 August at Mortain, The station, that we can see in the background, is in a valley at the foot of a granite outcrop where the small town of Mortain is built. The fighter-bombers took a terrible toll. The panzer attack was resumed on 8 August but was pinned down by air attack. Seen here is a 2.Panzer-Division vehicle, in the foreground, identifiable by its trident symbol painted on its wing, plus a Schwimmwagen, a Kettenkrad half-track and even a jeep.

9 August, American observation officers have set up an artillery observation post near Barenton (south-east of Mortain).

Medics giving first aid to wounded men. (NA)

The same destroyed column, seen from the other end, with the body of a soldier who did not manage to escape the strafing of the Jabos (fighter-bombers).

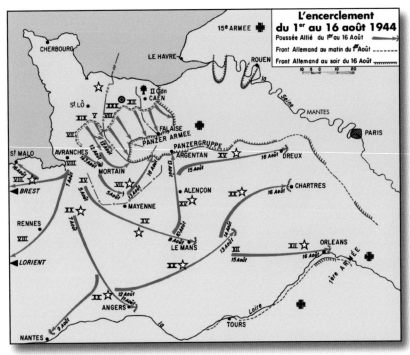

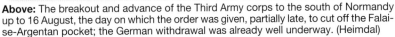

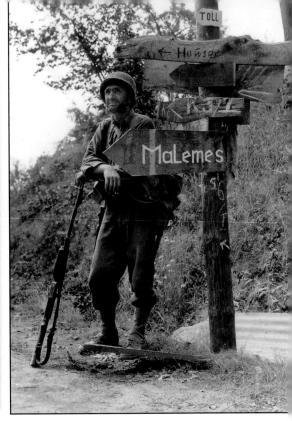

Above: The breakout and advance of the Third Army corps to the south of Normandy up to 16 August, the day on which the order was given, partially late, to cut off the Falaise-Argentan pocket; the German withdrawal was already well underway. (Heimdal)

Opposite: 16 August. Pfc. Louis L. Hespe takes a break at the crossroads of the Tinchebray, Domfront and Lonlay roads. He is standing next to signs left behind by the Germans. (DAVA/Heimdal)

Lieutenant-General
Omar Bradley

George S. Patton

From Alençon to Argentan

12 August was one of the most decisive days of the Battle of Normandy. Two XV Corps armoured divisions (5th Armoured Division led by Maj. Gen. Oliver and the Général Leclerc's French 2ᵉ DB on the right flank) took **Alençon** and reached the outs-

kirts of **Argentan**. A few American tanks and French troops of the 2ᵉ DB even entered the latter and there was now only twenty-three kilometres between Argentan and Falaise! But, the Canadians were not yet in Falaise and Bradley and Montgomery feared that the Americans would open fire on their Canadian allies as they advanced north from Argentan in order to close the pocket where a large part of the German army in Normandy would be trapped. Lt. Gen. Bradley ordered Patton to halt opposite Argentan and a fantastic opportunity was lost! On **13 August**, the German high command began the evacuation of its forces, those of the rear-echelon that were so important

Opposite: Two German soldiers, between Carrouges and Alençon, watching an explosion before continuing their withdrawal, circa 14 August. (BA)

in a war where logistics was paramount. Thus, in the evening, the 12. SS-Panzer-Division 'Hitlerjugend' (according to a report from its chief-of-staff), had already evacuated 10,000 men to east Normandy, keeping only in the front line a tactical group of 1,500 men, 20 tanks and sixteen 88 mm guns. It was the same for other units , such as the 17. SS Panzer-Division, the bulk of which had already left for the Lorraine to be rebuilt! On **14 August**, the commander of the 5. Panzer-Armee, General Eberbach, requested an order to pull back to avoid his troops from being wiped out. In the meantime, Bradley believed that the Germans had escaped and he decided to push towards the Seine. New counter orders arrived on **15 August** with the Canadians heading for Trun, but the Americans advancing straight to the east. On **16 August**, XV Corps was at Dreux, XX Corps at Chartres and XII Corps at Orléans; the advance was spectacular but the Falaise Pocket was still not closed and Hitler ordered a general withdrawal at 11.53 am. Therefore, between 13 and 18 August, 55,000 men, some 40% of the strength of the divisions under threat of encirclement, had withdrawn. Bradley was not, therefore, totally wrong when he thought that the bulk of the German armies had already escaped.

Finally, and some four days late, the closing of the Falaise Pocket could now begin. Montgomery had learned of Hitler's withdrawal order and at 3.30 pm on 16 August, decided to finish things once and for all, issuing the order to push on to Trun which the Canadians had just captured.

A photo from the same set on the bottom of the previous page showing Panther number 633 belonging to 6. Kompanie, Panzer-Regiment 33 of the 9. Panzer-Division which arrived, too late, as reinforcements. The division was in Argentan on 15 August. (BA)

From Rânes to Ferté-Macé, 15 to 16 August.

1 and 2. Men of the 39th Infantry Regiment, 9th Infantry Division, manning a bazooka in the Andaine forest on 15 August. Note the divisional emblem stencilled on the helmet, and the cloth shoulder patch of the same division sewn on to the sleeve. The Division was in action between Ferté-Macé and R,nes.

Tractable (14-16 August)

Operation Tractable had been preceded by Operation Totalize on 8 to 11 August, over the flat terrain heading towards Falaise, but it came up against a determined defence by elements of the Hitlerjugend, and the 4th Canadian Armoured Division had suffered a disaster on Hill 140 (see following pages).

On Monday **14 August**, the situation became clearer for the Germans as the southern front experienced a sort of respite with Patton having ordered Haislip to redirect the attack towards the Seine. Montgomery also believed that the bulk of the German forces had withdrawn. This was not yet the case, the German withdrawal was underway and there were still units in the Flers sector! In the northern sector of the salient into which the Germans were withdrawing, the Canadian divisions (2nd and 3rd Canadian Infantry Divisions, 4th Canadian Armoured Division, and the Poles of the 1st Polish Armoured Division, under command of the First Canadian Army), were ready to attack in the morning. Following artillery preparation at 11.37 am, the Canadian tanks attacked at **11.42** am but, in chaotic circumstances caused by the smoke and dust. The Canadian Corps made good progress, but was slowed down by skilled German defence and it was still five kilometres from Falaise, this day's objective according to Montgomery's order. At the same time, the Second British Army was heading to Trun.

On Tuesday **15 August**, the encirclement was delayed by orders and counter orders. Montgo-

Opposite: Lieutenant-General H.D.G. 'Harry' Crerar, the First Canadian Army commander. In this photo, taken in winter, Lt. Gen. Crerar wears a flight jacket issued to RAF and RCAF flight crews. This sort of vanity was typical of Commonwealth senior officers. (PAC)

Metal Polish cap badge. This insignia can be seen stencilled on the helmets of Polish units.

Polish tanks lined up on the start positions, awaiting their movement orders. (IWM)

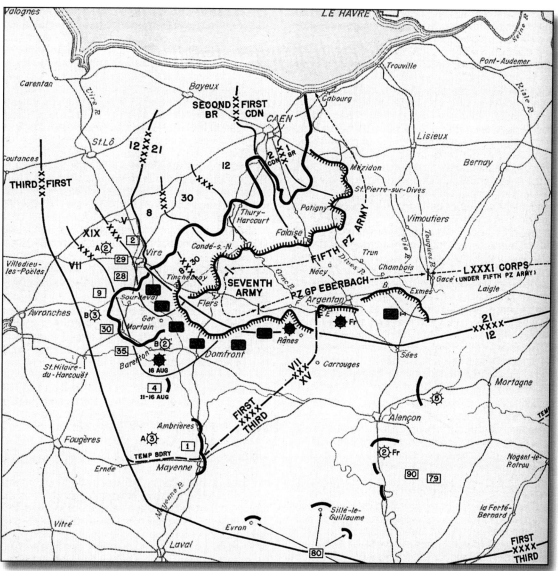

The movement of the front between 12 August (solid line) and 16 August (toothed line). During this period, the American army advanced up as far as Argentan before stopping, whilst the Germans withdrew east and defended the northern part of the front under pressure from the British and Canadians. This map shows the German withdrawal in the Mortain-Ger-Tinchebray sector, as well as that undertaken in the north (8th and 30th Corps sectors) following Operation Bluecoat. Finally, we can see sector where the First Canadian Army was in action. (From a US Army map)

The powerful 1st Polish Armoured Division in action from 8 August in Operation Totalize, then in Operation Tractable. (IWM)

207

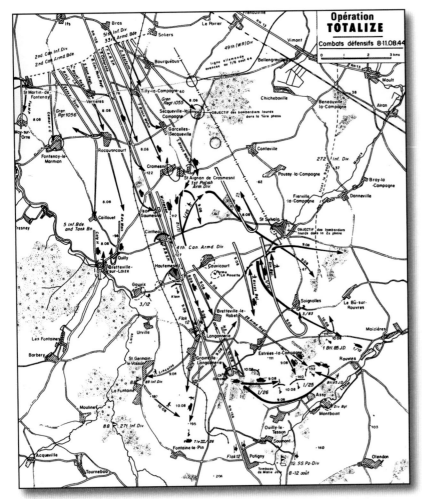

Phase I of the operation succeeded in reaching the road that runs alongside May, Fontenay-le-Marmion, Rocquancourt, Garcelles and Secqueville, and even Saint-Aignan which would play a vital role in the following phase. At the beginning of Phase II, the HJ counter-attack, launched with Tiger tanks, Panzer IV (I./12) and KG Waldm,ller, failed. However, over the following two days, the 4thCanadian Armoured Division would suffer a disaster at Hill 140 (to the east) and heavy losses at Hill 195 to the west. This disaster suffered by the Canadian tanks brought Totalize to an end. (Heimdal, according to H. Meyer.)

This colour photo shows an ammunition truck burning on the flat terrain near Cintheaux during the advance to Falaise. (PAC)

mery and Bradley met each other. Montgomery placed the American XVth Corps on the defensive south of Argentan whilst his troops marched towards Falaise. The Canadians tried in vain to advance, suffering heavy losses against a few Tiger tanks and elements of the 'Hitlerjugend' division (KG HJ).

On Wednesday **16 August**, the evacuation of the Germans in the salient continued and between 13 and 18 August, 55,000 men, some 40% of the strength of the troops under threat of encirclement, withdrew. However, at **3.30 pm**, Montgomery finally gave the order to the American XVth Corps to resume its advance. During this time, north of Falaise, Lieutenant-General Simonds (commanding the II Canadian Corps) issued the order to link up with the Americans. At 3 pm, the 2nd Canadian Infantry Division launched its attack on Falaise; the Saskatchewans entered the town at 5.30 pm, fiercely defended by elements of the HJ. The battle continued up to 3 am the next day.

Operation Totalize saw the first use of a new generation of armoured troop transportation, the 'Kangaroo', made from Canadian Ram tank chassis. The Royal Electrical and Mechanical Engineers had already made this type of vehicle in early July to be used for the repair of tanks left in No Man's Land. One of them is seen here bearing the symbol of the 30th Armoured Brigade Workshop of the 79th Armored Division.

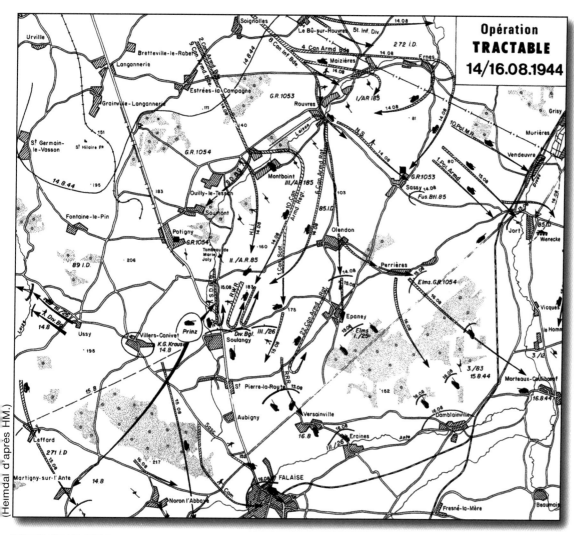

2nd Canadian Infantry Division. (N.B.)

3rd Canadian Infantry Division. (F.J.)

Divisional patch of the 4th Canadian Armoured Division.

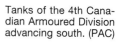

Tanks of the 4th Canadian Armoured Division advancing south. (PAC)

Closing the Pocket (17 to 18 August)

At 6.30 am on Thursday **17 August**, Major-General Leonard T. Gerow (Vth Corps) arrived at Alençon in torrential rain in order to relaunch the American offensive and at last take Argentan and link up with the Canadians along a line from Chambois to Trun. He had been ordered to take command of the XVth Corps divisions, the latter now having been attached to the First Army which was driving towards the Seine and Paris. On the evening of the previous day, the German salient was still forty kilometres long and all of the sectors in this salient were within allied artillery range! However, during the night, a withdrawal had been undertaken behind the Orne and was, according to M. Blumenson, a remarkable success. The main crossing point to the east was at Putanges. But, although the withdrawal over the Orne was coming to a close, the threat to the Germans was in the north of the **Falaise** sector where the last fighting for the town was taking place. At 3 am, the Saskatchewans had reached the railway crossing on the road leading to Trun, but fighting was still taking place in the western part of the town. The Camerons arrived in Trinité square in front of the town hall at 7.30 am and by 12.30 am were at Saint-Clair south of the town. In the town there were still areas of Hitlerjugend resistance, particularly in the girls' school where they held out all day long. Other HJ elements were positioned north-east of the town in the Damblainville sector. However, to the east, from the Jort brid-

This map shows the progressive withdrawals of German troops within the salient. On 17 August they withdrew behind a major obstacle, the Orne valley with Putanges being an important crossing point. This operation was a remarkable success undertaken in dramatic conditions. Falaise fell to the heavy attacks but Argentan still held out. (H. Fürbringer/ Heimdal.)

Putanges had been a vital crossing point over the Orne on 17 August. This photo, taken three days later, shows a British Sherman tank of the 11th Armoured Division, crossing the Orne on a Bailey bridge placed over the arches. The bridge was blown by the Germans after their withdrawal. (IWM)

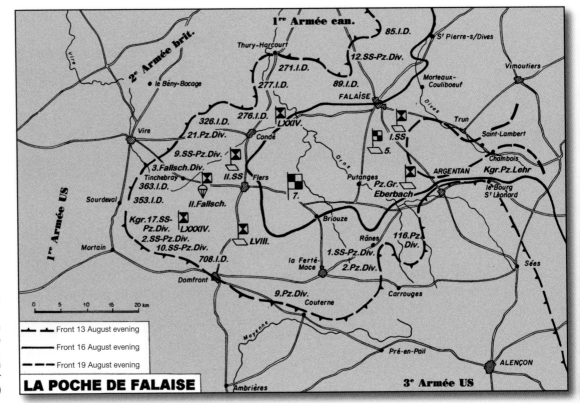

LA POCHE DE FALAISE

Front 13 August evening
Front 16 August evening
Front 19 August evening

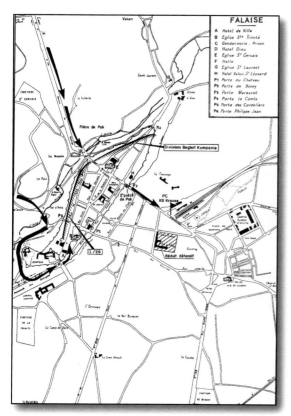

On this map of Falaise, the old town can be seen behind its ramparts with the fighting of 16 August (grey line), then the defensive perimeter of the girls' school with Rue des Ursulines to the south.

gehead, elements of the 1st Polish Armoured Division were advancing towards Trun and against KG Luck. Thus, for the Germans, the threat was in this sector. The stranglehold at Falaise had been broken, but the Canadians were still advancing very slowly. The main attempt of an allied breakthrough was made in the Trun sector and was given over to the Polish 1st Armoured Division. It was here that the fate of the Battle of Normandy would be played out. In the south, in the **Argentan** sector, the situation was better for the Germans; the 116.Pz.Div., which was holding the front, had been reinforced the previous day by the II.SS-Panzer-Korps. Facing them were the 80th and 90th US Infantry Divisions and the French 2e DB which were, according to the

116. PD chief-of-staff, luckily inactive . However, the II.SS-Pz.K also withdrew and **Bourg Saint-Léo-nard** was captured at 6 pm, this being a vital objective built on high ground.

In the north, on Friday **18 August**, the 4th Canadian Armoured Division advanced towards Trun, with the 1st Polish Armoured Division having the east of Chambois as its objective with the task of linking up with the US 90th ID. In the Argentan sector, the situation was also worsening for the Germans, even if the attacks led by the 80th ID against Argentan were repulsed. In Le Bourg-Saint-Léonard, the 90th ID posed a threat to Chambois. The exit was narrowing dangerously for the Germans.

Falaise, 17 August 1944. Sherman tanks arriving from the town centre (Sherbrooke Fusiliers), accompanied by the Fusiliers de Mont Royal, advance along Rue des Ursulines, parallel to Rue des Prémontrés, to the right of the girls' school where the HJ held out. They are seen here at the beginning of the street which escaped damage. (PAC)

17 August 1944, a mixed Canadian tank and infantry squad, with Shermans of the Sherbrooke Fusiliers and infantry of the Fusiliers de Mont Royal, advance into Falaise in order to quell the last areas of German resistance formed by 'Hitlerjugend' grenadiers. They are seen here advancing in Rue des Prémontrés along the axis of advance situated to the left of the girls' school. The buildings seen on the left are no longer there. (PAC)

In this period colour photo taken on 18 August, a Canadian infantryman smokes a cigarette with a 2nd Canadian Infantry Division military policeman, next to the fountain in Saint-Gervais square. Note that the soldier on the right is wearing a medal on his shirt. This is quite likely a medal given to large French families who had brought up their children well. He probably picked up this medal without knowing what it meant, from a house abandoned by its inhabitants. The German signs from unit 884 of the Feldgendarmerie are still in place.

Captain Laughlin E. Waters, commanding officer, in 1944, of E Company, 359th Infantry Regiment. He was the first American officer to meet with the Poles and thus establish the link up between the two armies.

L.E. Waters in 1994.

Saturday 19 August
The link up

This day was decisive for the Germans. Throughout the night of 18 to 19 August, the mouth of the salient, the bottleneck, had remained open and the German troops continued to withdraw in good order. On Saturday morning, the salient was ten kilometres in length and twelve wide, containing the remnants of four panzer divisions (1.SS-Pz.Div., 10.SS-Pz.Div., 12.SS-Pz.Div., 2.Pz.Div. and 116.Pz.Div.), elements of the 2.SS-Pz.Div. and what remained of six infantry divisions (84.ID, 276.ID, 277.ID, 326.ID, 353.ID, 363.ID) as well as various other elements, including the paras of 3.FjD and numerous combat groups. All of these elements now had to maintain the exit open before they were trapped inside. All units had been ordered to withdraw to the west of the river Touques. For these last units, the crossing of the Dives was due to take place the following night.

But this day would also be decisive for the Allies who would succeed in cutting off the salient and isolating the last retreating German units in a pocket. It was the **Canadians** who first resumed their advance. In the morning, a 4th Armoured Division tactical group comprising of B Company, Argyll and Sutherland Highlanders of Canada and C Squadron, South Alberta Regiment, led by Major D.V. Currie, reached **Saint-Lambert**. Late morning, the same day, the **1st Polish Armoured Division** sent two tank regiments and its reconnaissance group towards **Chambois** which it reached at around 7 pm after heavy fighting. Towards **7.45 pm**, Major W. Zgorgzelski of the 10th Polish Dragoons, linked

This photo, symbolising the link up of the two armies, was taken by an American war correspondent at Chambois the following day, 20 August, and shows (left) Lieutenant Wladyslaw Klaptocz of the 10th Polish Dragoons and Major Leonard C. Dull who had led the attack with his battalion against Fel and Chambois (including Captain Waters' company). Sadly, there was no war correspondent around late afternoon on 19 August to capture posterity the moment when the Major Zgorzelski and Captain Waters made the first link up. (US Army/ Coll. Heimdal)

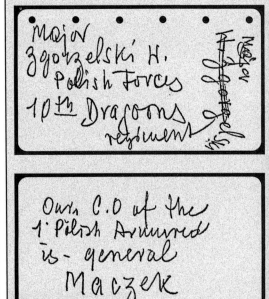

Notebook page written on by Major Zgorzelski. (Coll. Waters)

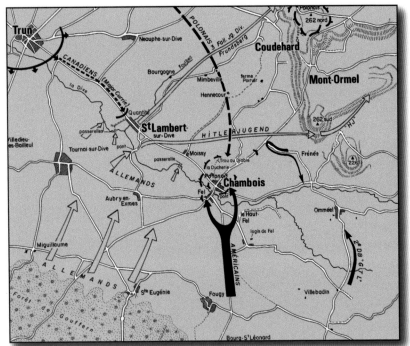

The Pocket is closed, 19 August. In the north, the Canadians are in Trun and have pushed as far as Saint-Lambert. In the south, the Poles of Major Zgorzelski and the Americans of the 359th IR have linked up at Chambois which they hold. The tactical combat group of the 2e division blindée advanced as far as Mont Ormel then turned back; this French armoured division was firing into the pocket with its artillery. However, the Germans could still get through via Saint-Lambert as far as Moissy and they would find an obstacle in their path: the Poles, who were established on Hill 262 north (Boisjos) that they named Maczuga, thus closing the exit. But the Germans managed to infiltrate via the north of Boisjos and by Hill 262 south, thus skirting around the obstacle. The Pocket was closed, but it was not blocked. (Heimdal)

L.E. Waters at the spot where he met Major Zgorzelski, he is seen here talking about it with G. Bernage in 1994. (Heimdal)

up with Captain Laughlin E. Waters (34) the commanding officer of G Company, 359th IR, 90th ID, which had advanced from Le Bourg Saint-Léonard with tank support from the French 2ᵉ DB tactical combat group. The pocket was closed. However, contrary to orders given by the 90th ID, the 2ᵉ DB tactical combat group withdrew behind the Dives at nightfall. The consequence of this was that the Chambois/Vimoutiers road was no longer cut between Saint-Lambert and Mont Ormel. Also, because of the slopes of Hill 262 between the road and French positions, this road could not be swept by the 2ᵉ DB's artillery. This breach would play a vital role over the following days for the last withdrawal of German forces.

Major D.V. Currie, commanding officer of the C Squadron, South Alberta Regiment. He was awarded the Victoria Cross (the first of the campaign for the Canadians).

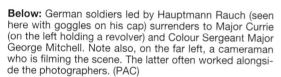

Below: German soldiers led by Hauptmann Rauch (seen here with goggles on his cap) surrenders to Major Currie (on the left holding a revolver) and Colour Sergeant Major George Mitchell. Note also, on the far left, a cameraman who is filming the scene. The latter often worked alongside the photographers. (PAC)

The bridges of Saint-Lambert. This famous painting (IWM) shows Typhoon fighter-bombers attacking German tank columns withdrawing through Saint-Lambert-sur-Dive. The painting depicts a few panzers that have been hit, burning in front of the church in Saint-Lambert, the tower of which can be seen above the fires. Two successive bridges over the Dives were the main crossing points for the retreating Germans. The two other crossing points were, in the final phase of the retreat, the fords at Moissy and Quantité.

Edouard Podyma in 1944 (HQ Squadron of the Polish 10th Armoured Brigade) and in 1994, with Georges Bernage on Hill 262 at Boisjos where he fought. (Coll. Heimdal)

Opposite: Two Polish tanks destroyed at Boisjos. (Coll. Granvalet.)

SS-Oberführer Heinz Harmel, commanding the 10. SS-Panzer-Division. In Saint-Lambert, he urged his men on to break out. (C/H.)

In a wood west of Saint-Lambert, men of the 1. SSPz.-Div. 'Leibstandarte' await their order to withdraw. Despite the allied artillery fire, it was the order and discipline of the German army that saved this withdrawal from becoming a rout and which made it a real success. (Munin.)

The breakout

By Sunday **20 August**, the final preparations for the German breakout had been carried. The first elements of II.Fallschirm-Korps (paras under the command of general Eugen Meindl) got underway the previous day at around 10.30 pm with the order not make any noise whatsoever and not use their weapons before daybreak. The paras crossed the Dives a few kilometres north of Saint-Lambert in the early hours and made their way to the east. Then, the 353.ID also crossed the Dives and it began to rain. When the morning mist lifted, the Polish soldiers on Mont-Ormel began to make out dozens of columns of German soldiers advancing towards them. Also, to their rear, the II. SS Panzer-Korps attacked as planned around **8 am** to clear the corridor. At the same time, the vanguard of the 3.FjD (parachutists) had reached Coudehard where they were halted by a violent allied artillery barrage. At around **midday**, Meindl and Hausser modified their plans. Following a two-hour bombardment, the Germans attacked Mont-Ormel, and the ground that they were holding, known to them as Maczuga (the mace, due to the contour of the summit) began to shrink. The paras linked up with forward elements of the Der Führer regiment and the road between Coudehard and Champosoult was opened at approximately 4.30 pm. Although they were under allied artillery fire, with the resultant losses, this was the way out to freedom. Another breakout, that of XXXXVII. (r.47) Pz-Korps was also carried out in the south,

between Chambois and Saint-Lambert, with the 1.SS-Pz.Div., 2.Pz.Div., starting at **4 in the morning** and in horrific conditions with men and horses killed and vehicles damaged. There was also KG HJ and other units, the 10.SS-Pz.Div. with SS-Oberführer Harmel urging his troops on in the church at Saint-Lambert. On the Maczuga, the Poles fired ceaselessly, risking being overwhelmed by the waves of attacking soldiers. The retreat of the II parachute corps continued throughout the **night of 20 to 21** with the rain coming down ever harder. In the south, the rearguard 116.Pz.Div. was assembled north of Goufern forest and the 80th US ID had at last succeeded in entering Argentan. By the evening of 20 August, the retreat of the II.Fallschirm-Korps and XXXXVII.Panzer-Korps was an undisputed success, but it was obvious that the second phase of the operation was going to be more difficult. The units still in the pocket would have to fight their way out of the enclosing trap.

In the early hours of **21 August**, Meindl gathered his men who were still holding Coudehard, a force of less than 3,500, of which only a few hundred were still combat fit. At around **7 in the morning**, they crossed the lines of the II.SS-Pz.-Korps near Champosoult and the soldiers of the 2.SS-Pz.-Div. spoke later of how they had been impressed by the paras who passed by singing in marching order. A few groups still crossed the Dives in the morning but, at around **midday**, the Allies were definitively positioned along the river and the pocket was closed. Isolated men continued to arrive at the exit, controlled by the Das Reich, but by **4 pm** there were no more. Approximately 45,000 German soldiers escaped the pocket, following the 55,000 others who had already withdrawn. Thus, the Germans had succeeded in evacuating a total of 100,000 men between 13 and 21 August. General Haislip's divisions were facing Argentan as early as 12 August. If the order had been given to attack, the 100,000 men, many of who were of elite units, would have been trapped.

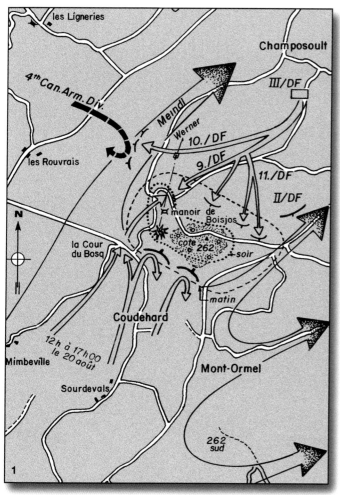

The ford at Moissy

1. Maczuga, the Polish defensive pocket, was counter-attacked in its rear and turned on its flanks by the flow of withdrawing German troops, particularly by Hill 262 south and Mont-Ormel, which were free, with Meindl's paras passing to the north. We can see that the defensive perimeter shrank in the evening. (Heimdal)

2. The river Dives, with banks approximately two metres deep, was an obstacle in the path of the retreating Germans who crossed it, mostly at Saint-Lambert, once Trun and Chambois had fallen into allied hands, but also at the ford at Moissy. As well as the foot bridge, the ford is passable, especially in August, and this allowed hundreds of vehicles to cross. Some of the latter were destroyed by strafing, artillery fire, or left behind by the Germans. (Heimdal)

3. Georges Bernage, accompanied by two Polish veterans, Edouard Podyma and Michel Kuc, look at the ford at Moissy in 1994. (Heimdal)

4. Two German tank crew have been burned alive whilst attempting to get out of their Panzer IV which was on fire. This is a brutal illustration of the battle which is rarely encountered in photos. (IWM)

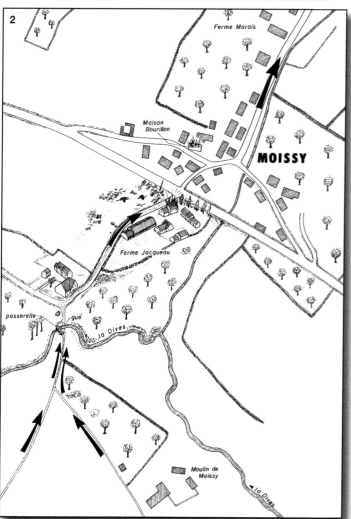

The ford at Moissy

Between the ford and
the crossroads at Mois-
sy of the Trun-
Chambois road, the
track running alongside
the banks of the Dives
passes next to the Jac-
queau farm. (see map
page 215). Horse-
drawn columns were
halted there and it is
blocked with dead
horses and abandoned
carts. (IWM)

Generalleutnant Otto
Elfeldt, the commander
of LXXXIV. Armee-
Korps, was captured
along with his staff
whilst attempting to
cross the Dives. (Coll.
Jasniak.)

The outcome of the Falaise-Argentan pocket

On **21 August**, the Allies counted the German losses with the number 'oscillating' between 25,000 (Montgomery's estimation) and 50,000 (the First US Army estimation), with some 6,000 German soldiers killed or missing. These numbers were relatively low considering the apocalyptic conditions of the retreat and corresponded more or less to two full-strength divisions. However, the Germans had lost a lot of materiel, even if they had saved the bulk of their men: 220 tanks, 160 guns, 700 artillery pieces, 130 tracked vehicles (SPW) and 500 motorised vehicles. 1,800 dead horses were also counted; the latter had greatly suffered. A vehicle riddled with bullets might be able to carry on if nothing vital is hit, but a horse hit with one bullet would not survive in such conditions. Only one of the generals commanding an army corps was captured. Of the fifteen divisional generals, three were taken prisoner. This makes an average of one general in five who did not escape.

The fact remains that the figures concerning the 'wiping out' of the panzer divisions have been used without any verification in the post war years. It is said that the 2. SS-Panzer-Division 'Das Reich' only managed to get out of the pocket with 15 tanks, 6 guns and 450 men; the reality is that 12,000 men of this division (although few comba-tants) reached the Seine. The previous figure only concerned the Kampfgruppe that held the pocket open, whereas the bulk of the rear-echelon ser-vices and technicians, who were of great value due to their skills, were already gone! The 12. SS-Panzer-Division is supposed to have only eva-cuated 10 tanks, not a single gun and four redu-ced infantry battalions; in reality, 11,500 of its men reached the Seine. Once again, everything that was not needed on the front line had been with-drawn. Also, the pocket remained open! Only the heroic Poles at the 'Maczuga' had tried to close it and there were not enough of them to do it. All they could do was form a breakwater which cau-sed heavy casualties to the Germans that advan-ced towards them, but they could do nothing to stop those who skirted around them to the north and, above all, to the south (Hill 262 south) where the French 2^e DB should have remained. So why are these figures exaggerated? The Allies needed to magnify their victory, the war was not over. As for the Germans, for those who had no regrets, Kurt Meyer being one of them (in his book, *Gre-nadiere*), they wanted to magnify the 'heroic sacri-fice' where most had perished like Samurai... As for the anti-Nazis, they could also highlight Hit-ler's madness. It is true that carnage on such a scale and the foul smell that followed it and which hung over everything for months, created a helli-sh scene which struck one's imagination. Several thousand men died in a few square metres but this spectacular aspect should not hide the fact that it was a failure for the Allies. It was not a Nor-man 'Stalingrad', but rather a Norman 'Dunkirk'. A few months later in the Ardennes, the Allies would once again encounter the panzer divisions that escaped from Normandy, and the war would continue.

On the road to Mont-Ormel

Prior to the last operations for closing the pocket, up to 19 August, the road from Chambois to Mont-Ormel was used by the withdrawing Germans. It was cut, for a short while, by the arrival of Polish troops, but when cleared, allowed the flow of German troops to continue up to 21 August. German vehicles, destroyed by planes, but above all by artillery, line the sides of the road and even block the way through. (IWM)

The German retreat (20-30 August)

Contrary to the often repeated opinion, the Battle of Normandy did not end with the 'Falaise Pocket'. The Allies would fight the German troops as far as the Seine, attempting to snare them in a huge encirclement planned by the Americans. Indeed, with the rear guard units escaping from the pocket, the two American armies advanced rapidly to the Seine. In the early hours of **20 August** and in pouring rain, the 313th IR, 79th US Infantry Division, left Mantes and crossed the Seine near Méricourt over a footpath that the Germans had failed to completely destroy. By the morning there were two battalions on the right bank and, in the temporary absence of any German reaction,

a pontoon bridge was in use by the afternoon. Thus, XV Corps (First US Army) had established a solid bridgehead near Mantes near the upper Normandy region. On **21 August**, XX Corps was between Dreux and Chartres, XII Corps in Orléans and Châteaudun with the Seine as their objective, to the south of Paris. The Seine was also crossed on the **22nd** at Melun, but the Germans put up a stiff fight. On the **23rd**, the latter succeeded in blowing the bridge.

In Normandy, after the final evacuation of the pocket, the entire German front had carried out its withdrawal, followed closely by the British and Canadian armies. But this withdrawal was undertaken by several hundred thousand men in a huge pocket with the Seine as an obstacle. This was a

Drocourt, 19 and 20 August 1944. With fighting still taking place in the Falaise Pocket, and with the bulk of the German armies falling back to the Seine, American units had already reached the river in order to try and carry out wider encirclement of German troops north of the Seine. The photos on this page were taken at Drocourt (9 kilometres north of Mantes) and nearby. This sector was held by the 49. Infanterie-Division. However, the Americans attacked Mantes with the 79th Infantry Division in order to cross the Seine to the east of Normandy. A 49. ID second-lieutenant is seen here reporting on the situation to his captain sitting in the side car (above). The Germans had just launched a successful local counter-attack against the Americans. However, the Americans crossed the Seine on the 21st and the 49. ID withdrew to a line between Chérence (to the east of La Roche-Guyon) and Magny-en-Vexin in order to cover the German retreat north of the Seine in Normandy. (photos BA)

Opposite: This 49. ID soldier awaits the American attack with determination. He is positioned in a trench and armed with grenades and a Panzerschreck, the German equivalent of the bazooka and a formidable anti-tank weapon. (BA)

considerable trap and much bigger than that of the Falaise-Argentan pocket, as there was only one bridge left downstream from Paris, apart from a seriously damaged railway bridge at Rouen. Generalfeldmarschall Walter Model, the man for hopeless situations, attempted to organize this retreat from his 5. Panzer-Armee HQ in Rouen. The threat was not on the heels of the retreating troops, closely pursued by the British who were at last advancing in Pays d'Auge; the 7th Armoured Division was in Lisieux on the **23rd**.

Above: Most of the bridges over the Seine had been destroyed, but numerous ferries meant that the river could be crossed in many sectors, from Quillebeuf to Elbeuf, and the Hohenstaufen at Duclair as we can see on the map on page 220. Luckily for the Germans, there were not many allied aircraft around and, despite the terrible scenes on the quaysides in Rouen, the crossing of the river was an indisputable success. (BA)

Opposite: Late August 1944, these three officers, from left to right, a Beamte (administrative officer), one from the Waffen-SS with his drill jacket and a Wehrmacht officer bearing the Infantry Assault Badge, are happy to have escaped the tightening net. This German retreat in Normandy was a new 'Dunkirk' and the bulk of the troops were saved during an exemplary retreat. The Allies would encounter them again later. (BA)

Below: The changing situation from 14 to 25 August. The operations for closing the Falaise Pocket took place from 16 to 20 August. XV Corps then headed towards the Seine to try and cut off the German retreat. This corps was attached, at this time, to the First Army, whilst the Third Army drove east towards the Lorraine, then Germany. The latter, however, was halted on the Moselle river and became bogged down in the Lorraine mud. (Heimdal map)

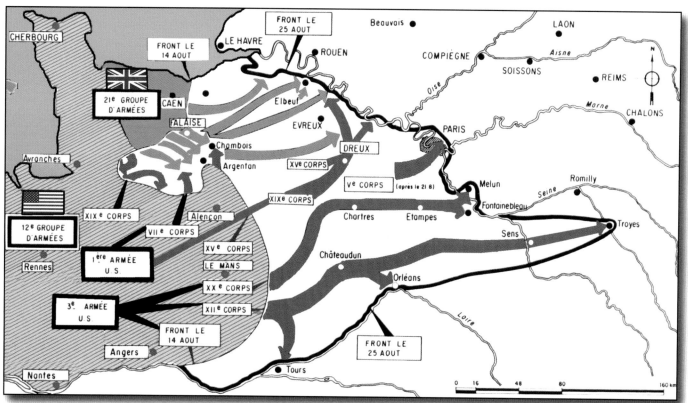

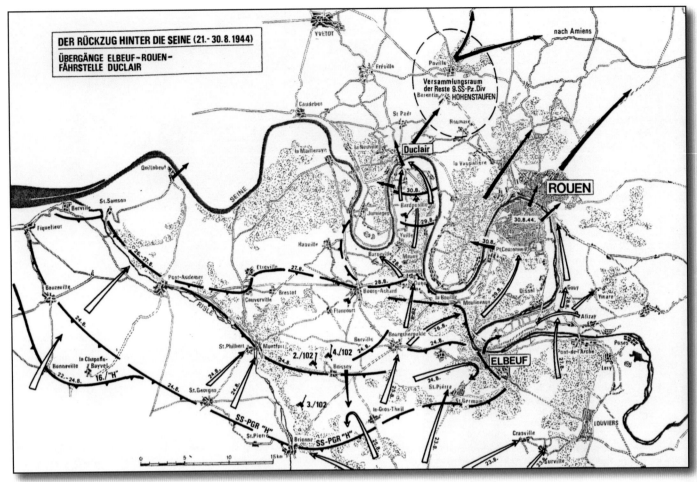

DER RÜCKZUG HINTER DIE SEINE (21.- 30.8.1944)

ÜBERGÄNGE ELBEUF-ROUEN-
FÄHRSTELLE DUCLAIR

The successive lines of withdrawal up to the Seine, showing mostly that of the Hohens-taufen. The crossing of the Seine was carried out at numerous areas including, downstream from Quillebeuf. The Risle line particularly stands out, making the most of a fairly deep valley, from 24 to 27 August. (Map by H. Fürbringer/Heimdal)

The three photos on these two pages are from the same report that were taken in the Roumois area on the roads leading to the Seine. Withdrawing columns have just come under air attack, a relatively rare occurrence in this sector as allied aircraft were already operating in other areas, allowing for a less dramatic withdrawal which saw 30,000 vehicles and 135 panzers cross the Seine. This Heer vehicle appears to mostly occupied by Waffen-SS men. We can also see the Hanreich sign on the windshield designating a Hitlerjugend officer. (BA)

The biggest threat was to the east of Lisieux where the British were also moving up towards the Seine on the left flank of the American XV Corps. Generalfeldmarschall Model, seeing this threat, rallied all of the available panzers in order to halt this advance in the Evreux sector on the evening of 22 August, and Vernon and Louviers the next day. Elbeuf remained an anchor downstream from Rouen for preserving crossing points as far as the mouth of the Seine.

The XII Corps vanguard units were in Bernay on **24 August** but, to the north-west, the 1st Canadian Army was advancing with difficulty against Germans who were withdrawing progressively. On this day, the II Canadian Corps crossed the river Touques. As for the Germans, they still had 50,000 troops south of the river and on **25 August**, Model gave the order to withdraw. The following night saw the forces still west of the river Risle withdraw to this river which formed an obstacle overlooked by sloping ground. On **25** and **26 August**, there was still a bridgehead south of Rouen, resting on a line passing through Bourg-Achard, Bourgtheroulde and Elbeuf. From west to east, cover was provided by elements of the 9.SS-Panzer-Division, 10. SS-Panzer-Division and 2. SS-Panzer-Division. Pressure was increasing and tension mounted on the banks of the Seine. However, as Major von Luck said in his memoirs, concerning the crossing of 27 to 29 August, the men waited calmly under cover for their turn to embark on ferries, barges or even rafts made from doors taken from the empty buildings along the river. Despite the difficulties, the crossing of the Seine was a success for the Germans, a fact that is underlined in a report written in early 1945 by the RAF Bom-

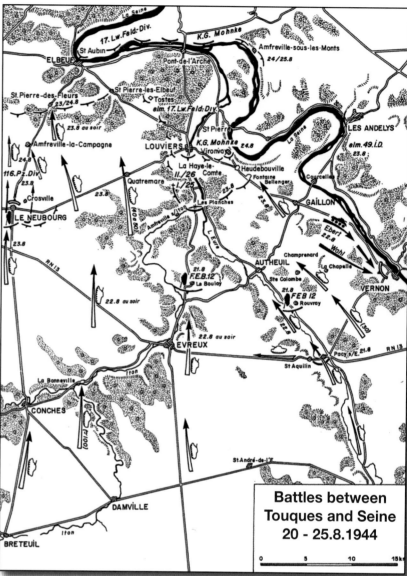

The same report shows two German soldiers waiting to start moving off again with, a little way behind them, burning vehicles. As the units approached the Seine, the amount of vehicles waiting to cross the wide river increased, as did the stress of this retreat. (BA)

Battles between Touques and Seine 20 - 25.8.1944

This map shows the German counter-attacks, mostly led by elements of the Hitler-jugend, against the British bridgehead at Vernon. This map joins up with that on the previous page, next to Elbeuf. (Heimdal map from information provided by H. Meyer)

The same vehicle as the one seen on the previous page is seen here surrounded by Waffen-SS men. We can see the column of trucks on fire along the road. (BA)

The photos on these two pages were taken on 22-23 August in Bourgtheroulde, a town with a vital road junction south of the Seine, both from the direction of Duclair and Rouen (see map page 220). Numerous tanks can be seen passing by the soldiers on foot; 133 tanks crossed the Seine. One of them can be seen here in the photos above at the crossroads in front of the Hôtel de l'Abondance, a Tiger I, number 213, second company of schwere Panzer-Abteilung 503 which had fought alongside the 21.Panzer-Division during 'Goodwood', then 'Bluecoat'. We can also see (below) two formidable Jagdpanther of schwere Panzer-Abteilung 654. Twelve of them, the only ones in Normandy, went into action during Operation Bluecoat (see page 197), causing heavy losses to British tanks. These surviving tanks are making their way towards the Seine. (Photos BA)

bing Analysis Unit. (The German retreat across the Seine August 1944): The Seine was not much of an obstacle despite nearly all of the bridges having been destroyed. Sixty crossing points and three pontoon bridges had been identified and another three built. In all, the report estimated that **240,000 men** had succeeded in crossing the Seine, along with **30,000 vehicles** and around **133 tanks**. All of the men who had reached the Seine had managed to cross it, with the same applying to 50% of the vehicles and 70% of the tanks that had reached the river. The success of the German retreat brought this battle to an end but, the Allies would

Above: A German tank man looks for Bourgtheroulde on a map of the Eure in order to find the roads which lead to the Seine.

Opposite: This young Waffen-SS soldier with a cigarette, accosts two young Normans to ask for a light. This is seen in the following photo in the set which has not been shown here. This scene shows a curiously peaceful moment, far removed from a rout and a panic-stricken retreat.

Below: Other faces are seen here, including two tank men, left and right. The man on the right is a sergeant belonging to schwere Panzer-Abteilung 503. Despite their apparent calm, their faces bear the the signs of the gruelling retreat. This remarkable photo is worth a thousand words. (Photos BA)

later come across these troops again, mostly in the Ardennes.

Thus, the **Battle of Normandy effectively came to an end** on **30 August**, but it would go into dramatic extra time on **5 September** when the Allies bombed Le Havre. Following the German withdrawal to Belgium, the port of Le Havre formed a Festung (fortress) and it was encircled by the British with the 49th Infantry Division. After blackmailing the Germans, the British bombed Le Havre on 5 September, resulting in 3,200 civilian deaths in a terrible bombardment that was qualified as 'pointless' by Le Havre resident, colonel Poupel, a member of the rescue teams in 1944. Three months after the landings, this battle ended with more than 21,000 civilian deaths in Normandy.

The human cost

Two million allied soldiers landed in Normandy between 6 June and 25 August 1944. In all, allied casualties reached 10% of their strength (206,703 men, of whom 124,394 were American, 82,309 British and Canadian), with 20,000 American and 17,000 British and Canadian dead. They faced a total of **740,000 German soldiers**. Losses for the German army reached 240,000 men and 210,000 prisoners, a total of 450,000 men, with another 290,000 German soldiers succeeding in withdrawing. Civilian losses were also very heavy with approximately 45,000 casualties, of whom 18,000 were killed, to which are added the victims of Le Havre, bringing the total number to almost 20,000 dead. Normandy was devastated by bombardments and fighting. Some towns were nothing more than a field of ruins: 86% of Villers-Bocage was destroyed, 77% of Saint-Lô, a figure that grew to 92% when the rubble was cleared and reconstruction began), 74% of Aunay-sur-Odon, 73% of Vire and 73% of Caen and so on.

120,000 buildings were totally destroyed and another 270,000 damaged, plus 43,000 hectares of farm land rendered temporarily unusable.

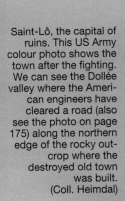

Saint-Lô, the capital of ruins. This US Army colour photo shows the town after the fighting. We can see the Dollée valley where the American engineers have cleared a road (also see the photo on page 175) along the northern edge of the rocky outcrop where the destroyed old town was built. (Coll. Heimdal)

The number of civilian deaths by department is as follows: Calvados, 8,100, Manche, 3,700, Orne, 2,100, Eure, 900, Seine-Maritime, 4,850. Most of the deaths were caused by air raids carried out against lines of communications in order to slow down the arrival of reinforcements, but the usefulness of which was more than relative. Indeed, the Germans had been able to quickly skirt around these areas thanks to a particularly dense road network. It was the civilians who mainly suffered from these raids. The deadliest raids took place on during the evening of 6 June and during the night from 6 to 7 June, destroying towns such as Lisieux, Pont-l'Evêque, Caen, Argentan, Flers, Condé-sur-Noireau, Vire, Saint-Lô and Coutance, already causing 3,000 civilian deaths in the first two days. In the days that followed, the bombs destroyed L'Aigle, Avranches, Valognes, Vimoutiers, Falaise, Argentan with Aunay-sur-Odon encountering an even more tragic fate, being bombed three times and thus tragically increasing civilian losses and totally wiping out the town! Artillery fire also caused heavy losses. It would take several decades to recover from all these ruins.

The battlefield

Some of the sectors of battlefield remain extremely evocative. In easy distance from Caen (161/163) are Rots and Bretteville-l'Orgueilleuse (116/123), Fontenay/Rauray (154/157), Hill 112 (168/171), Tilly-sur-Seulles (142/143) and Villers-Bocage (134/137), Trévières and Isigny (126/127), Carentan (132/133), Sainte-Mère-Eglise (124/125), Saint-Sauveur-le-Vicomte (138/139), Cherbourg (148/151), La Haye-du-Puits (160/161), Sainteny (166/167), Saint-Lô (172/175), Mortain (200/203), Putanges and Falaise (204/211), Chambois (212/217). Mont Ormel and its museum allow us to see across the entire sector of the Falaise Pocket.

Recommended reading

Editions Heimdal has published a considerable number of books over the decades on D-Day and the Battle of Normandy, some of which are now out of print. We recommend *Objective Carentan, Three Days in Hell (8- June), The Battle of the Cotentin, Caen 1944, Objective Saint-Lô, Cobra, Objective Falaise, The Corridor of Death*, but also the *Mur de l'Atlantique face au débarquement, Les panzers face au Débarquement, Les pilotes français du 6 juin, 50 aérodromes pour une victoire, La Götz von Berlichingen en Normandie, Le Commando Kieffer* - see our website www.editions.heimdal.fr

Printed on Pulsio Print prints at Sofia (Bulgaria) for Heimdal Publishing, Georges Bernage, June 2018